SECRET SERVANTS
A HISTORY OF JAPANESE ESPIONAGE

by the same author

Baltic Corner: Travel in Estonia
A Spy Has No Friends
The Patriot
Spies At Work: A History of Espionage
Lion With Blue Wings: The Story of the Glider Pilot Regiment
The Undaunted: The Story of Resistance in Western Europe
The Art of Spying

SECRET SERVANTS

A HISTORY
OF JAPANESE ESPIONAGE

By RONALD SETH

FARRAR, STRAUS AND CUDAHY

NEW YORK

To Sepha,
with private implications,
and with all my love

Contents

Contents

ACKNOWLEDGMENTS

While I was collecting material for my short history of world espionage, *Spies At Work*, I was struck by the almost complete lack of information concerning the espionage activities of Japan and I decided that, if I could, I would try to fill the gap. I therefore approached the Japanese Embassy in London, who referred my request for assistance to Tokyo. The Japanese Foreign Office replied, regretfully, that those intelligence records which had not been destroyed by Allied bombing appeared to be irretrievably lost.

I was on the point of abandoning my project when the Japanese Embassy in London informed me that the American government were holding a large number of Japanese Foreign Office documents in Washington, and that the Library of Congress had published a check list. Thereupon I switched my attention to the American Embassy in London, and through the vigorous and untiring efforts of my very good friend Dr. Bowen Evans of the United States Information Service, who has placed me deeply in his debt, I was able to consult this check list.

The list told me that it would be very well worth my while

ix

to pay a visit to Washington. This was arranged, and here I must acknowledge with gratitude the assistance of the Librarian of Congress and of various members of his staff, particularly Dr. Edwin Beale of the Department of Orientalia, which was given me with unfailing courtesy and without stint. I owe a similar acknowledgment to the staff of the State Department in Washington, D.C. and to the British Foreign Office in London.

The major part of my early material is taken from the Japanese documents to which I have already referred. In the latter part of my account I am indebted to about a dozen printed sources. In the bibliography at the end I have acknowledged both the documentary material (under the reference numbers provided by the Library of Congress check list) and the printed sources by the name of the work and the author.

R. S.

SECRET SERVANTS
A HISTORY OF JAPANESE ESPIONAGE

CHAPTER 1

The Beginning of the End

It was 7:55 on the morning of Sunday, December 7th, 1941.

In the attic of a small house overlooking Pearl Harbor, the great Pacific base of the American Navy, Ruth Kühn spoke to her father as she trained her binoculars on the eighty-six United States warships riding peacefully and unsuspectingly, at one of the largest natural anchorages in the world.

"They are coming!" she said.

Dr. Bernard Julius Otto Kühn gave a slight involuntary shiver of excitement. "All I hope is that they've managed to get the submarine inside the defenses," he replied. "If not . . ."

"They will do it," the girl said sharply. "Here they are! Be ready!"

From the northeast, out of the sky, it seemed, three formations of aircraft appeared. At first small specks against the deep blue, cloudless, sun-inflamed Pacific heavens, they grew momently as the drone of their engines crescendoed.

Through the finely precisioned Zeiss glasses, the girl saw the three groups presently veer away from one another. One made for the United States Army bases at Wheeler and

3

Hickham Field. Another swung toward the United States Naval Airfield at Kaneohe Bay. The third came steadily on toward the ships below.

Except for the noise of the aircraft, Pearl Harbor was silent.

In the ships, in the barracks and in the houses, officers, men and civilian workers of the base were breakfasting or standing formation or going on shift. Only here and there could Ruth Kühn discern casual groups of men.

Her mother came into the room.

"What do you want?" the girl snapped, without turning from the window.

"Are you sure we should not take clothes?" her mother asked.

"Nothing . . . only the money!" the girl retorted. "Go back to Hans! It is going to begin!"

Even as she spoke the windows of the little house rattled and the walls themselves seemed to tremble. Split seconds later came the roar of the first salvos of the aerial torpedoes, the thunder of bombs exploding and the sinister whine of diving bombers as the 105 aircraft of the Imperial Japanese Air Force launched themselves against the Pacific might of America in the harbor below and, farther off, at Wheeler and Kaneohe Bay.

Ruth Kühn spoke incisively to her father. Clearly he repeated what she said, and as he spoke he translated his words into light signals, which he flashed through the window by which he was standing.

"Direct hit on battleship . . . one destroyer on fire," Otto Kühn flashed on his signal lamp.

And on the other side of the town a clerk from the Japanese Consulate tapped out to the Japanese naval commander on his key the retranslation of the signals at the dictation of his chief, Consul Otojiro Okudo, who had his binoculars trained on the Kühns' attic window.

As soon as the Japanese attack began confusion assailed

the American forces. But it was only momentary. Despite
the fact that the aircraft warning system was not working
and that not a single regular reconnaissance or inshore patrol
had been maintained by the army or navy, the ship-borne
antiaircraft batteries had come into action.

But none of the land-based antiaircraft and coastal batteries came to their support, for they were unmanned; and even
if they had been manned, they would have been totally ineffective, for not one of them was supplied with a single
round of ammunition.

They did have the assistance of the few planes which were
able to become air-borne and of eighteen Navy dive bombers
from the aircraft carrier *Enterprise* which arrived fortui-
tously while the battle was in progress. But the aid these un-
prepared fliers could give was not very great.

With one fifteen-minute pause, the Japanese pressed their
attack until 9:45. When at last they broke off, out of their
total force they had lost only forty. But the losses they inflicted were such that besides immobilizing the United States
Pacific Fleet, in their ninety-five minutes of attack they had
given Japan naval and air supremacy in the Far East by making any immediate combination of American and British
Far Eastern naval forces an impossibility.

During eighty of those ninety-five minutes Ruth Kühn
had reported every success to her father, who flashed them to
Otojiro Okudo, who tapped them on to the Japanese commander, who, on the strength of them, issued his orders.

Why did she stop fifteen minutes too soon?

A little before 9:30 the door of the attic opened.

Ruth heard it. So did her father. Believing it to be her
mother again, she neither turned nor spoke, but continued
to scan the harbor which lay now under a pall of smoke.

Even when she heard the noise of a small scuffle she did
not turn. Only when she heard her father exclaim: "My
God!" and at once a strange voice, a man's voice, snap: "Put

up your hands!" did she whip around and find herself face to face with two American intelligence officers.

In the confusion that reigned in Pearl Harbor that morning—and only those who were there know what it was like—at least two men kept their heads. Hurrying to headquarters to discover how they might best help, these two men saw the light flashing from the attic window, realized that it was some sort of signal and decided to investigate. On the way they picked up a colleague.

Arrived at the little house, which the Kühns used as a week-end retreat, they surprised Frau Kühn as she soothed her frightened thirteen-year-old son, Hans, in the sitting room. While one of them guarded mother and son, the other two mounted quickly to the attic and took father and daughter even as they worked.

With their prisoners they took the packed suitcases standing ready in the hallway. At headquarters, when they were opened, the cases were found to contain only money—bundles and bundles of money, among them wads of Japanese currency.

Besides the forty Japanese aircraft the Americans destroyed they also sank three Japanese submarines which had been able to penetrate the harbor defenses. One of them was the submarine which had been sent to bear away Otojiro Okudo and his staff—and the Kühns.

How had the Kühns come to be spying for the Japanese?

Bernard Julius Otto Kühn joined the German Imperial Navy at the age of eighteen and was assigned to service in a cruiser. In 1915 his ship was sunk by the British and he was picked up and taken to England as a prisoner of war. To pass the dreary hours behind the wire he began to learn English, and made excellent progress.

After the armistice he returned to Germany and, having no profession, decided to take up medicine. Like so many of the disillusioned young in Germany during the twenties, the conditions which made it more than difficult for him to earn a living in his chosen profession turned him bitter. So when the Nazis came strutting into the streets proclaiming their promises to change all the harsh struggle for very existence in Weimar Germany into a utopia of National Socialism, they found in him a ready listener, and then an ardent adherent.

He met and became a personal friend of Heinrich Himmler and was given a job with the Gestapo. It was not a prominent nor even a lucrative job, but he was given to understand that it was merely a steppingstone to the position earmarked for him—chief of police in one of the great German cities.

One of the more peculiar traits of the extremely peculiar reichsführer and chief of the S.S., Himmler, was that he kept the promises he made to his intimates. His promise to Bernard Kühn, however, he did not keep. Instead, on August 15th, 1935, the good doctor found himself stepping ashore in the Hawaiian Islands accompanied by his wife and two of their children, Hans Joachim, aged six, and Ruth, aged eighteen.

And Ruth was the cause of this curious translocation!

The Kühn's elder son, Leopold, was in a good position. He held the post of private secretary to Dr. Joseph Goebbels, minister for propaganda and public enlightenment.

Early in 1935 Leopold's chief, the little clubfooted doctor, gave a gala party at the ministry for his staff. As Leopold Kühn had no fiancée or particular female friend, he took with him, as his partner, his sister Ruth.

Ruth was a really beautiful girl. The freshness of unsullied, still-burgeoning maturity was upon her, like the bloom upon a fine ripe peach. There were members of the Nazi Party at this time who still directed their domestic lives after an acceptable code of morals. Dr. Kühn was one of them. He brought up his sons and his daughter along the narrow path of moral rectitude. Ruth, though brushed with innocence, knew exactly what she must do to keep that innocence untarnished and, until this party at the propaganda ministry, fully intended that her innocence should be the main item in the dowry she would take to her fortunate husband.

When she was presented to the minister for propaganda he held her hand just a little longer than was really necessary, and she was too untutored to read the signs—yet. From the beginning the engagement was unequal and unfair. The ugly, crippled, almost dwarflike Goebbels could exude great charm, and one of his main weapons was his voice.

The present writer, after a series of vicissitudes which he has recounted elsewhere, found himself in the beleaguered city of Berlin in March 1945 when the Russians were but forty miles from the gates in the east and the Allied mobile forces were dashing up from the west. During his stay he attended one evening a meeting of several thousand dispirited, war-weary, bewildered Berliners who had congregated in the hope of receiving some encouragement from the minister of propaganda and public enlightenment.

When Joseph Goebbels stepped to the rostrum to speak only his head could be seen above the rail through the bullet-proof glass shield protecting him. Had it been anywhere else in the world, and with an audience of any but Germans, there must have been a demonstration of unkind merriment. But from the moment that the fanatic eyes flashed above the rail of the rostrum and their owner began to speak, a fantastically mellifluous voice controlled everyone within hearing. It was not the words he used, not the promises he made, for he had only the threadbare clichés of Nazism on which to fall back. Nevertheless the vast crowd was hypnotically hushed within seconds, not merely by the actual sound of the voice, but by the mysterious charm which it held.

Later in the evening at that reception ten years earlier, this little man had invited Ruth Kühn to dance with him—and despite his clubfoot he danced well. At close quarters, with his arms around one and the prestige of his position and the flattery of his invitation to enhance it, this charm must have been even more potent.

To the rake, virginity is one of the main attractions for sexual prowess for it erases temporarily the boredom of over-indulgence by its freshness and removes the necessity for perversion, which only too quickly jades the sexual palate. Against one so skilled the girl had no chance, and even if the charm and the art had had no effect there were few, even among moral Nazis, who would have dared to immolate themselves on the altar of chastity when the führer's staunchest friend wielded the sacrificial knife.

Within a short time Ruth Kühn, not yet seventeen, had become the deformed dwarf's mistress. She was only one of a number of the minister of public enlightenment's lights of love. He plucked them as they took his fancy and discarded them when the bloom began to fade, and under his blighting heat they faded soon. He was not discreet enough to prevent the particulars of his extensive amours from becoming public knowledge. The discussion of them provided diversion from the führer down to Gefreiter Schmitt. Frau Goebbels certainly knew of them, but the strange charm which bewitched the führer and Gefreiter Schmitt must have bewitched her too, for she never caused her husband the embarrassment of divorcing him or apparently ever threatening to do so; and at the end was content, both for herself and her children, to accept poison from his hand and to die in his arms as he fell back dead.

What happened exactly in the case of Ruth Kühn is now likely to remain a mystery for all time unless the woman—she is still alive in Germany—should ever choose to speak. Quite suddenly Goebbels not only cast her off but decided that she must leave Germany.

The head of the geopolitical department of Berlin University was General Haushofer, and the general's son, Karl, was one of Goebbels' closest intimates. The majority of students who passed through the general's hands entered the foreign service, usually becoming members of Ribbentrop's espionage service.

General Haushofer had had close connections with the Japanese espionage authorities since 1914, and as good fortune would have it, at the very moment of Goebbels' *contretemps* with Ruth the Japanese had asked if they could be given some assistance in acquiring the services of Europeans for their espionage organization. One of the great difficulties with which the Japanese spy masters have always had to contend has been the color and other physical characteristics of their own people, which makes them conspicuous in any area outside their own theater.

The coincidence of Tokyo's request with the German minister of propaganda's predicament could not have been more fortunate. When Goebbels explained his problem to his friend Karl, Karl's father could say that he could use not only Ruth but Ruth's family. Nothing could have been more satisfactory for the Little Doctor because it removed the embarrassing girl literally to the other side of the world. And thus it was that the Kühn family, with the exception of Leopold, who remained at his post as Goebbels' private secretary until he met his death on the Russian front, arrived in the Pacific.

Their "cover" was Dr. Kühn's supposed interest in the Japanese language and the ancient history of the Hawaiian Islands. They gave every appearance of being a typically united Teutonic family. Certainly they aroused no suspicions in the minds of anyone who ought to have been curious about a German family transplanting themselves so many miles from the fatherland. Not even the travels of Ruth and her father to the adjacent islands caused a single eyebrow to be raised. Indeed, it would seem that the Kühns had everything in their favor.

Friedel Kühn, the doctor's frau, was plump and bespectacled and treated her husband with the respect which has always been one of the good qualities of German women. But she had the pigeonhole type of mind which could sort and evaluate and store away even small details of military significance. While she gave every appearance of centering all her existence in the welfare of her family, she disarmed those who would have been on their guard had they ever thought what her true role really was. Even when she left Hawaii for two fairly protracted periods, her absence merely provoked expressions of commiseration for her family thus left without the prop of their domestic bliss. Yet, had the interested authorities only known, each time she was visiting Japan as a courier, carrying secrets of United States naval and military defenses in the Hawaiian Islands.

Despite her experiences at the hands of Joseph Goebbels, or perhaps because of them—for nothing enhances the beauty of maturity more than the awakening and satisfying of inherent sexuality—Ruth's appearance was more strikingly attractive than ever. She was fond of tennis and swimming and was an exquisite dancer, and these accomplishments, added to her natural grace, soon brought her invitations to every social event. The majority of these gave her contacts with American naval officers made hypersusceptible to female company by absence from home and the normal expression of those qualities inherited from the old Adam; and these contacts provided her with extremely useful information, all unwittingly disclosed by the aspirants for her favors.

Then, too, to observers the Kühns were clearly well provided with money. Since the source of their wealth was the Rotterdam Bank Association it was concluded—quite wrongly —that the doctor had made some very shrewd investments in the Netherlands. It is known now that in the six years 1935 to 1941 the Kühns received more than $100,000, and it is believed that this was by no means all their remuneration.

The Kühns were in the service of both the Germans and the Japanese, though the latter were unaware of their contact with the Nazis. Copies of all the information they supplied to the Japanese consuls in Hawaii, who were their con-

tacts, they sent to Ribbentrop's intelligence via General
Haushofer.

Early in 1939 the Kühns moved from Honolulu to the
quieter Pearl Harbor. It is now generally accepted that there
is no hotter bed of gossip than a woman's beauty parlor.
Either the Kühns or their superiors made this discovery two
decades ago.

As Ruth was very skillful at her own beautification, and
as there was no amenity of this kind for the navy wives in
Pearl Harbor, there was nothing strange to be seen in her
opening up a beauty parlor. This new venture marked the in-
tensification of Japanese espionage in the southern Pacific.

The success of the beauty parlor was as overwhelming as
it was instantaneous. At a meeting with Otojiro Okudo, the
consul at Honolulu, the specific requirements of the imperial
spy masters were explained to the Kühns. Their chief assignment was to supply the exact numbers of the United States
naval forces in the Pacific with their exact locations and
exact dates of departure and arrival at any given spot, with
particular reference to Pearl Harbor.

The innocence of little Hans, now eleven years old, was
to prove a very useful adjunct to the beauty parlor. The boy
was encouraged by his father to develop his natural curiosity
about and interest in ships, particularly in naval ships belong-
ing to the Americans. It was not long before kindly American sailors were inviting the boy aboard their vessels and
pointing out to him all the mysteries of their equipment.
What harm could there be in answering the spate of questions which Hans, like any normal little boy, asked, when he
would not understand a word of what he was being told?
But Hans was observant and had a retentive memory. When
he got home he was able to give an exact account of what he
had seen and heard.

The Kühns' next step was to work out a simple code and
light signal system by which they could transmit their information from the attic window of a small house they rented

above Pearl Harbor direct to a Japanese agent. The pace was
now increasing at such a rate that personal contact with the
Japanese as frequently as changes in the dispositions of
United States naval units now made desirable was dangerous. The signal system eliminated the risk.

The system was tried out on December 2nd, 1941, and was
a complete success. Otojiro Okudo now came himself to
Pearl Harbor and was able to transmit by radio to Japanese
naval intelligence, via his consul general, the exact location
of all American warships in Hawaiian waters.

As the Kühns, father and daughter, watched the Pearl
Harbor base filling up during the next few days, they had
great difficulty in keeping their mounting excitement in
check. And the excitement of their Japanese masters was
commensurate with, even if it did not exceed, their own.

In position by December 6th, the Japanese naval commander could congratulate his masters on their great good
fortune. The gods had given them a sure sign that they were
on their side by persuading the enemy to concentrate the
greater proportion of his naval forces in one spot so that, by
a simple plan, he could be attacked with the full weight of
Japanese aerial vengeance. The plan was to succeed, but the
people who were largely instrumental in its success provided
the sacrifice.

The Kühns were eventually brought to trial. The evidence
was all against them. The suitcases were produced and among
the other evidence were copies of their reports written in
German and even a copy of the signal code, which had all
been found in the house when it was searched.

The doctor, his wife and Ruth all attempted to claim the
leadership of the little ring. The Americans accepted the doctor's verision and he was sentenced to death. Friedel and
Ruth were imprisoned.

The doctor made a bid to save his life by telling all he
knew about Axis espionage in the Pacific. The Americans
must have found his information valuable, for on October

26th, 1942, his death sentence was commuted to fifty years' imprisonment.

But whatever the fate of the Kühns, Japanese espionage had scored a great victory. It was a victory for which espionage preparations had begun more than thirty years before the Kühns had arrived in Honolulu. In the library of congress, in Washington, D.C., there are two sets of Japanese Foreign Office documents titled *Honoruru Gumbi Chōsa, Investigation of the military preparations of Honolulu,* 1907 to 1926, and, *Hawai Rikugiu Jōhō-bu Shūhō, Weekly Intelligence Reports from the Army Intelligence Bureau on Hawaii,* 1922 to 1923, totaling 2,318 pages of documents altogether.

It is passing strange how events resolve themselves. Had Leopold Kühn been a normal young German he would have had a girl friend to partner him at his chief's gala party in 1935 instead of his young sister; or that young sister might have been neither beautiful nor possessed of the untouched virginity which attracted the deformed satyr of a minister of propaganda; or she might have possessed those skills which might have permanently satisfied the jaded palate of Goebbels. Any of these things could have prevented the Kühns from being exiled to the Pacific and spying for Japan. Instead, everything conspired to send this German family to this place, to work for these masters. In fact, the presence of the Kühns in Honolulu and their spying for Japan has a very great significance.

First, it underlines the close affinity that Japanese espionage has always had with the German. When Japan abolished its "closed door" policy in the mid-nineteenth century and began to develop from a medieval feudal state into a highly organized modern nation and the policies which she adopted made an espionage system essential, it had been to the methods and organization of one of the greatest spy masters of all times to which she had turned. The Prussian, Wilhelm Stieber, had produced what was then not only the most powerful espionage system in the world, an instrument with which Bismarck and his monarch had been able to forge the German empire, but also the most up-to-date system.

Second, Pearl Harbor was the brilliant culmination of more than half a century of spying in Honolulu and was one of the greatest coups of a truly fantastic system of espionage. It is fantastic not only in the vastness of its organization but in the physical area of the globe's surface which it covered.

In this story we shall hope to reveal not only the methods and the vast ramifications of Japanese espionage from its beginnings in the middle eighties of the last century down to Pearl Harbor, but to describe its activities in places as widely separated as St. Petersburg and New York, and in such tremendous areas as Siberia, Central Asia, China, Manchuria, the Pacific, the West Indies, Central America and the United States, linking these activities with the development of Japan's policy.

But to put the whole picture into proper perspective we must turn first to the model.

CHAPTER 2

The Model

One day in 1848 King Frederick William of Prussia found himself alone and unaccountably involved in one of those disturbances which, in those days, were becoming an all too frequent occurrence in Berlin. The disturbance had been spontaneous; someone had recognized the king and called out an insult. This had attracted the attention of others and soon the credulous, timorous Frederick found himself faced by a hostile mob. It seemed for a moment as if he would receive physical harm. He looked about him but could see no way of escape.

Like many timorous men, the king had a certain courage. He could not escape; he would not harangue these ill-mannered subjects; he would stand and wait for the blows which he was sure must come. All he hoped was that the end would be quick.

At that moment a man detached himself from the crowd, which even in its anger stood a little way off in deference to his royal person, and advanced toward him.

"Down with the tyrant!" the man shouted. "Death to the king! Let's end it now!"

So long had the tyranny of the secret police been at work

that even now the leaderless crowd hung back, none of them
willing to do anything which would make him a marked man.

The man continued to approach, still shouting his threats,
his arm raised, though whether to strike a blow or to egg on
the crowd the king could not be sure. Now he was within
reach. His back was to the crowd. The king flinched a little
but held his ground as his would-be assailant pushed his face
close to his and shouted a last threat. "Don't be afraid, your
majesty!" the man then whispered quickly. "I'm a police
agent. My men are in the crowd. They will see that nothing
happens to you."

"Thank God!" murmured the king.

"Death to the tyrant!" shouted the man, and seizing the
king by the arm began to bustle him along the pavement.

Struck mute by the handling of the king's person, the
crowd on the pavement made way for them. As they came
level with a door a few yards down, the man made a sudden
movement toward it, threw it open and pushed the king inside, quickly following himself. When the door was locked
and bolted the man leaned against it, let out his breath in a
sudden rush and passed his hand across his damp forehead.

"Sire!" he exclaimed to the trembling king. "That was a
narrow shave! But I must beg your majesty's indulgence. I
am not a police agent, but I had to say something. It would
have been fatal had your majesty's courage failed you at the
last moment."

The king forgot his trembling and smiled at the man.

"You certainly saved my life," he said softly, "and I am
grateful to you. May I know the name of my gallant, quick-
witted rescuer?"

"Wilhelm Stieber, sire. At your majesty's command, always."

"Wilhelm Stieber!" replied the king. "I shall not forget."

Wilhelm Stieber was born on May 3rd, 1818. His father
was a minor official in Merseburg, Saxony.

Wilhelm had not yet reached his teens when Herr Stieber was transferred to Berlin. There he educated his son with a view to ultimate ordination in the Lutheran ministry.

Before he had completed his education, however, Wilhelm had decided that he had no vocation for the ministry and turned his attention to the study of law. In the law he found at last the best use for his intellectual powers, qualified without difficulty and within a short time had become one of the most sought-after criminal lawyers in Berlin.

His clients were the riffraff of the criminal world, petty thieves, petty forgers, confidence men, rapists. They were the little, maladjusted men who took to crime as the only mode of expression they had—so far as they could see—of kicking against authority, cruel, unjust authority which was ceaselessly vigilant in harrying them, the underdogs.

Stieber's personality was such that he was able to get inside the minds of these little men, and when he assumed the title of champion of the underdogs they were willing to accord it to him. They did not know—for years they were never to discover—that their champion, in circles more influential in the realms of authority, was one of the most ardent monarchists.

Stieber never acted as attorney for the prosecution. He was always attorney for the defense. And his success in this role was phenomenal. Between 1845 and 1850 he successfully defended 3,000 clients.

What was the secret of his success as a lawyer? Was it his brilliance of intellect and oratory? Was it his superior knowledge of the law? It was certainly knowledge. But it was not knowledge of the law, extensive though this was.

When Stieber told the king that he was not a police agent he was not speaking the strict truth. He was not, admittedly, the normal kind of police agent, but he was in the pay of the police. He was, in fact, an *agent provocateur*, employed to smell out proscribed radicals, the enemies of the monarchy and the monarchists.

Besides this, he was editor of the *Police Journal*. Thus he had constant dealings with the police, and from these contacts and from the material supplied to his journal he was able to gain information in advance regarding the evidence which the police intended to bring against his clients. So he went into court fully prepared to meet with rebuttal and legal argument the facts and arguments put forward by the prosecutors. And, surprisingly, it never appeared to occur to the police that they were supplying the material for his success.

He used his role as champion of the underdog as a cover for his role as *agent provocateur*. He was not, he never would be, a man who acted from altruistic motives. A lawyer who consorted with the scum of the underworld, a shady "mouthpiece," would never be expected to be a monarchist. If he were, why should he devote his efforts and skill to defend, and only defend, those who were "agin the government."

But as well as being a cover, his association with his petty criminals was a source of information for his activities as *agent provocateur*. The proscribed radicals, even though they might be honest, decent men, and men of substance who had never stolen a penny from their grandmothers or even momentarily been tempted to do so, were, nevertheless, criminals. What they were doing, what they were saying, where they were to be found, all circulated along the grapevine of the underworld and came to Stieber's knowledge. So he smelled them out and was as successful in that as he was in the courts.

But Stieber was an ambitious man. It was not his intention always to be an *agent provocateur* and defender of petty thieves. He had his attention fixed on high places, and one or more of those high places he intended to fill.

His brilliant, quick-moving intellect also made him an opportunist. But quick to seize every opportunity, even he must have been overpowered by the prospects which suddenly opened up before him, so it seemed, on that day in 1848—he was then only thirty—as he stood in the crowd, looking at the lonely, frightened king.

On that day Stieber put his foot on the first rung of a tall ladder of success the moment he whispered in the king's ear. Frederick William was grateful to his gallant protector and did not, like some infamous princes, forget him as soon as he was safe once more within the protecting walls of his palace at Potsdam. Until the king went quite mad in 1857 and had to be put away, he heaped reward upon reward on Stieber.

In 1850 Stieber was appointed a commissioner of police. In the following year he visited England, ostensibly for the prince consort's Great Exhibition in the Crystal Palace in Hyde Park, but in reality to check up on the activities of Karl Marx and other German radical exiles then living in London. In 1852 he went to Paris where, posing as a liberal, and in his old role of *agent provocateur*, he obtained a list of radicals still living "underground" in Germany. His return was marked in Germany by the wholesale arrests of these men and women.

During the years which followed he became such an ardent supporter of autocracy that he almost outrivaled the autocrat himself. This ardor he translated into action against the radicals, thereby strengthening the king's position and so keeping green the king's sense of gratitude toward him.

But an autocratic policeman tends to make as many enemies as an autocratic monarch, and when Frederick William's brother became regent on the king's retirement, Stieber quickly discovered that the regent was not among his admirers. He was dismissed from his post and was fortunate that the support he had received from the now mad king could still save him from even worse revenge.

Deciding that it might be wiser for his physical well-being to leave his ungrateful country for a time, Stieber went to St. Petersburg. There, between 1858 and 1863, he assisted in the reorganization of the Russian secret service. He chose

St. Petersburg because it was the one place where he could legitimately expect to be helped. A few years before he had been able to hush up a scandal involving the wife of a Russian attaché in Berlin.

There is one aspect of this phase of Stieber's career which at first sight appears extraordinary. But when we come to know him better we shall see that it fits snugly into the jigsaw of the man's genius. While in disgrace and helping the Russians in St. Petersburg, he collected all the military information on which he could lay hands and sent it to Berlin, where it was found to be of great value. Optimist and always superb opportunist, he believed that he had encountered only a temporary setback and that the time would undoubtedly come when he would be restored to his rightful place. When this happened what he was doing now would be remembered to his advantage.

Nor had he too long to wait. In 1863 Stieber returned to Prussia and almost at once was recommended and introduced to Prince Otto von Bismarck by the proprietor of the *Norddeutsche Allegemeine Zeitung*.

At this time Bismarck was busy laying his plans for the aggrandizement of Prussian power and role on the European stage. He had reached that point in his planning where he had decided upon the elimination of Austria as a first step in the right direction.

A careful man and, of his kind, wise, Bismarck began to put his preparations in train. A first requirement of any action against the Austrians was the acquisition of the knowledge of their country's state of preparedness and military potential to resist attack. He suggested that Stieber might care to organize this intelligence for him.

It was exactly the opportunity for which Stieber had been waiting and hoping. He was certain that if he could bring off a brilliant *coup* he must be reinstated in his former position. Confident in his own capabilities and believing that the more he did personally the greater his success would be seen to be, he decided that he, and he alone, would conduct the operation, unless he found himself compelled by the enormity of the undertaking to have assistance.

So it happened that on a June day in 1863 the little Austrian village of Brunsbruck ran to the doors of its cottages, shops and workshops attracted by the cries of excited children who were running beside a small, horse-drawn cart as it slowly made its way down the village street.

The smiling, forty-five-year-old driver was a stranger. The good people of Brunsbruck had never seen him before, and this fact alone was sufficient to bring them to the street. But when he drew up his cart before the village inn and announced that he had sacred statuettes for sale, they left their doors and came crowding around him as the children had done.

The peddler was a good salesman. He was persuasive in his talk, he was witty, he cracked jokes that were new—at least to them—and which appealed to their country sense of humor, and before they knew where they were, they were buying one of the Sacred Hearts, or a Madonna, or a Holy Child which he was displaying for their inspection. He did not seem to be greedy, either. His charges were less than half those normally charged by door-to-door hawkers for sacred statuettes "blessed by the Holy Father himself."

When everyone was satisfied for the moment, he drove his cart round to the back of the inn, where he took the horse from between the shafts, tied her up and adjusted, for her convenience, a nose bag of sweet-smelling fresh hay. Then, having seen that her wants were satisfied, he went into the inn to attend to his own.

The taproom was practically empty. Only two or three men were sitting with steins in their hands, talking a little and drinking more quickly than usual because there was more work to be done. The peddler picked up the stein which the landlord had drawn for him and walked over with it to a table at which two men were sitting.

"Good day," he greeted them. "It's a pleasant village and pleasant people you have here."

The men grunted their appreciation of his appraisal and approval. He was a friendly man for a stranger. As soon as he spoke to them their country shyness and awkwardness with city-dwellers—they were always so damned superior—disappeared. Within a few minutes they felt that they had known the man for years.

"Any news?" one of the men asked.

"Not much." the peddler answered. "In the capital the army struts about as usual. Countess von Weber has been brought to bed of a boy, though the count has not been in Vienna for 372 days and she has never left the city. . . . Oh, it's the same old story!"

"What do they think about Prussia in the capital? Do they think Bismarck has got his eye on us?"

The peddler shrugged his shoulders.

"Why, yes. They believe he's bound to want to annex us, but they're confident our army is better than any Prussian army."

"Then they're expecting war?"

"Some time or other, they say it's bound to come; but not yet. And the longer we have, the better our defenses will be. Have you ever seen anything like this?" Suddenly he changed the subject. He drew from his pocket two or three cards on one side of which were drawings. He handed one to each of the men. For a moment or two there was silence, and then both men began to chuckle. And the chuckles grew into loud guffaws.

"Are these from the city?" one asked.

"Of course," the peddler answered. "The latest thing. There's scarcely a man of quality, or who can afford the price, that hasn't one, or two, or three."

"Who draws them?"

"A young artist I know."

"Does he have models, or does he do it out of his head?"

"His aunt keeps a brothel. He has made small spy holes in the walls of some of the rooms. He draws from life."

"Great heavens! And you really mean people . . ."

The peddler nodded. "Like to have one?" he asked.

"I could never afford it. How much?"

The peddler named the price—a few pence. The men handed back the cards. "When do you leave here?" one asked.

"Oh, not until tomorrow, if the landlord can give me a room."

"We have no money with us now. But we'll be here to-night. Save us one or two."

"I have plenty. I'll get them out and you can take your choice."

That evening the landlord of the inn did a roaring trade in beer as every man in the village and from the countryside around, it seemed, crowded into his taproom; and the peddler did a roaring trade in his pornographic drawings.

As he sold the drawings he drew the men into conversation. They answered him willingly. With their minds' eyes gloating on the new acquisitions, now secure in secret pockets, and their minds far away, they answered his questions, unconscious of the fact that they were telling this stranger how many soldiers were billeted in the neighborhood, which regiments they belonged to, how they were armed, what strong points there were round about, exactly where they were situated. And when bed called them at last they were equally unconscious of the peddler noting in a book, in a personal code, all the information he had gathered during the evening.

As, next morning, he drove away, his customers, both those who had bought his sacred statuettes and those who had purchased his pornography, waved him farewell as he passed them on the road to the next village, calling to him to return soon with newer wares; for his visit had been a red-letter day in their quiet lives.

So he went on his way with his sacred statuettes and his

pornography. It is not such an outrageous mixture of wares as would at first sight appear. Mankind is divided into two sorts—the pure and the impure. His Sacred Hearts brought him into the kitchens, his drawings into the taprooms. In both he was popular. In both he learned much.

For two years the peddler traveled the roads and byroads of Austria, questioning the unsuspecting, noting in his small black book, received everywhere as a friend by reason of his personal charm. Then, at the end of two years, his task completed, he returned to Berlin and to his master, Prince Otto von Bismarck, the Prussian king's Iron Chancellor, and laid before him a full and detailed account of Austria's armed strength and the disposition of her forces. It was as complete a picture of Austria's military preparedness as it was possible to gain without direct access to general staff blueprints.

By 1866, which was judged the opportune moment, the Prussian military leaders have devised a timetable which they were able to follow rigidly, based upon the peddler's information. The result was the Seven Weeks' War, terminating in the complete defeat at Sadowa of Austria's military might, and strewing upon the battlefields many of those who had bought the peddler's pictures.

Between police work and military espionage there is fixed a great gulf. Allan Pinkerton, the famous American detective, failed miserably when asked by President Lincoln to organize a system of military intelligence. The great spy—and great spies are a very small, select band—can combine the two sets of qualities required for success in both branches. Stieber very soon proved that he belonged to this select band.

In the Seven Weeks' War against Austria, which was fought strictly on the basis of the intelligence supplied by him, Stieber himself played an important and active role. In the months of preparation he organized an entirely new section of the secret police and went into the field with it as its commander. We recognize this new force to be the forerunner of the intelligence corps; and it is preserved still in the

German military organization as the *Geheimefeldpolizei*, the secret field police.

Though primarily organized to protect the persons of the king, his ministers and generals, Stieber's secret police were also to prevent foreign spies from obtaining Prussian military secrets. It was, in fact, counterespionage; and counterespionage in those days was a new concept. This was the first of Stieber's contributions to modern spycraft. It was a contribution which was to appeal most strongly to the Japanese.

The originality of Stieber's mind *vis-à-vis* espionage is demonstrated by other innovations and introduced by him. They are commonplaces today, but the measure of Stieber's greatness as a spy and a spy master is the fact that those innovations sprang from his mind.

There was, for example, military censorship, under which no dispatch, letter or telegram might be sent from the front unless it had first been censored by Stieber's staff. Alexander the Great had first used censorship of mail when his armies, thousands of miles from home, were threatening to revolt in the deserts of Persia. But he used censorship so that he might discover who the disaffected were and remove them.

Always aware of the necessity for secrecy concerning his movements and plans, Alexander had consistently forbidden his soldiers to write home to their families. Now, faced with wholesale mutiny, he directed that all officers and men might write one letter home and promised that they should be carried to Greece by special couriers. The men were delighted and poured out their hearts to wives and sweethearts.

The couriers set off, but twenty miles or so on their way they were met by trusted soldiers of the general. These took and read every letter and noted the names of all those who complained. They returned with their lists to Alexander and in a few days all the dissidents had been removed.

But this was not Stieber's motive. The motive was tied with yet another of his innovations. This was false propaganda, in which he was excelled only by his notorious successor, Dr. Joseph Goebbels, Hitler's minister of propaganda and public enlightenment.

Stieber argued, and the validity of his argument cannot be denied except on moral grounds, that the judicious manipulation of unpleasant facts may be used to boost the morale of one's own people and to weaken the morale of the enemy. The uneasiness which was caused in certain sections of the British public between 1939 and 1942 by Lord Haw-haw's (William Joyce's) broadcasts from Hamburg to England serve as an excellent illustration of the insidiousness and danger of this kind of attack.

In Stieber's day there was honor among high commands and they were honest in describing losses and defeats in their communiqués. Now, when the communiqués had to be submitted to Stieber, he played down the losses and suggested victories, if need be. It was ridiculous, he argued, to let the enemy know how many men he had killed because he was sure to know your strength when you began, and by a simple arithmetical calculation could gauge your strength or weakness after engagement. It was equally ridiculous to depress the people at home by telling them how many of their husbands and sons had been killed or were missing or wounded. Such news only distracted them from their essential duty of providing supplies.

As a result of the great success of the Seven Weeks' War Stieber was restored to favor, and appointed a privy councilor. Napoleon I had held the view that an agent was fortunate if he received financial rewards for his labors. Steadfastly he refused to award the Légion d'Honneur to his spy master, Schulmeister, also one of the select band of great spies. The Légion d'Honneur was the only award and reward Schulmeister coveted, and again and again throughout his career he urged his friends to persuade the emperor to bestow it on him. King William, however, was of quite another opinion. He believed that an agent should be awarded

the decorations granted to combatant soldiers if his work
merited such honors.

Since the removal of Napoleon I from the European scene
the fortunes of France had been in a state of flux. After making himself dictator by a *coup d'état* in 1851, President Napoleon had had himself elected emperor by a plebiscite in
the following year.

Napoleon III's ineffectual rule, accompanied by many un-
democratic restrictions, had set the French seething with
restlessness once more. Like other dictators we know of, he
decided to embark upon a program of conquests in the hope
of deflecting thereby the attention of his subjects from difficulties at home. In this he was encouraged by his ambitious
Empress Eugenie, a former Spanish countess.

After allying himself to England in the Crimea between
1854 and 1856, he later won Savoy and Nice by taking sides
with Piedmont against Austria. He followed this by adding
Algeria, Senegal and Indochina to France's overseas possessions. Encouraged, and ambitious himself, he then announced
his intention to push the eastern frontiers of France to the
Rhine.

For the next few years he began to prepare the way with
a propaganda barrage which did not deceive Bismarck so
much as it deceived himself. The Iron Chancellor used the
time to make his own preparations.

Soon, however, it looked as if Napoleon, *vis-à-vis* his
boastings of what he intended to annex from Prussia, was
vox et praeteria nihil. Bismarck, who had been planning to
give the French the lesson of their lives, felt himself constrained to take action, in which he was helped by Stieber.

By this time the Spanish throne had fallen vacant. Napoleon nominated a candidate; so did King William of Prussia. The Prussian candidate was elected.

Napoleon feared a Prussian-controlled Spain on his south-
western frontier because it raised the ancient and modern
bogey of encirclement. He therefore demanded that the

Hohenzollern prince should be removed. But when this was not done, still he only blustered. Determined, however, that Napoleon should have his war. Bismarck called on Stieber for aid.

The Prussian king was asked to put the Prussian views to the French ambassador. In those days diplomats did not always use codes, and when the ambassador's telegram to his government was received, as it had to be, by Stieber's censorship department, Stieber withheld a certain portion of it. The resulting message entirely distorted what the king had said. When the telegram was published in France every Frenchman was roused by it to truly Gallic wrath. Pressed by public opinion and assured by his generals that his army was "ready to the last gaiter button" when actually it was badly trained and only partly mobilized, Napoleon declared war on Prussia. If Napoleon had had half the information about his armed forces that Stieber had, he must have held his hand even then—unless he had been quite crazy.

For the two previous years Stieber had been infiltrating his spies into France until literally every nook and cranny was known to him. He had personally made a thorough tour of the future enemy's terrain, noting all kinds of information likely to be useful to Prussia's military leaders.

No spy master or chief of intelligence had ever gone into a similar task so exhaustively as Stieber. In the invasion zones his agents listed the stock of every single farm, so that when Prussian billeting and mess officers went about their tasks they would know exactly how many cattle, how many sheep, how many chickens and how many eggs Farmer Lebrun could supply for their needs. Stieber kept his lists up-to-date, and if Farmer Lebrun produced five heifers where the list said eight a fortnight before, he was called upon to explain what had happened to the missing three.

Stieber also knew the exact amount of the savings of the leaders of urban and rural communities. The state and dimensions of roads and byroads, the size and capacity of bridges,

the sites of stores of arms and ammunition and the type and
quantity held in them, numbers and types of transport, sites
and strength of strong points—all were listed. Nothing appeared to have escaped him.

He claimed that his agents in France alone numbered forty
thousand! The claim cannot be allowed, for such a number
would have required a headquarters staff and organization far
greater than Stieber maintained at any time. Nevertheless, his
army of spies must have exceeded by three or four times, or
even more, the number of spies ever employed by any other
spy master anywhere in the world at any time up to then.
It was a new concept of espionage. As his modern successors
were to invent a new type of war—total war—Stieber, a half
century earlier, invented what very nearly approached total
espionage.

His personal qualities were a blend of tireless application to
the task in hand, cunning, subtlety and utter, even ferocious,
ruthlessness. He demanded similar qualities in every single one
of his agents. He insisted that everyone who was even suspected of having a knowledge of Prussian military strength
should be liquidated. He decreed that when a company of
Prussian soldiers passed through a village they should be
preceded by outriders who were to warn all the inhabitants
to get indoors and close their shutters. Any peasant who
peeped from behind his shutters while the company passed
by was to be seized, tortured and hanged.

But while he demanded such excessive security, Stieber did
not complain if sometimes his agents were caught, tortured
and hanged. It served them right for being careless.

Stieber was in the closest contact with and deep in the
confidence of Bismarck. The Junkers, however, hated him
and never missed an opportunity for snubbing him. But no
insult seemed to affect him and he compensated his ego by
treating the conquered with arrogance, striking terror into
them by dire threats which he would have had no compunc-
tion in implementing had his victims not capitulated.

The French suffered a defeat at the hands of the Prussians in 1871 which still eats more deeply into the hearts and national pride of Frenchmen than the *débâcle* of 1940.

The Prussians established their headquarters in the Palace of Versailles. Thither the French leader, Jules Favre, was summoned when he expressed the desire, on behalf of his colleagues, to treat for the capitulation of Paris. The Prussians stipulated that Favre must come to Versailles alone, unaccompanied even by a personal servant. He was expected to have discussed the French side of the matter with his colleagues so fully that there would be no necessity for him to refer the Prussian terms to them. It was accepted that he was to be their envoy extraordinary and plenipotentiary, with the emphasis on plenipotentiary.

There is no record of what Favre may have felt about this invitation. But the propaganda of the day had attributed to the brutal and licentious Prussian soldiery the same sort of bestial atrocities which were laid at the door of German soldiers in Belgium in World War I—girls not yet in their teens raped by a score or more at one session, months-old babies impaled on pitchforks or bayonets and held, while still alive, in the flames of the burning thatch of what would have been their homes. But Favre must have wondered what particular brutalities the Prussians at Versailles had in store for him.

His surprise may be judged, therefore, when on arrival at Versailles he was welcomed courteously, if stiffly, by a Prussian colonel and conducted to a pleasant suite of rooms. When the surprise had worn off he doubtless imagined that this was part of the technique. They would lull him with politeness, fair words and creature comforts and then suddenly blast him sky-high when he was least expecting it. But even these thoughts were dispelled when the servant allocated to him to be his valet during his stay at Versailles was brought to him. He saw Gustav Olendorf to be a quiet, graying man in his early fifties whose eyes smiled at him even if his countenance was servant-solemn, who moved quietly about his duties and proved so efficient in his service that Favre would have liked to have engaged him to serve him always.

Favre had brought with him a portfolio which he insisted upon carrying up to his suite himself when the servant who was attending to his baggage would have taken it from him. When the colonel had withdrawn, having impressed upon him that if any of his needs had been overlooked a word to the valet would repair the omission, Favre walked over to the escritoire on the far side of the room between the two great windows and deposited his precious portfolio in it.

"I have prepared a bath for monsieur in the bedroom," the valet informed him in excellent French. "I thought that after the dusty journey from Paris monsieur would find it refreshing."

He followed Favre into the bedroom and helped him off with his clothes and before the Frenchman stepped into the large hip-bath tested the temperature of the water and added a little more cold.

"I understand, monsieur, that tonight monsieur is to be permitted to compose himself," the valet said as he unpacked Favre's valise. "I shall serve dinner in the sitting room. Perhaps monsieur would find it more comfortable if I put out his *robe de chambre* for him?"

"Yes, by all means," replied Favre, thankful that he was to be given the opportunity of sleeping before his meeting with the Iron Chancellor.

Presently the valet excused himself. "I have towels warming," he explained. "I will go and fetch them."

While he was gone Favre wallowed, as far as the dimensions of the bath would allow him, in the pleasant warmth of the water. He chuckled to himself as he remembered his past fears. Perhaps these Prussians were not so bad after all; perhaps they would not be too excessive in their demands? That valet was the devil of a time gone! Surely he wasn't warming the towels at the other end of the palace? Ah, there he was!

The valet returned, deftly soaped and rinsed the envoy extraordinary and plenipotentiary and held up a towel as large as a sheet, which he wrapped round him as he stepped from the bath. When the Frenchman was dry the valet held out his *robe de chambre* for him, placed his slippers conveniently and put ready his tasseled nightcap.

Dinner was excellent. The bottle of Château Neuf du Pape could not have been better chosen. As the valet hovered discreetly at his side, anticipating his wants, he chatted good-naturedly with the man. Where did he live? Was he married? How many children had he? Any grandchildren? He, Favre, had five. Where had he learned to speak French so well? Was he glad that his country had defeated France? But that was not a fair question. He had no wish to embarrass the good fellow.

After dinner Favre seated himself in an armchair by the fire and the valet placed a bottle of cognac and a glass by his side.

"Has monsieur any orders?"

"Bring me my portfolio from the escritoire, if you please, and then I have nothing more," Favre told him. "Try to find out what time the conference is tomorrow and wake me in good time."

"Certainly, monsieur. And if monsieur has any need of anything now or later, if monsieur rings I will come at once. My room is *à côté*."

"Thank you. But I'm sure there will be nothing. Good night."

"Good night, monsieur."

When he was alone, Favre poured himself a glass of brandy, took a sip and then opened his portfolio. From it he took a sheaf of papers. They were minutes of the fateful meetings with his colleagues, and *aides-memoires*, and the proposed French terms, the progressive phases through which he was to negotiate until the limit was reached. For the dozenth time he went over them, refreshing his memory, almost learning them off by heart.

At eleven o'clock he put them away in the portfolio, yawned and stretched, placed the portfolio in the escritoire, locked it and pocketed the key. Then he went to bed.

It was almost midday when he awoke next morning as the valet pulled back the curtains and let in the high-noon sun. He sat up in bed, slightly alarmed.

"What time is the conference?" he demanded.

"His excellency sends his compliments, monsieur, but pressing affairs prevent his excellency from meeting monsieur today. The conference is postponed until tomorrow."

"Pressing affairs?" Favre began. "But what is more pressing . . . Oh, well!" He resigned himself to the twenty-four hours of idleness; and after the tiring regime of the last weeks he was not sorry.

The valet attended him as impeccably as ever. The fellow had dark shadows under his eyes as though he had not slept. But if he had not slept, lack of sleep did not seem to impair his service.

Next morning the valet awakened him at nine.

"His excellency asks you to meet him at eleven o'clock," he said, looking even more drawn and haggard.

Precisely at eleven the envoy extraordinary and plenipotentiary entered the conference room and found himself face to face with his country's greatest enemy.

"Pray be seated, Monsieur Favre," Prince Otto von Bismarck invited him.

Favre sat down, put his portfolio on the table before him and opened it. Before he had had time to withdraw the papers the Prussian chancellor began to speak. As Favre listened, with every minute that passed he found himself growing more and more amazed and bewildered. It was a miracle! Bismarck apparently knew everything that had passed between him and his colleagues.

There was no argument, no negotiation. How could there

be, when all his bargaining power had been vitiated by the foreknowledge of this stern man? He signed, and returned to Paris bewildered; so bewildered that he overtipped the valet.

In Paris Favre reported to his colleagues, who shared his amazement at his revelations. But neither Favre nor his colleagues nor anyone else except the "valet" and Bismarck would ever know what had happened until, many years later, the "valet" wrote his *Reminiscences*.

In recounting this episode, Stieber says: "I often wonder what Favre's reactions would have been had he known that the valet who helped him with his bath and served him his dinner was none other than I, Wilhelm Stieber, minister of police and chief of espionage.

"When I went to fetch the towels which I had warming, I went to the escritoire where I had seen Favre put his portfolio. It was not then locked. I took a quick glimpse at the papers, sufficient to show me what they were. Then when Favre had gone to bed I opened the escritoire with a duplicate key and sat down to copy out all the papers which were in the portfolio.

"But as the new day broke I had finished only two-thirds of my task. I hurried to the chancellor, taking what I had, and explaining the rest. Prince Bismarck said that he must have the rest and to put off the meeting until tomorrow, which would give me the opportunity of finishing the work that night.

"So throughout the second night I worked until half past four. By the time for the meeting, the chancellor had read and mastered the documents.

"I remember standing at the top of the steps watching the carriage taking Favre back to Paris disappear in the distance, and though almost overcome with weariness from lacking two nights' sleep, I could not help but smile as I yawned and clinked the coins which he had given me in my hand."

Among the prisoners taken by the Prussians was a certain

General de Cissy. Though a bad general, de Cissy had been an active man and he found the restrictions of his confinement exceptionally irksome. Like the majority of regular soldiers, he had no secular resources. But as a Frenchman, he had a liking for one diversion above all others, in common with his compatriots.

Under the existing code of treatment for prisoners of war, and particularly for prisoners so elevated as General de Cissy, the conditions of confinement were much more refined than they are under the Geneva Convention today.

Then it was not held against a prisoner if he gave his parole not to escape in return for certain privileges. Parole, once given, was accepted at its face value by the detaining power and was regarded as binding on the honor of the prisoner.

Having given his parole, therefore, General de Cissy was permitted a certain freedom of movement in the city of Hamburg, which was the place of his imprisonment. Looking round for an object of diversion, his choice fell upon a very beautiful young German aristocrat, the Baroness de Kaulla.

Despite his advanced years, or perhaps because of the long experience those advanced years had bestowed on him, the general was an ardent wooer and a skillful lover. The baroness, not entirely inexperienced herself, knew a good lover when she met one, and the liaison settled down into a *modus vivendi* which both participants found entirely satisfactory.

In the course of time the general was released from captivity and returned to France, though there were occasions, after he had been informed that he was to be released and before his actual departure for the motherland, when it had seemed that he would never be able to part from the consolation which he found to be so devoutly to be desired. However, patriotism prevailed even over love despite Chaucer's prioress' pronouncement, *Amor vincit omnia*; and patriotism was rewarded. The general was appointed minister for war.

By 1875 the French were harboring thoughts of revenge

on the Prussians. The armed forces were being reorganized; the chiefs of staff were planning the campaign to come.

As his excellency left the war ministry one evening at the close of a long day's devotion to preparations for revenge, an urchin ran up to him and, thrusting a note into his hand, after making certain that he was General de Cissy, ran off into the dimness of the street.

Puzzled, General de Cissy returned to the lobby of the ministry where there was a light by which he might read. He slit open the envelope clumsily and withdrew a sheet of paper and scarcely comprehending what it meant read that the Baroness de Kaulla had come to Paris and was waiting for him at the Hôtel des Étoiles, now alas no more.

In the weeks and months that followed, the frantic idyl of Hamburg was renewed. Madame de Kaulla moved into an apartment of her own and engaged servants. Like most regular soldiers the general had little money besides his not very princely salary. She waved his regrets aside. She had money to spare and was prepared to spend the last *sou* for the consolation of his love.

As soon as his work was done he hurried to her apartment. Often he was weary with grappling with the plans which must be prepared; often perplexed by the problems which confronted him without any visible solution. His mistress received him with an embrace, drew off his coat, drew off his boots, drew him gently down to the sofa, put up his feet and brought him a glass of champagne. Then, sitting on a footstool beside him, she would soothe his hot brow with her cool hands while he discussed his problems with her. It was even more banal than these words!

But among the reorganized units of the French armed forces special attention was being paid to secret service. French espionage and counterespionage had once been among the most successful secret services in Europe. But after the great heights to which Napoleon I's spy master, Schulmeister, had brought it, it had fallen into decay, like many other institutions of the empire. Now it had been decided that Stieber must be fought with his own weapon.

So, before many months had passed, the general's and the baroness' idyl was brought to a rude termination by the intervention of the deadly prosaic *deuxième bureau*. The bureau had discovered that Stieber had become aware of the Hamburg liaison and when the general had returned to France and been appointed to high office he had threatened the baroness with the promise of awful consequences to her family if she would not agree to go to Paris and renew her *affaire* with her admirably situated lover.

This was perhaps the one occasion on which Stieber's flair for reading character let him down. There was no need for threats. The basis of the baroness' relationship with the general was purely sensual. On that account she could even overlook the little matter of his being French. She was quite prepared to do as Stieber asked so long as he made it worth her while. Delighted with such sweet reasonableness, Stieber, who was never stingy with his agents, excelled himself in the allowance he gave her.

So she had come to Paris, and before she was deported at the instance of the *deuxième bureau* she had supplied Stieber with such full information regarding French plans and intentions that the French never recovered the lost ground and revenge had to be forgotten.

Stieber employed many women among his agents: barmaids, waitresses, domestic servants and prostitutes. The Baroness de Kaulla was not the only women of aristocratic antecedents, if no less doubtful morals, whose name figured on his payroll, though she is, perhaps, the most famous of them.

After the Franco-Prussian War had terminated, Stieber set about organizing a system of permanent resident spies abroad on a scale never before conceived.

Waiters in foreign hotels, workers in factories, hairdressers, itinerant German bands, prostitutes of particular skills which

made them attractive to the jaded sexual palates of high-ranking naval and military personnel and civil servants, all had
their place in his organization. Money was poured into the
project on a scale comparable—when the results achieved by
both in their effect on world activities in their own day and
age are taken into account—with the vast sums being spent
by the American government on atomic research. All Europe
was aware of the existence of Stieber's secret army, impressed
and frightened by it; and, for the most part, did little to
counteract it.

Within Prussia itself Stieber's secret police were almost as
numerous, and certainly as ubiquitous. There were many citi-
zens who were discontented with the doctrine known as the
"Prussian Idea." This doctrine aimed at suppressing completely and utterly the liberty of the individual. (Had the
Nazis any really new ideas and practices at all?)

Many victims of the "Idea" could visualize only one way
of restoring individual freedom—the permanent removal of its
chief exponents: the emperor and his chancellor. In his later
years Stieber, as minister of police, was constantly being
called on to protect his masters from assassination. To deal
with this situation Stieber introduced yet another of his innovations, a diabolical plan but one which illustrates how clearly
he understood the characters and weaknesses of his enemies.

In Berlin Stieber set up an establishment to which he gave
the name, The Green House. To say that it was a brothel
owned by the minister of police and therefore enjoying complete police protection may be startling enough. But Stieber's
Green House was much worse, much more evil than a brothel.

Selecting his permanent staff with great care, he chose
women skillful in pandering to all known male sexual aber-
rations and capable of responding with equal skill to any that
might be conjured up by a particularly abnormal imagination
or craving. Besides such women, he enlisted the services of
boys and men, and those knowledgeable in the use of drugs
such as opium and hashish.

Then choosing his clientéle with equal care, he introduced to The Green House men in high positions, judges, front-rank civil servants, leaders of society, including at least one royal prince, and men whom his underworld grapevine had informed him either were or were suspected of being anti-monarchist conspirators or opponents of the "Prussian Idea." No man could visit this establishment without an introduction from Stieber.

He did not necessarily give the introduction himself, but selected his victim and had the existence of The Green House brought to his notice; in the case of a man whom he knew to have unusual appetites by one of his lesser minions approaching him in a quiet, dark street and, after a brief muttered conversation, thrusting a card of introduction into his hand; or by one of his own high officers, who would strike up an acquaintance with the man and at the close of a convivial evening suggest a visit to a new brothel he knew of.

These latter victims were generally normal men. If they refused the invitation once, a kind of pressure was put on them until they did accept. But Stieber has said that very few did not take up the first invitation.

The madame of The Green House had already been primed as to the guest's special proclivities. If he was already indulging in any depraved behavior he was matched with a partner skilled in that special behavior, and who could intensify his appetites by allied but more advanced wantonness.

Men of normal appetites were allowed to satisfy themselves normally and then, little by little, they would be introduced to variations from the normal until eventually, scarcely conscious of what was happening to them, they would suddenly discover that without the ministrations of The Green House they could not be satisfied. The same pattern was followed with those who were drug addicts already, while those who were not were transformed into addicts.

Briefly, Stieber took the depraved and thrust them ever deeper into depravity; while he took the normal and turned them into depraved beasts. Once the transformation had been achieved he began to turn the screw.

There was nowhere else in Berlin, nowhere else in Germany, perhaps nowhere else in Europe, where the habitués of The Green House could obtain the relief they could get there. When this point was reached, Stieber suddenly confronted them and threatened both to cut off supplies and facilities and to let their families and friends know what they were doing, unless—

The "unless" in the case of civil servants meant revealing all the secrets of their departments, knowledge of which would place Stieber in a position of power in Prussia second only to, if not on a par with, Bismarck himself. In the case of antimonarchists and those opposed to the "Prussian Idea," it meant identifying their fellows and their conspiracies.

There were a few who preferred to commit suicide rather than to betray, but these, compared with those who told Stieber all they knew, and acquired information for him, were an infinitesimal number. Though Stieber has admitted in his *Reminiscences* that he could have acquired the information by normal espionage, the success of The Green House exceeded all his hopes. He maintains that The Green House was quicker and surer than normal methods, and that he could never have obtained the power over the individuals that he did acquire in any other way.

The Green House was one of Stieber's later innovations. He outlived William I and remained in office after Bismarck had been dismissed.

Some time before he retired and settled down to write his *Reminiscences*, after fifty years' service as a spy, he received in 1876 a visit from some strange little men with almond shaped eyes who had come from the other side of the world.

They had come to him, they said, because they had been told by Prussian officers who were helping to organize and train their army, that Prussia had the finest espionage system in the world. Where they lived, they also had enemies, and they realized that their main protection against those enemies would be to know their intentions and secrets. This they might achieve only by espionage. But they had no espionage system; and if they were to organize such a system, naturally it would be foolish not to have the best. Would he advise them, and perhaps teach them his system?

Stieber, though a Saxon by birth, was a Prussian by environment and inclination. He had all the Prussian arrogance and pride, and a weakness for flattery. His *Reminiscences* are most revealing of traits. But his pride in his espionage system was not without justification, and the Japanese had not erred in going to him. Stieber would advise the Japanese; he would explain to them his espionage system in all its ramifications, even The Green House.

He found them apt pupils, and before he died in 1892 he had seen them introduce his system, with modifications and even some innovations, into their sphere of influence as effectively as he had battened down Europe with his own spies and counterspies.

CHAPTER **3**

Background to Espionage

While Wilhelm Stieber was defending his underdogs in the petty courts of Berlin and saving his king from the violence of the Berlin mob, while he rode through Austria peddling his sacred statuettes and his pornographic drawings and was counting the chickens of Farmer Lebrun in France, while he was learning the secrets of General de Cissy and trapping his opponents in the depravities of The Green House, on the other side of the world in an archipelago of islands known as Nippon, or the Land of the Rising Sun, a phenomenon was emerging.

Nippon, or Japan, as it was soon to become universally known, had been a secret land for many centuries. It had kept itself cut off from the rest of the world except for a few Dutch traders and some Buddhist monks who brought their religion from Korea.

It had an emperor who was considered by his people to be a god, and people who considered themselves to be children of the sun goddess. They believed that their country was the fairest on the earth, since it had been created by the gods, and themselves to be the chosen people of the gods, since they had been put there to inhabit it.

43

In the middle of the nineteenth century they were still a feudal state. But though the emperor was their grand seigneur, they were ruled by self-appointed tenants-in-chief, called shoguns. Below the shoguns were the lesser orders of tenants, the daimio, or barons, and the samurai, or knights, the hereditary bearers of arms. Below them came the serfs, the farmers, the merchants and the peasants. Their economy was tied to the rice production.

They were not an inspired people. They had taken their language, their form of writing, their philosophy, even one of their religions, from the ancient civilized Chinese. They had been torn by civil wars for more than four hundred and fifty years until, in 1600, the power was seized by a family called the Tokugawa, who, at the end of fifteen years of ridding themselves of their enemies, brought real peace at last to their country.

With peace, the Tokugawa shoguns reorganized the basis of their power, not on armed force, but by controlling the economy, by making the emperor even more of a recluse than he had ever been before, holding him completely incommunicado from all the daimio, and by clipping the power of the daimio by various means.

Peace brought inevitable changes to the social structure of the country, for it had a direct effect on the role of the samurai, the fighting men. Since the samurai were allowed to follow no other profession but arms, and since there was no longer any opportunity for practicing their profession because of the restrictions laid upon the daimio, their employers, they found themselves with nothing to do. The shoguns, therefore, encouraged them to turn to scholarship, and this in turn gave rise to an intellectual class, destined to produce a highly refined and artistic civilization.

Under the Tokugawa the merchants began to flourish as never before. Soon the wealth of the country began to flow into their hands and strict sumptuary laws had to be introduced to control them. But these laws they managed to evade, even as they evaded paying their taxes.

These new developments could very easily have undermined the authority of the shogunate. The Tokugawa shoguns realized this. Fearing most of all the conjunction of the internal changes with the few outside contacts they had, in 1639 the shogun closed Japan to all foreigners except the Chinese and the Dutch.

Now while the peace which the Tokugawa shoguns brought to the country provided suitable conditions for the development of a national culture, the strict closure of Japan to all foreigners had a restricting influence on the general development of the nation. For at this time Western culture was bursting into full flower, and the exclusion of those European merchants who had just begun to take an interest in this strange country denied to Japan the inevitable influences which they would have brought with them.

Eventually the country ran into financial difficulties. Forced loans were levied on the merchants and the coinage was debased, thereby creating inflation. The economy was soon completely undermined and the sufferings this brought with it led to agrarian uprisings.

In fact, everything was against the shoguns, and gradually a movement was created to end the exclusion of Western merchants, which was seen to be the cause not only of the economic disasters now falling on the nation, but of the general retarding of the nation's medical, scientific, artistic and military resources. But even without this internal movement, outside factors and influences would ultimately have broken down the barriers.

In the late eighteenth century the Russians were becoming more and more active on their Pacific seaboard and in Kamchatka, Sakhalin and the Kurile Islands. Then Western trade with this part of the world began to expand, accentuating Japan's position, which was further accentuated by the appearance of the steamship in the middle of the nineteenth century, with its need for bunkering facilities. But it was the Chinese defeat in the First British-Sino War which inserted the thin end of the wedge.

The shoguns were impressed, and though still determined to keep their country closed, in 1842 they did at least open up specific ports to foreign ships for taking on water and supplies.

The necessity for opening up Japan had been in the minds of the Americans ever since 1815, but it was not until 1846 that Commodore Biddle arrived in Edo Bay to attempt negotiations. The commodore's politeness the Japanese construed as weakness, and his mission failed.

Then on July 8th, 1853, Commodore Perry sailed into Edo Bay with a strong squadron. Going ashore with an impressive guard, he presented a letter from President Fillmore demanding trading rights, bunkering stations and protection for shipwrecked American sailors. Remaining with his squadron in the bay for a week so that the Japanese should have no mistaken ideas of American strength, he then sailed away, announcing that he would return in the spring of 1854 for an answer.

The American letter caused considerable consternation at the shogunate. So perturbed were the authorities that they took the unheard-of step of sending a translation of it to each daimio, asking for opinions. The daimio advice was that the demands should be resisted to the last degree, short of war. But when Perry returned in 1854 and made it quite clear that it was either a treaty or war, the Japanese yielded and on March 31st the Treaty of Kanagawa was signed.

Once opened to trade, it could only be a matter of time before foreign cultural influences made themselves felt. This process was hastened by the willingness of young samurai to risk death for a chance of acquiring knowledge, for an edict of 1636, forbidding all Japanese to leave Japan, was still in force.

Within a short time the Americans, English and French

had insisted on wider treaties. These, signed in 1858, granted to the United States, France and England the right to establish supply bases for their navies at Yokohama, Hakodate and Nagasaki.

Their signature was the sign for outbursts of antishogun and antiforeign feelings which were soon translated into actions. Those daimio who secretly had long been opposed to the Tokugawa shogunate defied the shogun's orders and went direct to the immured emperor. Foreigners were attacked and British and American officials assassinated. In 1863 the United States Legation at Edo was burned down.

In June of that year the shogun, who had been summoned to Kyoto by the emperor, was compelled to issue an imperial order to drive all the foreigners out of the country. One daimio, the lord of Choshu, attempted to obey the order and fired on ships passing through the Straits of Shimonoseki, which were in his demesne.

The British retaliated immediately by bombarding the capital of Satsuma. The following month, September, an Allied fleet destroyed the Choshu forts. Impressed by this, the Satsuma and Choshu daimio began to press for a policy of Westernization.

Under the pressure of these events the shogun was deprived of much of his authority. The process was continued until, in November 1867, the governing shogun, who had not long succeeded to the shogunate on the death of his father, handed his resignation to the young Emperor Meiji.

Early in January 1868 direct imperial rule was re-established and the former shogun was ordered to surrender all his demesnes. The new regime spent the first few years in making numerous changes in the administrative structure. The senior posts were divided among the court nobles and daimio, but the actual exercise of power came into the hands of a very capable and ambitious group of samurai. Thus, from the very beginning of her modern history, we see that the military clique were a great power in Japan.

On April 6th, 1868, the emperor, in an ancient ritual, announced a charter oath to the nation's ancestral gods and goddesses. This oath was entirely revolutionary in its concepts and paved the way for the reforms which were rapidly effected. Its fifth clause, by implication, forbade antiforeign feeling and activity and directly foreshadowed a policy of Westernization.

Important among the first reforms were those reorganizing the social structure, those permitting freedom of movement throughout the country to all, the right of farmers to plant any crops they wished, the right of every man to choose his own profession, the withdrawal of the right of vendetta from the samurai and the guarantee to all men, of whatever class, of equality before the law.

The social reforms abolished the military caste system, and this made it necessary for new armed forces to be developed. It was in this sphere that Western ideas were first adopted.

In our understanding of the Japanese character as we shall see it at work, we must take note very carefully of another tool forged in this period.

The religion which the Japanese had invented to meet the requirements of their beliefs about themselves, and which was peculiar to Japan, was known as Shintoism. We have referred briefly to the Japanese claim to be of direct divine descent. This cult was started by Jimmu, who made himself first emperor in 660 B.C. Jimmu claimed to be the great-great-great-grandson of the sun goddess, who was herself the daughter of the creators of heaven and earth.

When the earth was created out of chaos, the sun goddess's grandson was sent down, with a suitable retinue, to govern it, and made landfall on Mount Takachiho, in Japan, which was the first country to be formed. At the foot of this mountain Jimmu was born, and passed his youth and early manhood.

The emperors of Japan, including the present emperor,

Hirohito, have all, therefore, sprung from divine parentage; and despite the repudiation of divinity by Hirohito under orders from General MacArthur, vast numbers of his subjects still refuse, in 1956, to surrender what has been for them, for twenty-five centuries, one of the basic dogmas of their religion.

Since Japan was the first country to be created, this automatically made it the most beautiful country on earth, the country chosen by the gods before all others and, therefore, together with the person of the emperor, to be revered by its inhabitants.

The people themselves were also of divine descent, though in lesser degrees, since they were the descendants of the retinue of the grandson of the sun goddess when he came down to Mount Takachiho. This, of course, was as it should be, for only those of divine descent could be worthy inhabitants of the country chosen by the gods.

These ideas, as with the Hebrew concept of the chosen people, were kept flourishing by the national religion which sprang from them. Shintoism, which means The Way of the Gods, was accepted with unquestioning faith by all classes and ranks of Japanese. Its basic principles were ancestor worship and nature worship.

At the head of the deities—gods and goddesses who numbered many hundreds of thousands—was the sun goddess. After her, since they were her direct descendants, were all the past emperors and the present occupant of the imperial throne. Then came deified spirits of dead warriors and scholars who, by their deeds and works, had added glory to the country and people. After them came a man's own ancestors.

Mountains and rivers, earthquakes and storms, winds and seas, fire and floods—all that was beautiful and terrible in nature—were given their places in the divine hierarchy. They were worshiped with no less devotion and awe because they could be seen, touched and experienced.

So deeply ingrained in the national character did Shintoism become that when Korean missionaries brought Buddhism to Japan in the sixth century A.D., in order to impress the benefits of their religion on the Japanese people they decided to assimilate Shintoism rather than attempt to replace it. This was a brilliant move, for it made possible, two centuries later, what was the most wholesale, and most amazing, conversion in the religious history of mankind. The Japanese court, and the people *en masse*, accepted Buddhism—and at the same time continued to practice Shintoism.

From the late eighteenth century it had been a revival of Shintoism which had been one of the chief factors working for the overthrow of the shogunate. To concentrate the loyalty of the people on the emperor and government, there could clearly be no better device than a religion which was as ancient as the race and in its dogmas so ready-made to achieve this object. But to be most useful to the regime Shintoism had to be lopped of its Buddhist outgrowths, and an attempt was made to do this. It was soon discovered, however, that the two religions were so interlocked in the average Japanese mind that the attempt was dropped lest Shintoism should be harmed.

Instead, the authorities began attempts to establish a new state religion in which emphasis was placed on the divinity of the emperor. The attempts were extremely successful. By 1930 the new religion, known as State Shintoism, had more than 15,000 priests and more than 100,000 shrines, the chief of which was the Grand Shrine at Ise, dedicated to the sun goddess.

No matter to what religion he belonged, attendance at these shrines was the yardstick by which the loyalty of every Japanese to his emperor and country was measured. The educational system—originally modeled on the French, and subsequently on the German systems—and propaganda were employed to disseminate the state religion.

It had three basic tenets, and it is these which must be

constantly borne in mind in any consideration of Japan's activities from the Meiji Reformation in 1868 down to 1945. The tenets were:

1. The emperor is divine and derives his divinity from his great divine ancestors, possessing particularly the physical and spiritual attributes of the sun goddess.
2. The gods have Japan under their special protection. Therefore, its people and its very soil and every institution pertaining to it are superior to all others.
3. These attributes place upon Japan a divine mission to bring the whole world under one roof, so that all humanity may share the advantages of being ruled by the divine emperor.

In (3), in a nutshell, is Japan's foreign policy, for the fulfillment of which her domestic policy was fashioned and geared from the moment of awakening.

When Commodore Perry presented his ultimatum in 1853, Japan was 250 years behind the Western civilizations in almost every facet of national existence, and particularly so in her economic and industrial structure. The Meiji leaders realized the importance of having a modern economic structure, and realized too that this could only be based upon a modern industrial structure.

In the last years of its existence, the shogunate had arrived at something like the same point of view and before 1860 a shipbuilding yard and an arsenal had been established. By 1866 English cotton spinning machinery and technical instructors had been imported and a beginning had been made on the famous Yokusuka Naval Yard.

These establishments the Meiji leaders took over and added developments of their own—silk reeling, tiles, cement, woolens and bleaching powder, all of which were intended to be guides for future private enterprise. Postal and telegraph services were set up in 1871, and by 1893 2,000 miles of railway tracks had been laid. The Bank of Japan was founded in

1882, and within twenty-five years an extensive modern banking system was in full operation.

Almost it seems at the wave of a wand such an amazing advance had been made in the textile industry, due to cheap machinery and cheap female labor, that Japan was supplying one-quarter of the world's cotton yarn. An almost comparable advance was made in the heavy industries and the manufacture of machine tools. The merchant marine also expanded steadily and the shipbuilding industry was capable of building warships before the outbreak of World War I.

Side by side with these industrial and economic developments the army, under the expert tuition of German officers, and the navy, under no less expert guidance, had been transformed into fighting services almost equal to those of any Western power. The institution of these services rounded off the Japanese picture, so that we see the amazing phenomenon of a medieval state emerging completely as an industrial and military power within the space of a single generation.

Her new condition naturally produced for Japan a number of serious considerations. Overriding all, of course, was the injunction laid upon them by the third tenet of State Shintoism, to "bring the whole world under one roof"—the Japanese roof. No time limit had been set for the achievement of this by divine ordinance, but she now found that being a modern power placed cheek by jowl with the ancient conditions on the mainland of China presented her with responsibilities toward herself.

China had once been the great Asiatic power in the Pacific. Though now on her last legs, there were indications that she was not going to surrender her position to upstart Japan without a struggle, however ineffective that struggle might be.

A much more serious threat, however, came from the Russians in Siberia. Naturally, they saw in Japan a rival to the power which they themselves hoped to achieve, and had to a certain extent already achieved, in the northern Pacific.

They were even now regarding the confusion in Manchuria and Korea with conspiratorial eyes. An expansion of their influence in these countries would greatly weaken Japan's own position.

It was not only a weakening in her political position which Japan saw in the challenge of both China and Russia. If the influence of both or either, and particularly Russia, expanded, this would constitute a direct and serious threat to her economic position and strength. The Asian mainland was the obvious market near at hand for her products. If Russia should at any time exclude her from this market she would be dealt a blow that would stunt her growth, with very serious consequences.

So, both from the point of view of divine command and from the more realistic view of economic security, China and Russia were the obvious enemies. Not until the threat of both was removed would Japan be able to breathe freely in the direction of the Asiatic mainland. To remove the threat would require recourse to physical measures; in other words, there would have to be war. She had the army and the navy for this very purpose.

But while they were teaching her to organize and administer a modern army, her German helpers were also impressing on her the need for preparation before waging war; and a particular instrument of this preparation, as the Germans knew very well from personal experience, was espionage.

Japan was not entirely ignorant of espionage. Under the autocratic shogunate it had been absolutely necessary to employ agents to keep an eye on would-be rebels. Though she had cut herself off from the outside world, she had not been so foolish as to keep herself in ignorance of what was happening in China and had sent a few agents there. But this espionage was something quite different from the form and scope which the German military instructors were advising. There was soundness in their arguments, too. If Bismarck could build an empire using espionage as one of his chief agents, if Napoleon I had won his victories by careful espionage preparation, then Japan must have such an instrument to pave the way for her own future, inevitable warlike activities in Asia.

Since she would be beginning from scratch and had all the world to choose from, she could choose the best. And the best at this time in the field of espionage was Wilhelm Stieber's system. So, as we have seen, in the middle seventies they sent pupils to Stieber, and he and his assistants taught them all they knew about espionage.

The Japanese in every other aspect of their development had been copyists entirely, though copyists *par excellence*. Wilhelm Stieber had been an inventor and innovator in the realm of espionage, up to this time without peer. Yet, curiously enough, the Japanese were to introduce innovations into the art of spying which were to outclass some of Stieber's; and one of the most important of these innovations was the patriotic societies.

CHAPTER 4

Accent on Patriotism

Fuzzo Hattori was fifteen years old. He was a child of the New Japan, having been born in 1878.

His father was an artisan employed in the Yokusuka Naval Yard, skilled with his hands but not overintelligent.

His mother was the daughter of a small shopkeeper and still bore the traces of her young beauty, though she was long past the age when Japanese women surrender themselves to the care of their families rather than to the pleasures of their husbands. She was an obedient wife. She had been brought up to be that. She was content if she could feed and clothe her children. That was the sum total of her ambitions for, like her husband, her intellect was not sharp.

As often happens in the union of a not wildly intelligent couple, one member of the family, the fourth son, the young Hattori, was quick-witted, keen-minded, deep-thinking. Though only in his early teens, he had for some time been displaying these surprising qualities.

One spring day in 1893—the retired Wilhelm Stieber was at this time coming to the end of his *Reminiscences* and of his life—Fuzzo Hattori, in a brief period of leisure, took his new kite to the park for its maiden trials. It was not good weather to give the kite a fair test, for the breeze was light, and he had not properly gauged his toy's balance. As he struggled with it with growing annoyance, attempting to correct its erratic sideways oscillation, suddenly a voice behind him said: "Let me try, young man."

Turning, Hattori saw a little plump gentleman smiling at him and holding out his hand for the string.

"If you wish, sir," the boy answered, and gave the little gentleman the string. But the little gentleman was no more successful than he had been.

"Did you make it yourself?" the stranger asked presently.

"Yes, sir."

"You've got the thing top-heavy. You must shave the support at the top. I used to be an expert maker of kites when I was a boy. Come home with me and I'll show you how to do it."

The boy hesitated. He had heard of boys being picked up in parks by middle-aged gentlemen. He wasn't like that. He already had his eye on his neighbor's thirteen-year-old third daughter, who visited him in his sleep and did unrelatable things to him.

"Oh, come!" the stranger said, as if reading his thoughts. "You have nothing to fear from me. I have six sons of my own." And he smiled his smile and the boy was reassured, and a few minutes later he was taking his first ricksha ride, sitting beside the little gentleman.

"What is your name?" the man asked.

"Fuzzo Hattori, sir."

"Mine is Mitsuri Toyama."

Toyama watched the boy to see if his name meant anything to him and saw that it did not.

At the house, Toyama took the boy into his study, and for the next hour they worked together on the kite; and as they worked, the man questioned the boy about his parents and his home, his work and his interests, and made the discovery

which the older Hattoris had made—that for the son of a
poor family the boy was a freak, that he had brains.

When at last the boy had to go, Toyama invited him to
come to his house again, and there was something in the man
which unconsciously attracted the boy. He promised to return. In a short time the visits became weekly occurrences,
and later, twice or thrice weekly. On these visits Toyama
would offer the boy tea and he would talk. As he talked, the
boy listened attentively. Toyama spoke of the new Japan,
and of the third tenet of State Shintoism, and of the future
that lay ahead.

"We must bring the benefits of our divine emperor's rule
and our own superior way of life to all the other people of
the world," Toyama said. "It is the will of the gods. It will
take a long time and will be a hard struggle, for our enemies
will resist with all their might. So we must make a start now
and use every effort to prepare ourselves for joining battle."

The boy nodded, and the man went on: "First we must
make ourselves strong and rich and powerful. This we shall
do by building up our industries and our army and navy.
But while we are doing this we must also be finding out all
we can about our enemies."

And on another occasion: "Every Japanese man and
woman must dedicate himself and herself to this task. Every
woman by bearing and rearing all the children which her
husband can beget upon her. In this way we shall have the
people for our factories and our armies."

Toyama's precept was so heeded by the people that between 1874 and 1913, that is, in a generation and a half, the
population of the Japanese archipelago rose from 27,000,000
to 51,000,000, or nearly double. In the old days Japanese
women had been the most successful and extensive practi-
tioners of birth control at a time when the women of the
West, even the prostitutes, were for the most part ignorant
and innocent of any feminine method of contraception, and

the men only knew *coitus interruptus*, which the majority of
them refused to practice.

Toyama went on: "Every man must devote all his talents
and his energies to the help of the fatherland. He must do
so not in any spirit of seeking rewards for himself. His reward will be when he holds, subject to his will and to his
favors, all the other peoples of the world."

The picture he painted was an inspiring one, and with all
that he said the boy found himself in full agreement and was
prepared to dedicate himself to his country.

"First," said Toyama, "we must control those enemies
nearest to us. China is decadent and weak and will cause no
trouble. But Russia is another matter. She recognizes the
weakness and decadence of China and intends to expand her
own influence over that foolish country. It is Russia whom
we must first subdue, and to do this it is now that we must
begin to discover her weaknesses."

Then one day the boy made a discovery. He could not
get to Toyama's house quickly enough, and when he arrived
he burst into his friend's study and threw himself at his feet.

"Honorable sir! Why did you not tell me?" he asked.

Toyama put out his hand and, cupping the boy's chin,
lifted up his face.

"What should I have told you?" he asked in his turn,
smiling.

"That you are the founder of *Genoysha*," the boy said.

He beckoned the boy to the cushions beside him.

"Yes," he said. "I am the founder of *Genoysha*."

Half a dozen years before, in the late 1880's, Mitsuri Toyama had hit upon the means of putting into practice his
theories of discovering the weaknesses of the Russians. Calling together a number of his rich and influential friends, to
whom he expounded his ideas, he invited them to join in
the founding of a patriotic society which would put his
thoughts into deeds.

Without a single dissentient, his friends agreed, and there

came into being the first example of one aspect of Japanese espionage organization, though it has a near relationship with the revolutionary societies which flourished in Russia under the later tsars. As time passed these patriotic societies, as they were called, were to become one of the most important features of Japanese espionage activities.

Toyama and his friends gave their society the name of *Genoysha*, which means The Black Ocean Society. They took the name from the strip of water which separates Kiyushu from the mainland and is called *Genkainada*, the Black Sea. The patriotic societies were secret only insofar as their specific activities were concerned. They were known to the public and their general objects were proclaimed, but their methods and their results were jealously guarded from the public eye and ear.

"Tell me about *Genoysha*," Hattori said.

"*Genoysha*," replied its founder, "has an eight-pronged program which is aimed at discovering and exploiting the weaknesses of our enemies the Russians. If I tell you more, you must swear by the sun goddess herself that you will never divulge what I say to another living soul."

"I swear by the sun goddess, our divine emperor and by all my ancestors!" Hattori assured him solemnly.

"In Sinkiang and Russian Central Asia, we have been told," Toyama went on, "the people are in great distress because of the financial and taxation policies of the administration. The people are unsettled and have many grievances. We have sent men, whom we have trained, into these areas to discover the true facts and how, if they prove to be true, we may use them for setting the people against their masters.

"Other men we have sent to study the agricultural system of that region and how it may be improved. When the society is satisfied that this, too, can be used as a weapon against the Russians, we shall contribute money which will be used to ensure a progressive development there. As soon as the people see what we can do for them they will turn to Japan for guidance and forsake the Russians. Naturally, the Russians will resist, but with the people on our side Japan's task will be easier.

"Yet other men we have sent to explore the defenses of Russia, Tibet, Burma and India in Central Asia. At the same time they are to study and report on the conditions of the roads.

"All our agents, as we call them, on whatever work they are engaged, are to seek out and make friends with the Moslem and Buddhist priests in those areas. Through them, when the time comes for Japan to begin her struggle, we shall have the support of their followers. They are also to make contact with the local and Chinese nomadic groups for the same purpose, and with important personages who may be useful to us."

He paused and looked at the boy, who was regarding him in wonder.

"It is a great work," Hattori said. "I should like to be an agent of *Genoysha*."

So the day had come at last, the day for which Toyama had been working ever since that afternoon when, while helping the boy with his kite, he discovered him to be intelligent, quick-witted and serious.

"And so you shall," he said simply. "How old are you now?"

"I am sixteen and one month, sir."

"When you are seventeen you can begin."

And for the rest of Hattori's visit they laid plans.

Within a month Hattori had married the third daughter of his neighbor, and Toyama, who gave as his wedding gift a sum of money such as Hattori's father had never dreamed of and a promise of a monthly payment should Hattori ever have to go "on a journey" for him, was present at the festivities.

"She is made for childbearing," Toyama whispered to the

young husband when he had seen the fourteen-year-old bride prepared for the bridal bed.

She was fertile, too. Within nine months she gave to Japan her first son. As she lay in her husband's arms on his seventeenth birthday, she confessed to her lord in a whisper that though she was suckling her one-month-old son she was pregnant again.

Three days later her husband "went on a journey," and they were not to see each other again for five long years.

When he left his wife, Hattori went to the house of Mitsuri Toyama, and from there they went together to the headquarters of the Black Ocean Society. Waiting for them were half a dozen men whom Hattori had never seen before, solemn men who greeted them silently with bows.

"I present to you Fuzzo Hattori," Toyama said, "who has expressed the wish to work for our society to the greater glory of Japan and our divine emperor. If it is your pleasure, I will administer the oath to him."

"Does he know our rules and what is expected of him, and does he believe himself to be strong enough in body and in spirit to carry out the tasks we shall set him?"

The speaker was a little, bent man, whose kimono was worn and as old-looking as himself.

"I have instructed him myself, honorable sir," Toyama replied.

"Then if you are satisfied, we are satisfied," the old man exclaimed to a chorus of grunts of approval.

Toyama turned to the boy, his face solemn, his voice quivering slightly with emotion which one would normally have believed him to lack, and said: "Fuzzo Hattori, you face now the most solemn moment of your life. I have spoken to you about all that will be required of you. I have treated nothing as a triviality. If you should have doubts about your desire to undertake all that we shall ask, now is the time to say so. We shall think no worse of you if you withdraw now; but if you decide to go on and then find that your vocation is not a true one, for our protection death may be the only solution."

Without hesitation, the young man answered: "I have no doubt, honorable sir, that my vocation is a true one. But if it should happen not to be, then I should wish for death, which would be preferable to loss of face."

Toyama held out his hand and took Hattori's.

"Very well," he said. "Repeat after me, in the presence of these witnesses, this solemn oath."

And firmly, without faltering, giving the impression that he was transfixed with the sense of his mission, Hattori repeated the oath.

"I swear by the sun goddess, by our divine emperor who is the high priest of the Grand Shrine of Ise, by my ancestors, by Mount Fujiyama the sacred, by all the rivers and seas, by all the storms and floods, that I here and now dedicate myself to the service of the emperor and my country, without seeking personal reward except the merit I shall lay up for myself in heaven. And I solemnly swear that I will never divulge to any living man except those who are set in authority over me, whom I will obey though they may order me to kill myself, anything that the society may teach or show me, or anything which I shall learn or discover in any place where I may be sent or find myself. If I break this oath, may my ancestors disown me and may I pass eternity in hell."

When Toyama unclasped his hand Hattori bowed to the assembled men. They returned his bow in silence. No one wished him good fortune; no one sent him on his way with a kindly word of encouragement. He bowed again to Toyama, turned and left the room.

The first stage of his journey brought him to Sappiro, in Hokkaido, the northernmost island of the archipelago. Here he reported at a school which the Black Ocean Society had established for the training of agents.

On the Asiatic mainland, the society had founded a headquarters at Hankow and another establishment on Russian territory, an ostensible jujitsu school at Vladivostok. In 1893 a member of the headquarters staff had been transferred from Hankow to Sappiro, as it was thought that with a central school of this nature, situated on the security of their native soil, the agents under training would make more rapid progress than they did under conditions which restricted their leisure moments.

At the Sappiro school Hattori concentrated upon learning Chinese and the dialect of the area to which he was to be sent. Besides this there were courses in jujitsu, in the art of deception, in security and in the Japanese equivalent of intelligence.

At the end of eighteen months he was regarded as sufficiently trained to be sent out on his mission. But before he went into the "field" he must report to headquarters in Hankow for his final briefing—and a special course of conditioning.

Attached to the headquarters at Hankow was what was called The Hall of Pleasurable Delights. It was a much more attractive name than Stieber's Green House in Berlin, and it had a multipurpose character.

Within The Hall, every oriental version of all the vices could be experienced. Set up originally for the purpose for which Stieber had founded The Green House—the obtaining of intelligence by blackmail from decadent Chinese notables—its second function was to serve as a meeting place for agents operating in Sinkiang and Russian Central Asia.

Once he had entered the field, the agent was never again to contact any of his superiors directly except on their instructions. Any agent who had a report to make was to go to The Hall of Pleasurable Delights, engage the services of a prostitute and hand to her his report. She would know what to do with it, and there is no more secret place for handing over a report than a bed.

But The Hall of Pleasurable Delights had a third purpose.

In the West, in these modern times, it is the fashion to discount sex as a weapon of espionage. Gone, they say, are the days of Delilah and Mata Hari. Men, they say, are now more conditioned to sex and are unlikely to reveal their secrets under its influence. Then in the next breath they contradict themselves and forbid their agents to indulge in promiscuity while engaged on a mission, since there is no greater danger to, no more certain undermining influence of, security.

The Japanese, on the other hand, have never been so muddleheaded. They knew that if they laid upon their agents an injunction to refrain from dalliance they would be obeyed, so deep-rooted was the discipline, the devotion to duty, with which their men were imbued. But they knew, too, that enforced celibacy of this kind can be harmful to a man's morale, particularly when the opportunity is to hand. So, in The Hall of Pleasurable Delights they prepared their agents for every variation from the norm of conventional sexual behavior he might be likely to meet, and taught him special skills by which he might acquire the confidence—here synonymous with *love*—of women able to aid him in his mission.

With agents who were to have the "cover" which Hattori was to have, there was yet a further reason why a course in The Hall of Pleasurable Delights was essential. Any man who is to peddle pornographic literature and drawings will be all the more successful if he had been conditioned to pornographic activities in the flesh.

For this had been chosen as Hattori's "cover." He was to emulate Stieber. He was to go into the towns and villages, the cottages and tents of Sinkiang as a Chinese peddler of pornographic drawings and—no, not sacred statuettes, but something even more efficacious for the health of the body than the soul—bottles of Black Ocean Panacea, guaranteed to cure all ills from ingrowing toenails to epilepsy.

For five years the boy whose kite had started it all sold his filthy pictures and his nasty medicine, talked with Moslem qadis and Buddhist monks, made love to the daughters of local headmen, talked of defense works and roads and the grievous burden of taxation and oiled the palms of men whom he believed would be useful to his masters. Once he returned to The Hall of Pleasurable Delights to report, once to the jujitsu school at Vladivostok.

The latter he found to be an even greater success than The Hall of Pleasurable Delights. Those who were responsible for it knew that they would never attract the stupid Russians unless a course of twenty lessons in jujitsu included, free of charge, twenty hours of dalliance with the most practiced female dispensers of delight in the Orient, and the most cunning wheedlers of information in the pay of the Black Ocean Society.

But in addition to being a machine for acquiring intelligence, the jujitsu school was the base for Black Ocean agents in eastern and central Siberia, especially those deployed along the route of the Trans-Siberian Railway, which was then in the process of being built. In this aspect of its work, it was far more successful than the Hankow school. Its personnel were now supplied exclusively by the Sappiro training school which, in its *métier*, was so successful that from its foundation it never lost a single agent except from natural causes.

When he arrived in Vladivostok in 1898 Hattori found congregating there and almost ready to set out, a photographic expedition—disguised, naturally—whose destination was Khabarovsk, the most important Russian center after Vladivostok. It had been trained and sent by the Sappiro school and was the second such expedition, the first having successfully completed its mission in the previous year. Hattori would have liked to accompany them, but his new assignment called for his return to Russian Central Asia. When he returned from this mission in 1900 he found his recall to Japan waiting for him.

Back in the fatherland he became private secretary to Toyama and begat on his nineteen-year-old wife nine more children before she prematurely reached the change of life at thirty-five. Then, so that his patriotism should never be in doubt, he took a concubine, a young girl of thirteen, by whom he produced six more children for the emperor before his own powers began to fail, when he handed her over to his second son.

The case of Hattori is by no means a special one. In the same way that Toyama had sought him out and influenced him, so the other members of the Black Ocean sought out suitable "agent material," played upon their patriotic feelings with great skill and eventually inveigled them into the service of the society.

Thus, like Hattori, every agent of the society was hand picked, and though none perhaps had quite the same advantage as Hattori in becoming the favorite of Toyama, they worked with a selflessnes which to our Western eyes is almost unbelievable. Probably no other espionage organization in the world has had such loyalty, such devotion or such patriotism in its agents, or such material to work upon.

Hattori sets the stamp; all the others were molded in his likeness, as he was molded in the likeness of those who had preceded him.

2

The founding of the Black Ocean Society set the fashion for other patriotic societies with diversified objects but one main aim—to discover and work upon the weaknesses of the Chinese and the Russians.

Two smaller societies which were founded shortly after the Black Ocean amalgamated in 1898 to form the East Asia One-Culture Society. As its name implies, it operated ostensibly in the cultural field. Its pronounced aim was to formulate and spread a common system of writing, and on this a Sino-Japanese *rapprochement* was to be formed. Its activities, however, were not confined to China.

A school was founded in Shanghai known as the Tung

Wen College, which was to train members for work in East Asia. By 1908 the college had no fewer than 272 graduates working in China, Burma, India, Annam, the Philippines and Mongolia. In 1937 it was still functioning. By then it was occupying buildings of Chiaotung University and was supported by army funds. Its real activities were widely known and the Chinese openly referred to it as the Japanese spy college. In 1939 it had four thousand members and was still extremely active at the time of the capitulation in 1945.

One of the outstanding members of its staff was reputed to be a certain Qurban Ali. Qurban Ali had come to Japan in 1924 at the invitation of Ki Inukai, one of the founders of the college. He had already a long record of subversive activity against the Soviet Union and had been prominent in Manchuria. He was an expert in Turki, and became an instructor in Turki languages at the Tokyo Military College. Later he transferred to the Tun Wen College where, besides languages, he also gave instruction in the technique of subversive tactics.

But the most important of all patriotic societies was the Black Dragon Society, founded in 1901 by Ryohei Uchida. It derived its name from the Amur or Black Dragon River, which forms the boundary between Manchuria and the Soviet Union. Again the name gives the hint of its chief aim —to drive all the Russians back across the Amur River, out of Manchuria and Korea, and wherever else they might be in the Pacific, outside Siberia. In other words, its activities were to be directed toward waging war with Russia; and its aim was the success of Japanese arms in that war.

All its charter members were already experienced in espionage in continental Asia. Uchida had organized the Black Ocean's jujitsu school at Vladivostok; Sugiyama had been director of The Hall of Pleasurable Delights in Hankow; until he died at a ripe old age in 1944, Mitsuri Toyama, the archpatriot, founder of the Black Ocean, was for many years adviser to the Black Dragon besides being the director of the

Imperial Rule Assistance Association, Japan's official, unified political organization.

In 1944 the Black Dragon had an estimated membership in excess of ten thousand and had a long record of activity which spanned such widely separated points of the globe as the United States and Latin America to Ethiopia and North Africa. Among its members, up to its dissolution, it had an unknown number of high government officials including at least one prime minister, Koki Hirota.

The last president of the Black Dragon was Yoshihisu Kurusu, who was also a director of the Imperial Rule Assistance Association. It was Kurusu, and not an official of the government, who on June 3rd, 1943, broadcast to President Roosevelt and Mr. Churchill the threat of the dire consequences which would overtake the Allied forces if they did not surrender unconditionally to Japan. This was an indication of the tremendous power which the society exerted throughout its career.

The Black Dragon, like the other patriotic societies, maintained its own establishments. In Tokyo it had two schools which catered to all aspects of espionage under the cover of innocuous sounding names: the Nationalists' Training Academy, at whose head in 1944 was Giichi Fukushima; and the Tokyo and Osaka Foreign Language School.

Among the lesser but still important societies was *Dai-A-Gi Kai*, The Reawakening of Greater Asia Society. Founded in 1908, it had a fourfold program which included the study of economic, geographical, educational, colonial and religious conditions and organizations in China and Central Asia, the sending out of agents, the founding of branch societies and the dissemination of oral and printed propaganda. At the beginning of its existence its headquarters were in Mukden, but after the Chinese revolution of 1911 it moved to Manchuria. It had branches throughout China, in Siam, Afghanistan, Turkey, Persia and India.

Of later patriotic societies the White Wolf and the Turan

Societies are important. The former was founded in 1924 and seems to have evolved from the arrival in Japan, three years earlier, of a representative of the Pan-Turan Society of Budapest. The Turan Society was the offspring, born in 1933, of the union of certain elements of the Black Ocean and Black Dragon Societies. The White Wolf and the Turan Societies were both probably affiliated with the Gray Wolf Society of Turkey and the Pan-Turan Society of Budapest, both of which were composed predominantly of Moslem refugees from Russia, particularly Russian Turkestan.

There is an ancient belief that the Turkic and Mongol peoples had a common ancestor in the White and Gray She Wolf. The stress of these two societies was, therefore, racial rather than religious, and the ultimate aim of their subversive activities against Soviet Russia was the establishment of an independent Pan-Turkic and Pan-Islamic state in Central Asia. They had a dual interest for Japan. Any trouble they could cause Russia was worthy of being encouraged, and control of them would ensure Japan's complete authority on the Asian continent, when the day came.

3

Though the patriotic societies were private and independent of each other they were, nevertheless, related to one another and to the Japanese government by various ties. We have seen, for example, that Mitsuri Toyama, who was the hero of every Japanese expansionist both inside and outside the government, was the founder of the Black Ocean and adviser to the Black Dragon. There were also Chinashi Hirayama and Choichi Kaji, who, while being charter members of the Black Dragon, also helped to organize and subsequently advise the East Asia One-Culture Society. Though not actually members, two very prominent party leaders, Shigenobu Okuma and Ki Inukai, collaborated in many of the undertakings both of the Black Ocean and Black Dragon.

All the societies—and there were many others to which reference has not been made, since their influence tended to be local and their activities more restricted—placed the emphasis on patriotism. Nevertheless, they shared a common, predatory purpose—the control of Asia (and eventually the world) and the bestowal of Japanese cultural, economic and administrative benefits on all those unfortunates who were not descended from the sun goddess and her retinue.

They permeated the political life of the entire nation and exerted a continuous and extremely powerful pressure on the exponents of Japanese aggression. They did this in a variety of ways. They helped those sympathetic with their aims to high government or army posts; they eliminated those who opposed them. It is notorious and true that almost every political assassination in Japan during the thirties and forties—and there were many—could all be linked with our friend Mitsuri Toyama, though the links might be such that had he ever been arraigned before the courts the evidence against him would never have secured a conviction.

The societies recruited their members from every walk of life. They demanded, first and foremost, extreme zeal for the ideas and ideals which they represented. Should such zeal be lacking, no matter how outstanding the other qualities and qualifications of the applicant might be, he was rejected. It was this extreme zeal which made the societies both important and dangerous beyond the boundaries of Japan.

Those members chosen for the more important work were trained in languages and subversive tactics. These represented the cream of the rank and file. The milk, however, was also regarded as an equally essential ingredient. To it was assigned the role of collecting information, and it was composed of shopkeepers, tourists, salesmen of literature and pornographic drawings and medicine, wrestling instructors, fishermen, businessmen, students of Islam and of the English language, professors, priests and archeologists.

The whole approach to espionage was based firmly on patriotism. No reward was offered to the agent and none was expected, except the merit which his activities would lay up for him with the gods. Thus, the records of the societies are packed with the biographies of "little" men who earned a place of honor by their unspectacular, unobtrusive lifetime of devotion to their particular brand of patriotism. What they learned and passed on to their leaders was by their leaders passed on to the government or to the military forces, into whoever's jigsaw the "piece" most snugly fitted.

In a country such as Japan which has an age-old military tradition and which, in modern times, indulged in peacetime conscription, it is never possible to draw a clear line of distinction between civilian and fighting man. In the same way, it is not always possible to separate the activities and functions of the patriotic societies from those of military intelligence. Throughout the whole of this period of Japan's history there was a close cooperation between the work of the societies and formal intelligence; and their activities were more often than not complementary.

In 1932 the patriotic societies—note, *not* the government—decided that the Moslem policy must be more vigorously implemented than hitherto and that it must be applied to a much more extensive field in the Near and Middle East.

Wakabayashi and Tanaka, who were protégés of Mitsuri Toyama and Ryohei Uchida and, following in Araki's footsteps, ostensible converts to Islam, were given the task of making the new policy effective. They enlisted the official support of General Araki and General Isogai. This was immediately forthcoming, with the result that groups of officers were taught the various languages of the Moslem groups and instructed in Islam. A number of the apparent converts subsequently made annual pilgrimages to Mecca. There they set up their tents among those pilgrims whose languages they spoke, and it was the easiest thing in the world to give and receive hospitality under cover of which they made useful contacts, spread propaganda and obtained useful intelligence with great success.

It would be wrong to suppose that all the agents of the patriotic societies were army officers. Admittedly, a high proportion of them were drawn from the armed services, though this was incidental to the soldiers being members of the societies. Reciprocally, the societies supplied military intelligence with many of its best agents.

Nor were the societies supported only by the military. The foreign office also closely, though with the maximum of discretion, identified itself with the policy of infiltrating the Moslem communities by propaganda and by cultural means.

The diplomatic missions to Moslem countries became the training ground for Moslem experts. In 1944 secretaries at the Japanese embassies in Kabul and Ankara were nominees of patriotic societies.

The projects supported by the foreign office funds were many and various. Among them were the East Asia One-Culture Society's school, and the foreign language schools in Osaka and Tokyo. Agents were directly supplied with money either by the foreign office itself or by embassies, legations and consulates in the Moslem countries.

The patriotic societies were early in the field. The role they played in paving the way for the first great success of Japan's trial of strength with Russia was an outstanding one.

The Japanese could not tell when the moment would come when it would be either necessary or profitable to go against the Russians. For their own part, they were ready to wait until they had completed their preparations, and the longer the time given them for this the better chances they would have of success.

Fortunately the Russians, while encroaching little by little into Manchuria, were not anxious, it seemed, to force a quick decision. They had realized, as much as Japan had realized,

that there would have to be a combat between them before
an ultimate decision could be reached.

Like Japan, they also needed to make preparations. Their
preparations were of quite a different nature from Japan's.
They were separated from their base by many thousands of
miles, so they must build up their strength in Siberia in
order to become independent of European Russia once the
war had started.

They were now bending their efforts to this achievement.
To make movement of material and men more rapid, they
were building the Trans-Siberian Railway and planning railways south of the Amur River, both of which projects they
began to speed up in the nineties.

Such a railway, stretching across what to the eye appeared
to be limitless country for the most part uninhabited, and
where it was inhabited only sparsely so, would be vulnerable
to attack. Further, not only would it be vulnerable to attack,
but would obviously be one of the primary objectives of a
potential enemy. So while they were constructing the railway they were also building fortifications, erecting forts,
strengthening the few already existing and setting up a fortified line in some depth. In addition, they were reorganizing
and strengthening their naval bases at Port Arthur and all
the main centers such as Vladivostok and Khabarovsk. They
were locating stores, ammunition and weapons depots. They
were constructing new electrical powerhouses.

The Russians, however, had not learned the value of espionage in preparation for war and sent very few agents to
discover what the Japanese were doing. The Japanese, on
the other hand, while building up their war industries at
home and getting a foothold on the Asian mainland—in
Korea and parts of Manchuria—had large numbers of agents
watching and reporting on all that the Russians were doing.
There was nothing that escaped them in Asia, all the way
across Asia, and into European Russia itself.

CHAPTER 5

Preparations for the First Trial

One of the Siberian towns which had had its importance enhanced by the coming of the Trans-Siberian Railway
was Iman. By the end of the 1890's the Russians had converted
it into a military center and had set up and maintained there a
garrison whose task was not only to protect the railway but to
build up the fortifications in the surrounding area.

For some reason which is not made clear, Iman had not yet,
in 1897, received the attention of Japanese spies which its position and opportunities for obtaining vital information about
Russian activities and intentions here warranted; warranted,
that is to say, in the opinions of several perspicacious Japanese
patriots, among whom was Ryohei Uchida.

In 1897 Uchida was still a member of the Black Ocean Society. To his way of thinking, the society was not paying nearly
enough attention to that part of Siberia in which Iman was
situated. He was pondering this problem one evening as he
was riding home from a meeting of the society. At the meeting he had put a proposal before his fellow members that a
resident agent should be sent there without delay, and he had
been disappointed and angry at the cool reception it had
received.

He had pointed out that besides its importance as a Russian garrison town, Iman also lay across the lines of communication of at least five itinerant agents working in more distant regions, each of whom had to present his report periodically in person at the jujitsu school in Vladivostok. This not only took time but removed the agent from his area of activity temporarily; but while he was gone important things might happen and he would miss them.

If they put a resident agent in Iman, besides gathering information about the Russians' doings in the area he could also collect the reports of the itinerant agents and send them by special courier to Vladivostok. It seemed a logical thing to do and yet his proposal had met with a strange lack of interest and the argument that at the moment the society had no suitable agent to send there; and besides, there were places more important than Iman.

Like his superior and friend, Mitsuri Toyama, Uchida was constantly on the watch for men who might serve their country under Black Ocean's direction. As his ricksha boy strode out, silently and easily, making no sound, Uchida reflected what he would do if only he could find such a man now. Even while he was muttering silently to himself, the ricksha stopped before his house. He paid the boy off and strode down the path leading to the entrance. As he did so, he heard the boy's quiet voice calling after him.

At any other time Uchida would have dismissed the boy impatiently, convinced that he would only be begging. But he did not do that now. On an impulse he stopped and turned round and asked the boy what he wanted.

The boy moved toward him and he saw that the eyes, creased slightly in a respectful smile, were bright with intelligence, so bright as to be strange in a ricksha boy.

In a few words the boy explained that he had heard about the Black Ocean Society and knew that Uchida was an important member. He wished he could be a member of the society and serve his country in some special way.

Uchida regarded him closely as he spoke and saw that he was not the youth he had thought him to be but a young man perhaps in his middle twenties. He asked him into the house and questioned him. He learned that the young man's name was Choichi Hirayama, that he was twenty-six and that though he had been married for three years, fatherhood up to now had eluded him.

"What would you do to help your country?" Uchida asked him.

"Anything that might be required of me, sir."

"Would you leave Japan and go into far places and among strange people?"

"If it were asked, sir, willingly."

Uchida grunted and looked at the young man in silence for a moment or two and then, abruptly, told him to strip. Without question, Hirayama loosened the cord about his waist and pulled off his jacket and let his drawers fall about his feet.

Uchida looked at the strong arms and shoulders, the flat belly, the powerful thighs and calves, the almost sculptured muscles of the back and arms, and saw not just the lithe figure of a ricksha runner but the smooth strength of the wrestler. In every movement that he made there was the alertness of the wrestler, too.

For the moment Uchida was content to go no further, but asked Hirayama to return the following evening. In the meantime he was to tell no one, not even his wife, that he had spoken to him.

The next evening the young man returned, and for most of the time it was Uchida who talked. It was so on many following evenings. But each time a little more of the plan was laid, and soon it was the turn of Choichi Hirayama to take the oath which Mitsuri Toyama had administered to his protégé, the boy with the kite, Fuzo Hattori, less than a year ago.

Before this happened, however, Hirayama had begun his training. He had sold his ricksha on Uchida's instruction and

with Uchida's financial aid had become the assistant of Nakamura, the owner of a small general store. From the aging
storekeeper he learned quickly the secrets of buying and
selling, and no one was ever more sorry to lose so apt a pupil
and so hard-working an assistant as Nakamura when Hirayama announced that the next week he must leave him.

At the same time, Uchida had insisted that Hirayama's
weak wife should leave her bobbins in the Motomura Cotton Mills. As soon as she had only to attend to the wants of
her husband, the seventeen-year-old overworked girl began
to put on the flesh her still-growing body so sorely needed,
and before her husband took the oath to the Black Ocean
and went to the training school at Sappiro, he was the father
of twin sons.

Since in Iman Hirayama was to set himself up as a Japanese storekeeper, his stay at Sappiro was not prolonged.
When he had mastered enough spoken Russian to eliminate
any initial language difficulties and had acquired the rudi-
ments of appreciating any information which might come
his way and had grasped the intricacies of operating what is
known in espionage jargon as a "letter-box," a reception
center for the reports of and special instructions to agents,
he returned to Tokyo.

With money given him by Uchida from his private purse,
he laid in a stock of goods which the experts had advised
him would find favor with the inhabitants of Iman. These
he crated and labeled, and when at last all was ready he went
to say farewell to his "benefactor."

And Uchida was pleased with him. "You have done well,
Choichi Hirayama," Uchida said. "I expect, and know, I
shall receive great rewards from you. But this last warning
I must give you. From now on, you must expect no further
help from me. If you fail as a storekeeper you fail as an
agent. And no matter how well you may succeed, you will
receive no reward from your country but its gratitude, for

the merit you will acquire with the gods would make even
the greatest earthly reward seem paltry."

With that last warning, but with great contentment and a
still greater determination to succeed, Hirayama set sail for
Port Arthur accompanied by his twin sons and his wife and
the third child just moving in her womb.

The transformation which had taken charge of Hirayama's
life since the night he had had the great honor and greater
good fortune of taking Ryohei Uchida to his home had done
nothing to dim the flash of his dark eyes and the warmth of
his quick smile.

When he opened his store in Iman the inhabitants eyed
both him and his shop with curiosity. They stopped and
peered in, but only the more bold entered and made trial
purchases. In their remoteness they were suspicious of anything new, and especially new, strange people who came and
settled among them.

For a time Hirayama saw himself stalked by the shadow
of failure, and doubts began to assail him as to the ability he
believed himself to have, under Uchida's coaching and old
Nakamura's cunning tuition, of attracting customers and
then winning their friendship.

He was pondering his problem one morning in his empty
store as he broke open a crate of goods which had newly
arrived. It was warm, and as he paused in his hammering he
took off his jacket. As he struggled with the fastenings of
the chest sweat broke out on his body and lit up the muscles
of his back and shoulders and arms until they looked like
polished stone.

With his back to the door of his shop, he did not see or
hear the entrance of Madame Gregorieva, the wife of Captain Gregoriev of the Iman garrison, until, as he straightened
up to rest a while, he became aware of her sibilant breathing.

Captain Gregoriev was forty-three, slim to the point of
skinniness, though the military tailor in St. Petersburg cleverly
managed to disguise his lack of manly appearance. But the

tailor could not deceive Madame Gregorieva who, at twenty-one, after two years of marriage, wished she had chosen a man instead of a uniform for a husband.

In contrast to his wife, the captain was a very busy man. His work at the garrison placed such a strain on his mental and physical strength that more often than not he fell asleep over his dinner and retired immediately the meal was over to his bed, where he recuperated his vitality with ten hours' solid sleep.

Madame Gregorieva, on the other hand, had nothing to do all day after she had given her orders to the servants but to wander bored from room to room or gossip over teacups with the wives of other officers.

As she stared at the little Japanese, with his wrestler's body, bending over his crates, the impact of her loss struck her with a new and disturbing force. When he turned and faced her she was almost overcome by her confusion.

"Madame, I am sorry, please excuse me," the Japanese was saying, bowing in that exaggerated way they had. "I did not hear madame come into the shop. What can I have the honor of showing madame?"

With a vast effort she controlled herself. "I would like to see your silks," she said.

She had entered the shop attracted by a bale of printed cotton he had on display. But her eye had caught the silks stacked high on shelves near the ceiling.

She made him get every bale down. She made him carry each bale to the door so that she might see the true shade in the daylight—and see, too, more clearly, his wrestler's litheness and his wrestler's strength.

At last, with Russian imperiousness, she ordered him to cut her twelve yards of olive green, though she needed only six for a gown. He would have delivered it to her house, but she made him wrap it, and with it in her arms she fled into the street.

She had gone less than a hundred yards when she met

Madame Prohkorova, the wife of Lieutenant Prohkorov, her husband's adjutant. They exchanged greetings and she told her friend what she had bought. She dropped her voice to a whisper and there was something in her voice which made Madame Prohkorova curious to see the little Japanese.

It was not until the fourth Russia lady had made purchases that morning that the truth began to reveal itself to Choichi Hirayama. Then he smiled to himself and laid his plan.

He used great subtlety. Only occasionally did he work in his shop clad only in his drawers, and they came more often than they would otherwise have done in the hope that they would this time be able to admire his fine physique.

When the other inhabitants of Iman saw that the Japanese received the patronage of the garrison ladies, then they knew that they might safely give him theirs. In a short time Hirayama's store was flourishing. It did not produce great wealth, but he was successful. Within two years he had opened a branch in Nikolsk, where he put in a Russian manager.

But before he did that, many things had happened. Peddlers and travelers of his own race called at the shop when they saw the sign above the door. He received them hospitably, for he could talk to them in his own language and they could give him news; and when they pressed small pellets of rice paper secretly into his hand he gave no sign. He knew what to do with them.

He became fluent in the dialect of the region, too, and the men of Iman took a liking to the quiet, smiling little foreigner. One of his particular friends was a schoolmaster who came to ask questions about his country and its customs. He suggested that he should teach the Russian's pupils wrestling, and it was not long before he was also teaching their fathers.

He was always ready to contribute a few kopeks to their charities, or give his services, or join in their activities. He was a man of ideas, too, they found; and they would have elected him to the city council had he not been a foreigner.

His wife, now plump and quietly happy, bore him a child

each year. He loved her even more than he had loved her when he had asked his cousin to go to her father and ask if he might marry her.

And he allowed himself to be seduced by the wife of Captain Gregoriev.

The first time it had happened he had gone to her house to leave some paper chrysanthemums for her. She had admired some he had decorating his shop. She had wanted those, but he had told her that they were poor quality and he would order some from Tokyo especially for her.

He was not entirely innocent in his motives. Since the day she had bought the silk she had made her wishes quite plain. She received him in her sitting room and as he explained to her how the flowers were made, she touched him.

Ten days later she came into the shop, and when they were alone she asked him why he had not visited her again.

"It is too dangerous, and unwise," he had said, turning away.

"My husband is away for five days," she said, commanding him. "I wish to make curtains of brocade. You will please bring what you have to my house this evening so that I may decide which goes best with my furnishings." She gave him no time to answer, but turned on her heel and left the shop. That evening, when it was dark, he got down the bales of brocade and carried them to her house.

At first he would not yield to her, and she berated him in her necessity.

"Where is the captain?" he asked.

"I told you—he is away for five days."

"Where?"

"At Kobolsk."

When he had first come to Iman Kobolsk, some twenty miles away, had been a small village. With the coming of the railway it had changed to an important center. What, he wondered, was the significance of the captain's visit there? When he left the captain's house that night he knew that the Russians were building a new fort at Kobolsk large enough to accommodate a garrison of two hundred men and a score of cannon.

In the coming months Captain Gregoriev's absences became more and more frequent and more prolonged. Whether Madame Gregorieva realized the significance of the price demanded of her or not, she did not seem to care. If she thought about it at all she would probably have blamed it on her husband. But there were none of her husband's activities at Kobolsk and other places round about which for long remained unknown to Hirayama.

Madame Gregorieva was not the storekeeper's only source of information. The wives of the other officers now met constantly at his shop and gossiped as they fingered the rolls of brocades and gave his fans a trial flutter, and their gossip was nearly all concerned with their husbands' work, the arrival of reinforcements, the postings to other strong points of this unit and that, the problems of getting enough ammunition for the small arms and artillery.

Such information Hirayama checked by skillful questioning of his friends the townspeople, who worked for the Russian Army. They gave him not only confirmation but fresh information; and all of it he sent down to Vladivostok with the reports of the peddlers and the medicine men who visited him after dark.

Soon there was not anything which the Russians in Iman and the surrounding region were doing and planning which did not reach Japanese intelligence. On the basis of this information the Japanese Army laid its plans for dealing with Iman when the time came, as we shall see.

What Hirayama was doing in Iman other Japanese spies were doing, though not perhaps with the same weapons or using the same methods, at almost every other place where the Russians were making their preparations. In the important Russian base at Port Arthur, the porters and stevedores and other dock laborers were for the most part Japanese agents. They were disguised as Chinese or Manchurians, and the Russians, even when they could recognize them as being Japanese, were not perturbed. The main thing was that they worked well, for next to nothing.

It has been estimated that one in ten of every coolie working for the Russians in Manchuria was a Japanese agent. Not all of them were Japanese. It was found that poor Chinese were quite ready to supplement the starvation wages paid them by the Russians by giving the Japanese snippets of information in return for one or two roubles; and these snippets rapidly built up into a vast mosaic picture of Russian activity.

Once the war had begun, and the Japanese found that espionage paid such handsome dividends, they employed more and more Chinese to spy for them. They took these men mainly from the Chinese who, in peacetime, had served the Russians as interpreters, clerks and couriers, but who had not fled when the Russians had retreated because they owned a parcel of land or had their families settled in the district. With their source of livelihood gone with the Russian armies back across the Black Dragon River, these people were very content to serve a new master. They had to live. The Japanese would give them fifteen dollars a month, which was better than having no rice.

The Russian high command had put two crack regiments to garrison Port Arthur, the 1st Tomsk Regiment and the 25th/26th Siberian Rifles. They had done so because they were not entirely misjudging the situation, and Port Arthur was a pivot of Russian strength.

Yet the 1st Tomsk Regiment and the 25th/26th Siberian Rifles were served entirely by Japanese agents. They cleaned the rooms of the officers, where they could read any notes a careless young lieutenant might leave lying around. They cleaned the offices, where files were not always kept under lock and key at night, and where much that was interesting could be gleaned from wastepaper baskets. They waited at table in the officers' messes, where subjects of strategic importance were discussed despite the ban on talking "shop" in the mess. They performed chores for the N.C.O.'s and private soldiers who, as in most armies, often knew more than officers of field rank.

Captain Gregoriev—and there were many Captain Gregorievs in Siberia at this time—employed a small army of coolies to dig and build and carry earth and stones as he built new fortifications and strengthened existing ones. Of course, he did not know that as soon as Hirayama had reported what was happening one in seven of all the coolies working for him and all his colleagues was a Japanese agent trained to study fortifications, estimate strength, draw plans and discover their weaknesses.

Like Iman, Na-Shao was an important strategic center for the Russians, who went to great lengths in fortifying it. As a first line of defense they sowed a field of electrical mines. They believed themselves to be very clever in using these mines instead of self-detonating mines which would blow up as soon as anyone trod on them or otherwise disturbed them. By using electrical mines, which they wired in several series so that not all of them should explode at once, they would be able to wait until the whole field was covered with Japanese attackers and then, by pressing buttons, they could wipe out the enemy at will.

At Japanese headquarters there was a map on which was marked the exact positions of all the detonating wire junctions with the main leads. When the time came, the commander sent out a party of men under cover of darkness who cut every single lead and rendered every single mine harmless. Also on the map was marked the exact position of the artillery batteries in the fort itself, with a note beside each indicating the type of gun and the amount of ammunition with which it was supplied.

The information had been supplied by Japanese agents who, under Russian instruction, had planted the mines and helped join up the wires; who had placed the guns in position and hauled up to each emplacement the supplies of ammunition. And when the time came, Na-Shao fell within the hour.

One in ten of the coolies who were working on the new chain of electrical power stations was a Japanese agent. By skillful subversive activity they were able to delay the completion of the program for a considerable time. They also prepared plans of every one, marking on each plan the vulnerable points of the plant. Armed with these plans, when the war started small parties of trained saboteurs rendered many of the power stations ineffective and caused great confusion among the Russians by the subsequent dislocation of the power and light supply.

The vast scope of Japanese espionage in Manchuria and Russia in this preparatory period is almost inconceivable. Even if Stieber's claim that he employed 40,000 agents could be allowed, his claim would pale into insignificance beside the vast secret force which the Japanese were employing in this area alone; and this was only one section of their effort. Almost equal numbers were being used in China, Burma, India, all across Asia and, in connection with the effort against Russia, in European Russia itself.

In the autumn of 1900 the Japanese War Office appointed Colonel Motojiro Akashi to be military attaché in France, Switzerland, Sweden and Russia. His appointment, which had been resisted by the war office at first, had been made at the insistence of Ryohei Uchida, now a prominent member of the Black Dragon Society, who had threatened that unless Akashi were appointed, the society might find it necessary to withhold the reports of its agents from the military.

A short time before he left Japan for Europe, Akashi was summoned to a meeting with Uchida and another leading executive of the Black Dragon, Sugiyama, who had once been director of The Hall of Pleasurable Delights in Hankow.

From these two members of the Black Dragon Akashi received his orders.

He was to visit France, Switzerland and Sweden just for long enough to make himself acquainted with the situation there. He was then to go to St. Petersburg, which he was to make his headquarters.

"Very soon now," Uchida said, "we shall find ourselves striking a blow against our enemies in Siberia. European Russia is very far distant from us, but it is there that policies are made and instructions are given concerning Asiatic Russia. We believe that we could acquire important information if we could have agents there."

Colonel Akashi bowed his agreement.

"There are, of course, many difficulties in the way of our achieving this, colonel." It was Sugiyama speaking now. "But we believe there is a way in which we could not only acquire information but cause difficulties for the Russian government.

"As you are probably aware, colonel, there is much dissatisfaction with the regime in Russia. For many years now, revolutionary societies have been formed and have operated in secret to bring about the overthrow of the tsar and the elimination of his government.

"If we could make contact with some of these revolutionaries we could, I think, in return for offers of money and materials with which they could be helped to carry out their activities, obtain from them information regarding policies and military strength in East and Central Asia. For these revolutionaries have their agents in high places."

Again the colonel accepted the validity of these views.

"There are two leading revolutionaries," Uchida informed him, "whose identity and capabilities have been revealed to us. One is a priest of the Russian Orthodox Church, a certain Father Gapon. The other is an electrical engineer called Eugene Azeff. If you can make contact with either of these men, or better still, with both, we are sure you could achieve a high measure of success, colonel."

Once more the colonel assured them that he would devote himself faithfully to this end, and for the next hour or so the three men discussed details of what Akashi could offer the secret revolutionaries of Russia, how he should report to the Black Dragon the information he acquired, what he should do to encourage the revolutionaries to intensify their pressure on the Russian government.

So, on the morning of the second day, the military attaché set off to take up his appointment, and some months later arrived in St. Petersburg. There he lost no time in making contact with the two revolutionaries, and in a few weeks could regard himself—if a little cynically—as their friend.

Akashi pressed forward with his plans and had a notable success and won for himself the reputation of being one of the outstanding agents of the Black Dragon.

The peak of the early success he achieved on February 4th, 1904. On this day, two days before their formal declaration of war, the Japanese attacked the Russian fleet at Port Arthur.

At the moment of the attack Akashi was addressing the Russian Socialist (Revolutionary) Congress which was being held secretly in Stockholm, and to which he had been invited through the good offices of Azeff. As the guns of both fleets fired salvos at one another, Akashi was telling the congress: "I am authorized by my superiors to inform you that Japan is prepared to supply arms for revolutionary uprisings in St. Petersburg, Odessa and Kiev."

It was the most successful speech of the congress.

Had Colonel Akashi known the characters of the two men who were to make his success possible he might have hesitated before getting in touch with them, for they were two strange men indeed.

In the year after the Stockholm congress, on a Sunday in October, 1905, Gapon came out into the open and marched at the head of a large crowd to the Winter Palace of St. Petersburg, where the tsar was in residence, to present a petition to the tsar on behalf of the people. Troops opened fire on the demonstration and thousands were killed, but Gapon escaped abroad and lived for some time in London. Unfortunately, he fell victim to comfortable living and the revolutionaries lost confidence in him, and so did Akashi.

He returned to Russian secretly in 1906 but, finding that he was no longer acceptable to the revolutionaries, he turned traitor to the cause and offered his services to the police. This, naturally, upset the revolutionaries—and Akashi—and placed the priest at once in great jeopardy, and on March 28th, 1906, he was lured, by a trick, into an empty house in St. Petersburg and hanged.

The man who had most to lose by Gapon's defection was Colonel Akashi's other friend, Eugene Azeff, who, while working with the revolutionaries, was at the same time one of the most trusted and successful agents of the Ochrana, the secret police. In this role, he stands at the pinnacle of double-dealing as recorded in the annals of revolutionary, secret police and espionage history, of all times, throughout the entire world.

He had begun by working for the police as a student by informing on fellow students engaged in revolutionary activities, for which treachery he was paid the princely salary of fifteen dollars a month. From that he was promoted to Ochrana headquarters in St. Petersburg. At the same time he gained the confidence of the revolutionary leaders to such an extent that he reached a position of great trust among them. He planned and organized some of the most spectacular assassinations, even making bombs with his own hands. Not even when the assassins were arrested—on his information—before they could throw their bombs, did any suspicion fall on him! Equally, the Ochrana was blissfully ignorant of his association with the revolutionaries. He took money from both sides.

But Nemesis, though she may play a waiting game with such men, eventually strikes—and strikes hard. In 1908 both the Ochrana and the revolutionaries discovered him for what he was. Yet he escaped the vengeance of both sides, spent the rest of his life as a wandering fugitive and died in a German internment camp in 1919. It was Azeff who discovered Gapon's approach to the Ochrana. It was Azeff who planned and witnessed his execution.

Perhaps even more significant than his friendship with these two men was another Akashi made in St. Petersburg.

There was at this time in the Russian capital a noted Tartar Moslem, Abdur Rashid Ibrahim, who, besides publishing a Tartar newspaper called *Ulfet*, was adviser to the government on Moslem affairs. He and Akashi understood one another very well, and when the Russo-Japanese War eventually broke out they worked together in organizing Moslem resistance in the Russian rear.

As a recompense for the aid he had received from Ibrahim, when Akashi returned to Japan he arranged for the Tartar's son to be educated in Tokyo at the Black Dragon's expense. In 1906 and 1909 Ibrahim himself visited Japan and entered into even closer collaboration with the Japanese.

Akashi went from success to success, surprising even Uchida and Sugiyama, who, on the night of their meeting on the eve of the colonel's departure for Europe, had found Akashi competent, but not outstandingly so.

In World War I, Akashi was appointed assistant chief of the general staff. With the collaboration of General Sadao Araki, he encouraged Baron Ungern von Sternberg's project for establishing an autonomous Mongol empire. As a part of this plan, Akashi and Araki organized and directed the Japanese occupation of Siberia. He died in 1919, however, before the full fruits of all his schemes could be harvested.

Akashi was not the only Japanese working to discover all he could about the enemy's strength and intentions in metropolitan Russia. The Japanese Navy, working independently of the patriotic societies and military intelligence, had placed their agents at strategic points.

In the kitchens of imperial navy headquarters at Odessa, the great Russian Black Sea naval base, Alexander Alexandrovitch plunged his arms up to their elbows in dough. He had been making bread for the Russian Navy for many years now, afloat and ashore, and could carry out the operation with his eyes shut.

As he worked he looked about him and thought what a good place Odessa was to be in. He could not imagine what it would be like to live, for example, in Moscow, where there was, so he was told, no sea, no beach and very often no sun. But then he had been reared on the western seaboard of the Crimean Peninsular. The gentle sounds of the sea had been the first sounds he had heard, and they were the sounds he liked most of any. That was why he had chosen the imperial navy when the urge had come upon him as a boy to see what he could see of the world.

But of all the places he had visited, of all the oceans he had sailed, of all the men he had seen, none was like Odessa, the Black Sea and his own countrymen. He could not understand a man leaving his own country, cutting himself off from his own people for years and years on end, when there was no really good reason for it. Like that little Jap, for instance, at the table next to his kneading trough, cutting up cabbage for soup.

Without pausing in his pummeling of the mobile, almost living substance under his fists, he turned to Yasunosuke Yamamoto and said: "Suke, how long is it since you were home?"

The plump little man, not more than five foot one, looked at him with his face creased in a smile which was almost perpetual, his dark eyes gleaming from their up-tilted almond-shaped slits.

"Six years, Alexander Alexandrovitch," he said.

"Don't you ever want to go home?" the young Russian asked.

"No!"

"I can't make you out. When I was afloat I liked seeing all the sights and people, and how they lived, and I hope when my time here is up to see more, if only I can get aboard a battleship; but I'm glad to be home here in Russia for a spell, among my own people. There's no one like your own people for friendship, Suke. It's understandable really, because you know what to expect from them and they know what to expect from you. You can't have friendship without tranquillity. Don't you miss your friends?"

"No. But then I never had any friends."

"Not even in your own town?"

"Not even in my own town. You may think it is strange, but I don't admire my own countrymen."

"But why?" The surprise in Alexander Alexandrovitch's voice was the measure of his incredulity.

"They are narrowminded. They believe that no people are like them. That they are the chosen of the gods. That no one can do things like they do them."

"Well, that's natural. I think there are no people on earth like the Russians, though I wouldn't go so far as to say we're the chosen people. And I think that the Russian way of doing things is a pretty good one."

"But you don't say it's the only way."

"No. Different people have different ways of doing things; what suits me doesn't necessarily suit you."

"There you are, you see. But it isn't just that. I don't like the way things are going in Japan."

"How are they going?"

"Well, we've got a state religion."

"But so have we."

"But ours is not like yours. Every man in Japan must accept the state religion, and do you know what that religion says? It says that the divine mission of Japan is 'to bring

the whole world under one roof'—the Japanese roof, naturally—'so that all humanity may share the advantages of being
ruled by the divine emperor.' "

"You mean that the Japanese emperor is one day going to
rule Russia?"

"Just that."

"But . . . but . . ."

"I know it sounds mad, but it is more than mad, it is dangerous."

"You mean they really mean to conquer all the world?"

"Just that. They are planning for it now, and soon you
will see, they will start trouble, and they won't stop until
they have done what they want to do, or someone stronger
than they are defeats them. Now perhaps you can understand why I don't like what they are doing in my country,
Alexander Alexandrovitch."

"Well, I'm not very clever, but even I can see that it will
mean war. Do you really mean that they intend to fight the
whole world?"

"In the end, yes. But they will attack the countries one
by one."

"Then there is no need to worry. Because everyone will
see what they are doing, and . . . well . . . the tsar will stop
them for one."

"Don't be so sure. Madness gives a person great strength.
It gives to a nation the added strength of fanaticism."

"Ah, now you're taking me out of my depth. What are
you doing this afternoon?"

Alexander Alexandrovitch knew that he would never talk
like that about Russia, whatever the Little Father did. But
he felt sorry for the little man who had no friends. Alexander Alexandrovitch was almost the only man in the kitchens
who would have anything to do with the Japanese. The
others said that a man who talked like that about his own
country was a traitor. But there were two sides to that. If

you could see that the rulers of your country were doing bad things, why then . . . you could stop them!

He was on the point of saying so to Yamamoto when another thought struck him: hadn't the people been trying to get the tsar to change his government for years, and still couldn't make him? Perhaps the ordinary man had no power against those in power.

"What did you say?" he asked.

"I said I thought I might take a walk along the sea front this afternoon," the Japanese repeated.

"May I come with you?"

"I shall be honored, Alexander Alexandrovitch."

So when they were free the Russia naval cook and the Japanese cook went for a walk, the Russian in his uniform, the Japanese, who was a civilian employee of the Russian Admiralty, in a smart European suit.

But somehow they did not walk along the sea front but found themselves strolling along the jetties of the naval harbor. There were one battleship, three destroyers and several corvettes tied up there. They represented perhaps a few per cent of Russia's naval forces.

"Does Japan have any ships like those?" Alexander Alexandrovitch asked.

"Many, and all of them the very latest types," Yamamoto answered.

"But none as new as the light cruiser *Grand Duke Dimitrov*, I'll bet."

"I don't know how new she is."

"She's just completed her trials. A friend of mine is in her. He says there's no other ship in the whole fleet can touch her. Do you know she can do twenty-five knots?"

"That's a high speed, but to get that speed they must have sacrificed most of her armament."

"Don't you believe it!" And the young Russian reeled off all the details of the tsar's proudest addition to his fleet.

The little Japanese listened, putting in a question here and

there. His face was impassive, belying the excitement growing within him with every sentence the young man spoke.

"Let's walk along the shore," he suggested presently, "and
then perhaps you will do me the honor of taking a glass of
vodka with me?"

"I was going to suggest the same thing," Alexander Alexandrovitch replied, and in his sentimental Russian way he
thought he might be able to supply some of the friendship
which the Japanese wanted—you could tell he wanted it—
but never seemed to get. In time, perhaps he might be able
to tell his friend that he would get along much better if he
was not always running down his country and his countrymen however much he was against what they hoped to do,
intended to do.

The following morning Yamamoto came late to his vegetables.

"Sleep too long?" Alexander Alexandrovitch asked.

"No," the Japanese smiled. "I had some leave due and I
thought I would take some of it. I'm going off tonight."

"Where do you plan to go?"

"I thought I might take a trip to Istanbul. I've never been
there."

"You certainly ought to see the Golden Gate," Alexander
Alexandrovitch assured him.

So that evening Yasunosuke Yamamoto took the train and
three days later disembarked at—St. Petersburg.

Hailing a *droshky* he ordered the driver to take him to
the Imperial Japanese Embassy.

The servant who opened the door to him bowed low.

"Will you tell Commander Yoshiro that I wish to speak
to him urgently?" he said.

"What name shall I tell the commander, sir?"

"Lieutenant Commander Yasunosuke Yamamoto."

Within three minutes the naval attaché was receiving him
as deferentially as the servant below.

"I came in person," Lieutenant Commander Yasunosuke

Yamamoto said, "because I have full particulars of the speed and armament of the *Grand Duke Dimitrov*. She has just completed her trials, as you no doubt know, but did you know that she leaves for Port Arthur on the twelfth of February?"

For some reason, instead of making the attaché look serious, as he had supposed it would, Commander Yoshiro smiled.

"In that case she will be too late," he said.

"Too late?"

"Yes, Lieutenant Commander Yamamoto. By then the war will have started with Russia, and might be almost over by the time the *Grand Duke Dimitrov* reaches the China Sea. Nevertheless, your information is very valuable."

"I knew it was valuable; that is why I came with it in person. I did not dare to risk it to the post. So we are ready at last!"

"Yes, we are ready."

Commander Yoshiro was right. By 1904 Japan believed herself to be in the position from which she might attack Russia with every hope of success. Fifteen to twenty years of preparation had not only brought Japanese industrial and military development to a high pitch, but a vast army of secret servants, more vast than that in the service of any other nation in the world, had uncovered Russia's military secrets and intentions in that area in which she could best be attacked. She was now to discover for herself what the old Prussian spy master, Wilhelm Stieber, had insisted was infallible truth—that well-made, extensive and patiently insistent espionage preparations can achieve half the victory before the first blow is even struck in battle.

CHAPTER 6

The First Great Victory

On February 4th, 1904, at the very moment that Colonel Akashi, the Japanese military attaché in St. Petersburg, was making the most successful speech before the secret congress of the Russian revolutionaries in Stockholm, telling them that his government was willing to provide them with arms for uprisings in certain specified centers, the Japanese fleet opened fire, without any declaration of hostilities, on the Russian base at Port Arthur. Formal declaration of war was not to be made until two days later.

The naval commander of Port Arthur was not taken entirely by surprise. Reading the signs, he had become convinced that it would not be long before the Japanese began the conflict and that the importance of the base would make it an early object of their attention.

The naval commander was Admiral Baron Fersen, a member of the German Balt nobility, one of the 272 great feudal landlords who divided up the Russian province of Estonia between them. The baron's family owned about 100,000 acres of good arable land and forest land, centered on a small village about thirty miles northeast of Revel—now Tallin—the capital of the province.

The administration of an estate of this size, one would have imagined, would have filled most of the baron's waking hours. But he had an urge to go to sea which could not be denied; so appointing a regent to control his affairs, he went off and joined the tsar's navy.

Partly because he was a first-class naval officer, but chiefly because he was a Fersen, his promotion was rapid, and at the incredibly early age of forty he was appointed to flag rank, and shortly before the war broke out he was advanced to vice-admiral in command of Port Arthur.

As the baron pondered how he might best foil the attempt he was certain Admiral Tojo of the Japanese fleet would make to render Port Arthur useless as a naval base, he hit upon a novel and brilliant idea.

He had searchlights taken off ships and rustled up any others that were available and had them placed at strategic points around Port Arthur, pointing out to sea. If Tojo then succeeded in getting through the mine field into the harbor —and on two previous small-scale raids he had shown himself capable of that; "You'd think he had a plot of the mine field!" Fersen grumbled, quite unaware that Tojo had just that—suddenly all the searchlights would be switched on. This would have the dual effect of picking out the Japanese ships for the Russian gunners, which was good; and it would so dazzle the Japanese gunners that they would not be able to find the range and so would be rendered completely in-effectual, which was even better.

Admiral Fersen's prediction of Tojo's attempt proved right. But that was all!

When the Japanese admiral chose a particularly dark night for his assault and Fersen received news of the enemy fleet's approach, he rubbed his hands together with delight. The darker the night the more effectively would the Japanese be dazzled by the searchlights.

Fersen gave the order that the Russian fire was to be withheld until the Japanese fleet was well within the harbor defenses.

At a signal from the admiral baron, all the searchlights were switched on, and there was the Japanese fleet all lit up, a sitting target for the Russian gunners! It was a magnificent sight!

Unfortunately, it did not last for long! Before the Russian gunners could find their range the Japanese gunners, instead of being dazzled, opened up with such perfect shooting that within three minutes the whole of Port Arthur was plunged in darkness as every single searchlight was put out by a Japanese direct hit.

Tojo had been supplied, days before he made his attack, with the exact position of every single searchlight, and his gunnery commanders had been able to draw up a plan which gave their gunners the absolute range for the searchlights allotted to each of them.

Even Tojo was surprised by the success he achieved. He had not expected the Russians to let him get so near before they opened their attack. By doing so they had made the success of the Japanese gunners all the more certain.

As for Admiral Baron Fersen, he continued to be puzzled by the failure of his plan until those more cognizant with Japanese ways of spying explained to him that those very coolies who had helped to place the searchlights in position were most likely Japanese agents, as in fact they had been.

The assault on Port Arthur was by way of being a trial run. When the news of Tojo's success was reported, those in authority in Tokyo gave the order to advance to their forces in north Manchuria, and formally advised St. Petersburg that Japan was in a state of war with Russia.

There was scarcely a single point all along the line which the Japanese had taken up that did not fall to their first assault. The Russians fell back steadily until they reached their second series of fortifications. But here again, the Japa-

nese knew exactly their strength and weakness, and exploited
their knowledge to the full.

Early in April the inhabitants of Iman and Nikolsk were
surprised to see displayed in the windows of Hirayama's
shops these notices: SALE: ALL STOCK OFFERED AT ONE QUARTER
USUAL PRICES.

Both Hirayama in Iman and his manager in Nikolsk were
at once besieged, if not with customers, at least by the curious.

"This war between your country and mine," he explained,
"is not good."

"We know that," one man shouted. "But what has that
got to do with you or us? Who makes war? It is not you or
us, but those who govern us."

Hirayama held up a scrap of paper.

"Look what I found under my door two days ago. It says:
'Go home, little foreigner. We don't want you here!' So I
go."

"We'll find the fool who wrote that," another exclaimed.
"And when we do . . ."

The crowd made plain what the speaker left unsaid. For a
moment Hirayama was afraid. Supposing they did find out
who had written the paper. He screwed it up and dropped
it surreptitiously on a heap of rubbish behind him and shook
his head.

"No, it is better that I go. War changes men. You will
see."

What he could not sell he gave away; and two days later,
with the wife he loved and the seven children she had given
to Japan, he left Iman.

The uniform the Japanese Army gave him changed his
appearance, but there was always the fear in his mind, as he
pointed the way to the forts which Captain Gregoriev had
built so carefully, and interpreted to his superiors the language the people of Iman had taught him, there was always
the fear that someone he knew would recognize him.

But nobody did, and when the war was over and Russia defeated, he returned to Iman and opened up his store again. And the people of Iman were glad he had returned and determined to make up to him the losses he had suffered through a war for which he was responsible no more than they.

So once more Choichi Hirayama flourished, and when the new war came his people were the allies of Russia, so he stayed where he was; and the war passed him over, as it passed over his neighbors.

Until one day in 1917, when there arrived at his house stealthily a certain Captain Kalmykov.

"But why do you come to me, captain?" Hirayama asked. "Of course you are welcome, but these people are your people. Won't they think it is strange you should take refuge with me?"

"They won't when they see what I am going to do," the captain answered. "The people here are not Bolsheviks. I shall lead them in their support of the government of the good Admiral Kolchak."

"But I still do not understand why they will not be offended that you live with me rather than with one of them."

"Have you opened the crates that came this morning?" the captain asked.

"Not yet."

"Then open them."

Still puzzled, Hirayama did as he was bid, and his bewilderment changed to speechless surprise. For the crates contained, instead of cloth and fans and embroidery, rifles and ammunition and gold.

"A gift from your government," Kalmykov smiled.

But for all Kalmykov's efforts, the government of the good Admiral Kolchak gave ground under every assault, both physical and ideological, of the Bolsheviks. The situation became so confused that the Japanese Army felt constrained to intervene to restore order, and Hirayama's shop became their headquarters in Iman.

Then, when order was at last restored, the people of Iman received another shock. The government which the Japanese put in power was not that of Admiral Kolchak, but of the Bolsheviks, and high in office was Captain Kalmykov. The people realized then that all the time the captain had been pretending to lead them against the Bolsheviks, he had been working to overthrow the government of the admiral. But they realized, too, that in this wicked work the captain's chief aide had been Choichi Hirayama.

This time they had no sympathy for the little Japanese, and he knew in 1921 that he must leave Siberia for good. But Ryohei Uchida had need of him still and sent him to open up another store on the Chinese Eastern Railway in Manchuria.

But by now a germ had attacked him far more viciously than his neighbors in Iman had done, and advancing age helped it. The flesh sloughed from his body, the muscles went flabby and held no strength any more, and his mind was no longer alert.

Two years later he was appealing to Uchida for permission to retire. The permission was granted and he returned to the fatherland, where he settled in a village north of Lake Biwa. There he died on December 10th, 1924.

He was fifty-five years old. Twenty-seven of those years he had been an agent. What he left was scarcely enough to support his widow. He had certainly not worked for money, but from the deep conviction of the rightness of his people's divinely bestowed role as rulers of the world.

Wherever the battle moved there were resident spies, like Hirayama, and the itinerant spies who knew the byways and unmarked tracks, the forts and the depots and the inclinations of the inhabitants, who put on the uniform of the advancing armies and interpreted and guided, making the way plain where otherwise it might have confused. But these

peacetime spies were not the only Japanese agents to prove
their worth.

By now Japanese military espionage had thoroughly organized a branch to move slightly ahead of the main body,
and had set up a highly systematic scheme for relaying the
intelligence gained by these agents and any others to those
officers for whom the information was of vital importance.

Along the whole front bureaus were established under the
command of officers whose business it was to control the
intelligence in their sectors, sift the information that came
through to them and pass it on to the general staff.

In the Russian lines there were secret bureaus correspond-
ing to these bureaus. They were managed by agents, Chinese
for the most part, but thoroughly loyal, whose business was
to arrange the sending of spies into towns behind the Russian
lines and to all Russian troop concentrations.

Each individual spy who worked in this way had attached
to him three or four runners by whom he sent to the Chinese-
controlled bureaus the information he had managed to acquire. As the Russian lines never exceeded fifty to sixty
versts in depth, a spy assisted by three runners could answer
an inquiry put to him by the Japanese in three or four days
and maintain an almost uninterrupted flow of intelligence.

When the information was received by the Chinese-con-
trolled bureaus they had to arrange for sending it through
the Russian outposts to the Japanese lines. The couriers used
for this purpose were mostly Chinese peddlers or poor coolies
of the lowest class, indistinguishable from the beggars who
swarmed all over Manchuria. Their intellectual capacity was
such that they did not properly realize what they were doing.
They knew that they must go to certain Japanese officers in
the Japanese lines; and they knew that they must not be
caught or lose the minute scraps of rice paper with the
strange marks on them. But that was about all. They received
the equivalent of one dollar a message at today's rates and

considered the risk they took well covered by that microscopic sum.

But the system had a surprising flexibility, too; surprising because the Stieber model had had everything systematized and cut and dried. Local commanders were encouraged to use their initiative to procure information that was vital to their plans, and often we find commanders prepared to organize their own small cells in order to discover exactly what the Russian commander facing them was planning. One such was Colonel Yamaguchi, who, in June 1904, was in command of the key town of Inkou, in northern Manchuria.

Inkou was important not only as a strategic base but because it was a junction for several branches of the Manchurian railway system. Sooner or later, Colonel Yamaguchi was sure, General Mishchenko, who was commanding the Russians on this sector of the front, would attack him.

"It is so important to them," he remarked to his second-in-command, "that Mishchenko will throw in every man he can lay hold of. Now, while I have every confidence in my men and know that each will fight until he is killed, that is no good if we are going to be defeated in the end. To compensate for our being inferior to the Russians in numbers, I intend to try to find out when Mishchenko plans to attack us, and if possible the details of his plan. So I, too, have worked out my little plan."

He clapped his hands.

"Bring in Fang and Ching," he instructed the orderly who answered his summons.

Fang and Ching entered and bowed. They were small men, though slightly taller than the colonel, and their faces were narrower, their cheekbones higher set and more pronounced. Fang carried a tray before him supported by a string that went around his neck. On the tray was an assortment of small gaily colored articles. Some of the articles were arrayed in an orderly fashion on one side of the tray while the rest were jumbled in a disorderly heap on the other side.

"Well, Ching," the colonel said, "what information has Fang for you this morning?"

Ching looked at the tray.

"General Mishchenko has called up two cavalry battalions and two infantry regiments from the rear. He has added two more artillery companies, one heavy, the other light, to the three he already had the day before yesterday."

The colonel had also been studying the tray.

"Right," he said, and smiled at the astonishment he saw on his second-in-command's face.

"But how does he know that?" the major exclaimed.

"Of course, this is only hypothetical information," the colonel answered. "However, if he can do it here, he can do it there. How does he do it? Simple. The green bundles of ribbon each represent a cavalry battalion. The red ribbons are infantry battalions, and each of those little boxes are infantry regiments. Every article on Fang's tray represents some formation or type of weapons in certain quantities. The way Fang set them out tells Ching when they have been added or withdrawn. Now, Fang, what are you to do?"

"I am to peddle my wares among the clerks of General Mishchenko's headquarters. I am to keep my eyes and my ears open. I am to make friends with the general's clerks. They are mostly my countrymen who, fools that they are, decided to go with the Russians, so it should not be too difficult. Each morning I shall go to the south corner of the main square an hour before noon."

The colonel turned to Ching.

"I shall go each morning to Fang to buy from him a ribbon or a box, and as I do so I will read what his ribbons say. I shall then send one of my runners with the information to you."

"Excellent!" exclaimed the colonel. "Go now."

Over the next ten days a runner arrived daily in Inkou, and from the information he brought Colonel Yamaguchi made his tally of his enemy's strength and discussed with his second-in-command what his plan would be if he were Mishchenko and had these forces under his orders for an attack on Inkou.

Then came the day when the first of the matchboxes arrived. It came in the morning by runner, and in the evening another came.

Despite his outward calm, the major could sense his commanding officer's inward excitement when he received the first matchbox.

"He has done it!" he exclaimed, his eyes flashing. "I never thought he would. But somehow he has managed it."

"What has he managed?" the major asked a little shortly, irritated by the colonel's mystery.

"When I have five more of these matchboxes I will tell you," the colonel answered, grinning provocatively, so that for the first time the major saw how bad the colonel's teeth were.

"He's like a child playing a silly game," the major complained to the colonel's adjutant, who was his wife's brother.

"When you become a colonel you enter your second childhood," his wife's brother replied. "So mind you don't get promotion, brother-in-law."

But when three matchboxes arrived the next day it was the major who displayed most impatience for the arrival of the sixth and last.

That evening at dinner the colonel announced to his officers that he wished them to hold themselves in readiness all next day to attend a conference with him immediately he summoned them. He did not know when this might be, but they must come at once.

They looked at one another with slightly raised eyebrows. None of them could supply a possible or even likely solution to the colonel's mystery.

The summons reached them in the mid-afternoon of the next day.

When they were assembled and seated in the colonel's

office they saw that he had arranged before him six match-boxes.

He rose, and picking up one matchbox and peering at it, he began: "Gentlemen, General Mishchenko intends to attack Inkou and the railway at six A.M. on June 27th. That's exactly a fortnight from now. He will attack the railway at the following points and with the following forces, and Inkou with . . ." And for the next half hour he outlined Mishchenko's complete plan, always referring to the matchboxes and to a few notes he had scribbled on a piece of paper.

"I have not yet worked out our plan of defense, but I shall do that now, with your assistance," he said when he had completed his exposition.

When the conference was over his second-in-command stayed behind and, picking up the matchboxes from the desk, looked at them carefully. There were a number of small ideographs on each, but none made any sense to him.

"A good idea, wasn't it?" the colonel smiled. "Fang is a clever man. One of these matchboxes on its own tells nothing to anyone. But the six put together reveal General Mishchenko's plan in detail."

At six A.M. on June 27th General Mishchenko launched his assault on Inkou and the railway; and no one was more surprised than he to find the Japanese in strength at every point of attack. There could not have been a leakage of information. He had not told his subordinate commanders of his plan until two days ago; and that would not have given the Japanese commander, if he had heard of the plan then, the necessary time to deploy his troops. Until he had told his subordinates of his plan, only he, his adjutant and his confidential clerk had known of it and all were to be trusted implicitly—he thought. But of course he did not know of the clerk's friendship with the peddler, who sold many interesting things besides ribbons and boxes. He was still puzzled when he found himself the next day pushed well behind the line from which he had started.

But besides the intelligence bureaus and the *ad hoc* activities of army commanders, there was yet another kind of organization. This consisted of a number of completely independent groups of three or four spies operating from a particular base. They were entrusted with the solution of some accurately defined problem, such as reconnoitering one specified section of the Russian Army, or the observation of troop movements.

These groups were always provided with considerable means which enabled them to set up a kind of "jam pot" center which would attract to it people of every class, who would gossip freely. The most frequently used "jam pot" was a baker's shop, for here soldiers of all ranks would call, since army rations were always inadequate and bread, besides being a staple food, was cheap.

Soldiers rank next in the line of gossips after maiden ladies and wives with too much time on their hands. From the conversations of their customers, and by means of casual, unsuspicious questions, the trained agent could pick up invaluable information.

It must not be thought, however, that the Russians put up no resistance to the espionage assault made upon them by the Japanese. It was not very long before the significance of what was happening at places like Inkou and Na-Shao dawned even on the Russians.

Shortly after the war began General Harting, who up to then had been chief of the political police, had been appointed by the Russian Army G.H.Q. to take over the supervision of Russian intelligence in the field. He was given a special grant of about 25,000 dollars for this work, which was a widow's mite compared with the vast sums with which the Japanese provided their espionage, and the result was not very satisfactory.

Local Russian commanders then set up their own private counterespionage echelons, which were much more effective. They became so effective, in fact, that they caused the Japanese to invent new devices for the communication of their information and for their couriers to conceal their messages. These would be buried deep in pigtails or hidden in the soles of shoes or sewn into the seams of clothing. These methods have now been so extensively used that they are no longer safe. In those days, they had never been attempted before. Information of very great importance had to be committed to memory and repeated orally to the officer in charge of a Japanese bureau, and this called for the necessity of employing a more intelligent class of agent.

But the greatest damage had been done before the war began and before the Russians decided to tighten up their counterespionage.

The Japanese introduced several innovations into their clandestine activity during their fight with the Russians. They were the first ever to use groups of saboteurs behind the enemy lines on an organized scale. Small groups of two or three agents, well-trained in the used of explosives, were sent to blow up the railways, electrical power stations and other installations of strategic importance. But perhaps the most striking innovation was their attitude toward spies and spying.

In the West it was not until the First World War that spies were freed a little of the contempt in which they were always held by *soi-disant* "decent" people.

As the pathetic German spy, Carl Lody, was standing on the scaffold in the Tower of London, he remarked to the governor of the Tower, who had visited him often during his confinement and who was now required to witness his execution: "I don't suppose, sir, that you would care to shake hands with a spy?"

To which the governor replied: "I will shake hands not with a spy, sir, but with a very brave gentleman."

And it was King George V himself who was the first to have the courage to declare publicly: "A spy is the bravest man I know," and who later conferred the first knighthood ever to be bestowed on a British agent on Sir Paul Dukes, who operated in Russia during the Bolshevik revolution and the first months of the Soviet regime.

The Japanese, however, from the beginning of their espionage activity had brought espionage within the scope of *bushido*, their extremely strict and elevated code of morals and conduct. Espionage, they declared, practiced in the service of one's country, was both honorable and fair; for did it not demand courage and daring, two of the virtues most highly prized by the samurai?

This code they extended to their enemies. A young Russian soldier, disguised as a Chinese, was captured, convicted of spying and executed. The Japanese were so impressed by his bravery and his ideal of devotion to his country that when he was dead they sent a letter to Russian headquarters in which they lavishly praised his behavior, courage and devotion.

The Russians reciprocated. When a Russian patrol on the East China Railway captured two Japanese officers disguised as Manchurians in the act of attempting to blow up the railway, they were court-martialed at Harbin and condemned to hanging. But when General Kuropatkin, the Russian commander-in-chief, heard that they were officers he modified the order, in deference to their rank, to death before the firing squad.

This approach to espionage was, of course, all of a piece with their general approach to service for their country and the ideal of patriotism. It encouraged many who might have hesitated to accept the risks of spying, anywhere, at any time, and it made them doubly dangerous. One of the best examples of *bushido* at work is provided by the *kamikazes*, the suicide pilots of the Second World War.

Nor was it only on the battlefield itself that Japanese espionage was so effective in all its manifestations.

When Admiral Fersen's ships had had their effectiveness whittled away to almost nothing by the first attack and when the armies in Manchuria and Siberia were falling back under the amazing pressure of the little yellow men, St. Petersburg decided that they must do something to relieve that pressure. An effective fleet in the Black Ocean should, it was argued, be able to intercept reinforcements both of men and materials being sent from the home islands to the Asian mainland.

Orders were, therefore, given to Admiral Rozhdestvenski to move his Baltic Fleet to the Orient. But before he could do this there were certain preparations which the admiral had to make.

While he was making his preparations one day in September 1904, Kenzo Kamakura and Seiko Akiyoshi, two clerks in the Potemkin Shipping Company's St. Petersburg offices, were taking special trouble with their dressing. Both had joined the Russian Orthodox Church some months previously and today Kenzo Kamakura was marrying a Russian girl, and Seiko Akiyoshi was to support him. As they giggled and twittered to one another, there was a knock on the door.

"It will be the florist with the boutonnieres," said Kamakura and, as he was still without his trousers, went on: "You're more presentable than I am; open the door, Seiko."

So Seiko, with his suspenders dangling behind him and his white tie half-knotted, went to the door to admit, not the florist's messenger, but two men.

"Kenzo Kamakura?" one of the men asked.

"No, I am Seiko Akiyoshi. My friend Kamakura is in the next room. You wish to see him?"

"Yes."

Kamakura answered Akiyoshi's call.

"You wish to see me, gentlemen? I am in a great hurry. I am to be married in one hour."

"I'm afraid you'll have to postpone your wedding," the spokesman said.

"But I can't do that!"

"Kenzo Kamakura and Seiko Akiyoshi, we are agents of

the Ochrana, and we are arresting you on suspicion of being Japanese spies."

"On what evidence?"

"You will learn that at headquarters," he was told.

As a matter of fact, the Ochrana had little evidence, but a search of the men's rooms revealed that they were supplying the Japanese Embassy with information about Admiral Rozhdestvenski's Baltic Fleet. It was also revealed that both men were lieutenant commanders in the Imperial Japanese Navy.

As the embassy in St. Petersburg received the information from the two spies they passed it on both to Tokyo and the embassy in Berlin. The embassy in Berlin, in turn, conveyed it to another lieutenant commander, who was touring Europe, and at this moment was at the Skaw, the northernmost point of Denmark.

It was only when Rozhdestvenski's fleet passed the Skaw that the Danes discovered the tourist to be sending code messages to the embassy in Berlin. It was too late then, but they arrested him on suspicion of spying.

All around the coasts of Europe and Asia at points where the Russian Baltic Fleet must call for bunkering the Japanese had placed spies, who immediately informed Tokyo of the arrival and departure of the Russian ships from each point. When the fleet sailed into the Sea of Japan, Japanese fishermen in speedier boats than the warships went ahead of them and warned the Japanese high command of their progress.

It was a fantastic chain of spying, but it was espionage on this scale, based on really firm and sure foundations, which played a very large part in the successful outcome of the war for Japan.

For a little over a year the Russians kept up the unequal struggle, but at last were compelled to sue for peace. They could not deal with the military reverses in Siberia and the Japanese-fostered unrest in their Moslem provinces and the ever-increasing revolutionary activity nearer home, also helped by Japanese money and arms.

Though they must have been expecting it secretly, the other nations of the world, and especially the Western world, were dumfounded when Russia threw in the towel. From now on they regarded the almond-eyed men of Nippon with a new respect.

As for the Japanese, they bowed to one another with great satisfaction. They had driven the Russians back across the Black Dragon River and weakened their power in Manchuria and in China. No longer would they have to worry about a Russian threat either to the edifice which they were continuing to build at home or to their own position on the Asiatic mainland. In this one sharp blow Japan had made herself the dominant power in this sphere of her influence. Never again would she have to fear the interference of the Russian bear. The rest of the world had believed that she was taking a gambler's chance when she attacked Russia. She knew that the element of chance was not excessive. She had laid her plan and worked to it, and it proved to have been well laid. She had proved by practice the theory that had been taught her by the now dead Wilhelm Stieber. As she began to plot the next phase of her plan, which would ultimately bring "the whole world under one roof" if she made sure that industrially and economically she would be in a position to give effect to her plots, she also made certain that her espionage preparations would be as effective, when the next battle was joined, as they had been in knocking out Russia.

CHAPTER **7**

The Final Touches to the Plan

It is necessary for us to go back a little way from the first great victory of Japanese arms and espionage to consider briefly what had happened in the political sphere. For it was against this somewhat peculiar background that she contrived to implement her "divinely" inspired policy of world domination.

The samurai, the hereditary fighting men, had been the thorn in the flesh of the reformers since the birth of the new Japan. It must be admitted that the rulers did not handle them very well.

In August 1876 they had been compelled to accept a lump sum payment in the form of interest-bearing bonds in lieu of their pensions, which were placing too great a strain on the nation's economy. The following year there was a general uprising of samurai which was easily quelled by the new conscript army, but those in authority realized that they must do something to keep them permanently quiet. They therefore acceded to the samurai demands that there should be some form of representative assembly. This led in its turn to the formation of political parties, and in 1890 the emperor and government instituted a parliament.

113

A Diet was established consisting of two houses, a House
of Peers and a House of Representatives. A peerage, on English lines, was introduced, but not all peers *ipso facto* sat in
the upper house, a number of them being elected by their
fellow peers for a seven-year term, while the princes and
marquises sat for life. The representatives were elected by
popular suffrage. Under the original constitution, property
qualifications were set so high that the suffrage was by no
means universal.

The emperor's position was reduced to that of a constitutional monarch. Theoretically, he combined in his person all
the legislative, executive and judicial powers, but he did not
exercise these powers except by advice. Compared with the
English monarch's constitutional powers, the emperor's were
even more restricted, for no political document signed by
him was valid unless countersigned by all the members of the
cabinet.

In this way, the emperor was identified with all the measures decided upon by the government of the day. Aligned
with the state religion, the main tenet of which was the divinity of the emperor, this identification gave unusual power
to the government. In practice, it gave the cabinet all the
emperor's political powers while, in turn, the emperor's in-
ability to do wrong by reason of his divinity was transferred,
by implication, to the acts of government.

Though outwardly the system had all the apparatus of
two-chamber democratic government under a constitutional
monarch, in practice it was merely a sham. The limitations
set upon the powers of the Diet hamstrung any effective government by them should their proposals not be in accord
with the intentions of the government. The Diet met only
once a year for a three-month session, and the government
had the power to convoke, prorogue or dissolve it.

There was one check upon the government in its exercise
of the vast powers theoretically assigned to the emperor.
This was the privy council, which, consisting of a president

and vice-president, twenty-four members and the cabinet, had to approve constitutional amendments, laws and supplementary constitutional decrees, as well as all emergency decrees, including emergency financial decrees, treaties, international agreements and the institution, when required, of martial law.

One power was confined to the emperor and remained outside the competence of the government. In his role as supreme commander of the armed forces, the emperor was advised in all military matters by the chiefs of the army and naval general staffs, and the army and navy ministers. By ancient custom the two latter offices were restricted to officers on the active list.

It was under this constitutional setup that the war with Russia, and all Japan's subsequent warlike activity, was undertaken, and it is necessary to have an understanding of this very brief outline in order to appreciate the background to the events of the next thirty years.

With the success that came to Japanese arms in the Russian war came the even firmer establishment of the conviction that the gods favored the expansionist policy. With this success in mind, in 1910 Japan formally annexed Korea without any opposition whatsoever from outside.

World War I was to prove a great blessing to Japan. Her development program had by this time put such a strain on her economy that she was on the verge of bankruptcy. She aligned herself with the Western Allies, who were only too ready to buy her cheap products, and this not only saved her from economic collapse but enabled her to press forward with her development program even more vigorously.

It also strengthened her position in East Asia. Here she had been aided by the Chinese revolution of 1911, which had weakened China so considerably that she had never recovered, nor was likely ever to recover. Japan took over the German leased territories in Shantung and in 1915 presented her Twenty-one Demands to the Chinese government, which accepted them. These gave Japan extensive rights, particularly in Manchuria and northern China.

With Japanese connivance Marshal Chang Tso-lin made himself the virtual ruler of Manchuria, and that country remained separated from China until 1928. In that year Chang was assassinated, and his successor proclaimed his adherence to the policy of Chinese nationalism, in so doing rejecting the advice of Japan. The outcome was the Japanese attack on Manchuria in 1931 and the setting up of a puppet state under Henry Pu-yi, the last Chinese emperor.

Two years later Japan attempted to set up a second puppet state by detaching the Five Northern Provinces. Here she met with her first failure and withdrew to lick her wounds, determined never again to fail.

In the events that led up to the seizure of Manchuria and in the actual seizure itself, Japan had the services of one of the strangest figures not only in her espionage history but in espionage history anywhere. His name was Kenji Doihara, often called, though with more than a tinge of facetiousness, the Lawrence of Manchuria.

CHAPTER 8

The Lawrence of Manchuria

One evening Kenji Doihara sat with his father and two of his brothers talking over the course of the war in Europe, which was not going well for the Allies, with whom Japan had aligned herself.

He was twenty-one, plumply round, not with puppy fat —he was too old for that—but with an incipient coarse grossness which was to clothe his bones more permanently as the years passed. Twenty years from now, had you sliced him neatly horizontally through the middle you would have probably expected to find him ringed like a tree, and counting the number of rings of fat you might have gauged his age. The innermost ring would have represented his first year of maturity, this year, of which this evening was a part.

Presently a servant came in and spoke to his father. "A message has come from the imperial prince," he said, "requesting that Kenji San shall call on him at once."

The father turned to his son. "You must go," he said. "Acquaintance with the imperial family can bring great honor to us."

As Kenji bowed to his father he stored these words in his

117

memory. He hoped that he would soon have need to remind the old man that he had spoken them.

At the prince's palace he found his imperial highness alone except for his chamberlain.

"I have received your package," the prince said at once, after their greetings were finished.

It was a superfluous remark, for set out before the prince were the half dozen photographs of a very beautiful naked girl, which he had sent to the palace that morning.

Looking down at the photographs, Kenji Doihara felt no shame. He remembered only that they had cost him his most prized possession, a little jade fawn that he had won from the son of a Manchu merchant. It was an exquisite piece of almost priceless value. He thought much more of it than he did of his fine German Zeiss camera, which made possible the pursuit of his main hobby.

He had tried every wile, every argument his cunning could devise, had run past the limit of his patience without losing it in anger. Then when these had been of no avail, he had thought of the jade fawn. Only when she was sure that he was not teasing her, but that he meant it when he said she might have it for her own if only she would take off her gown and let him photograph her, had she seen reason. Even then she had made him repeat his earlier promise that he would never show the photographs he took to any living soul.

Naturally he had repeated the promise. Just as naturally, as soon as he had developed and printed the photographs he had sent them by messenger to his imperial highness.

That had been his object all along. That was why he had sacrificed his jade fawn—to win the consent of a fifteen-year-old girl.

"And what is your imperial highness' decision?" he asked.

It needed all his courage to control his apprehension as he waited for the prince's answer. Supposing he had sacrificed the little jade fawn for nothing?

"You are right, Doihara," the prince said. "She is the most beautiful woman in Japan. I would like to know her."

Inwardly, Doihara's heart sang, but he pulled his features into a frown.

"Your imperial highness," he began, and his voice was sharp with resentment, "our family has been one of the leading samurai families for more than a hundred generations."

"What a touchy fellow you are!" the prince smiled soothingly. "I have a proposition to make. An honorable one. I wish your sister to enter my household as my first concubine."

"But my sister is already betrothed, your imperial highness," Doihara began.

The prince snapped back at him. "The offer I am making could be excelled only if the son of heaven himself made her his first concubine or if one of my unmarried brothers were to make her his wife, which the difference in rank prohibits anyhow."

"I am not my sister's father," he said quietly.

"I have asked you here to know if you will support my proposal, both to your father and to the girl," the prince said.

"Yes," said Doihara quietly, though how he could control his excitement he did not himself know. "Yes, I will do that, your imperial highness."

But it was not easy, either with the girl or with his father, and he might not have succeeded had not his brothers joined him, seeing in such an alliance the opportunities he himself saw. It was they who reminded his father that he had said: "Acquaintance with the imperial family can bring our family great honor." Here was an offer of much more than acquaintance. How could he think of rejecting it?

As for the girl, she would do as her father commanded. But she, silly child, would be a wife of a samurai rather than the concubine of a prince, even an imperial prince. She wished to beget warrior sons, not royal bastards. And she had done nothing wrong to deserve such punishment. It was Kenji who should be punished for persuading her to let him photograph her naked. He had promised . . .

His brothers looked at their brother. He stared back at them defiantly. They smiled at him, and he knew he had won.

A few weeks later Doihara called at the prince's palace, not to see the prince but the prince's first concubine.

"Well?" he asked cautiously.

"Oh, brother!" the radiant girl exclaimed. "I shall never be able to thank you."

"You are happy?"

"I cannot tell you how happy. The prince smothers me with kindness and showers me with presents. When he is here he never leaves my side."

Doihara moved closer to his sister and dropped his voice to a whisper. "Beware of the fickleness of princes," he warned her. "A year from now, when childbirth has distorted your beauty, he may look about him. . . ."

"You are wrong, brother," the girl cried. "He loves me. He will do everything I ask. Even my smallest whim. I never dreamed that life could be so wonderful. I shall never be able to repay you, brother."

Doihara did not reply immediately, but presently he said, slowly, watching her carefully to judge her reaction, "Sister, there is something you could do for me."

"Anything you ask, I promise you."

"Tell the prince that I speak nine European languages and four Chinese dialects without a trace of accent. Tell him that there is much I could do for the divine emperor and for the fatherland if only I could be sent to China in a responsible position. The prince has great influence with the government. He could arrange it if only he knew what I am capable of."

"Is that all you want, brother?" his sister laughed. "This very night the prince shall be told what a brilliant brother

I have. He will have to promise to send my brother to
China. . . . Have no fear, brother."

When they had drunk tea, Doihara left the first concubine happy and confident. As he made his way to the tea-
house of the Great Swords, he mused that it had not been
easy, but he would never have given up his plan until he had
succeeded. He smiled to himself. The most difficult part of
all was to persuade his sister to pose for him naked. If that
beginning of his plan had misfired . . . ? But he did not allow things to misfire. And now he only had to wait until
the summons came!

The summons was not long in coming.

Within a few months General Honjo, of the high command, was sent to Peking as military attaché and Kenji
Doihara, promoted to the rank of major, was posted as his
assistant.

There was very little to choose between the characters
of Honjo and Doihara. Both were entirely ruthless, utterly
without any moral values or scruples and relentless, if daring, plotters.

Now that Doihara had achieved his ambition of getting
to China, it was not long before he was putting the second
part of his plan into effect. His basic scheme was to create
a kind of moral desert on the Asian mainland. His slogan
would be, "Asia for the Asiatics," though for "Asiatics" one
should read "Japanese." He would accomplish his plan by
undercover means, undermining by plots, sabotage, assassinations, the promotion of vice of every kind, by bribery
and corruption the influence of the Chinese republican
government both in China and Manchuria.

As a beginning he would use the contacts which his position as assistant military attaché gave him. Before long
one of the high-ranking Chinese officials, who was not one
of his "men" but who saw what was happening, was able
to say: "Doihara probably has more Chinese acquaintances

than any living Chinese engaged in the most intense political activity."

The Honjo-Doihara combination was soon making its nefarious influence felt in Chinese affairs. It was during this early period that Doihara made the only great mistake of his career, though he managed to emerge safely even from that.

There was in China at this time, the early 1920's, a powerful movement called Anfu, meaning "Peace and Joy." It was so powerful that for a time it controlled the Chinese government. Honjo and Doihara supported the movement strongly.

How it happened is not clear, but presently it came to the knowledge of the better elements of the Chinese government that certain important members of Anfu had sold concessions in Manchuria to the Japanese, who already had many concessions there, without the official approval of the government and had pocketed the proceeds. Though this was not known, Doihara had been the prime mover in the business.

The matter became public knowledge and the nation rose against the government in a solid, angry body. There were demonstrations and riots and demands that the government should resign. A number of patriotic students stormed the Presidential Palace, their intention being to seize the person of President Hsu and compel him to dissolve the government. Hsu, however, believed that their real intentions were more violent and was panic-stricken. As he paced the palace, a frightened, trembling man waiting with oriental fatalism for the noisy students to break in and kill him, Doihara suddenly appeared before him.

"You are in great danger, Mr. President," Doihara said. "You should not be here."

"I know I am in great danger," the distracted Hsu cried. "But what can I do? Where can I go? There is nowhere in the palace where I could hide and they would not find me!"

Anfu had proved a broken reed. After this it would no longer be of any use to Doihara. But he might still pluck the chestnuts—the Chinese government, and more particularly the president—out of the fire, and, who knew? perhaps have those that mattered even more tightly in his hands. The first thing to be done was to rescue the president from his present dangerous predicament.

"Stay here, excellency," Doihara said firmly. "And do not move from here until I return."

The firm voice and the lack of fear steadied Hsu. He was a strange one, this fat little Japanese officer. He was a cunning one, too! But what could he do? He, Hsu, was trapped here in the palace. To judge from the noise, the mob had got into the grounds.

Within a few moments Doihara returned. Accompanying him were two servants carrying between them a large wicker basket with a lid.

"It will be a little cramped, excellency," Doihara smiled, "but it will be better than being torn apart alive by these young hooligans."

"Do you mean I am to get in that basket?" Hsu exclaimed.

"Exactly, your excellency. It is a clean laundry basket, though the little laundry in it is somewhat soiled. Quickly, excellency!"

He almost picked Hsu up and bundled him into the basket, covered him with soiled linen and tied down the lid.

"Follow me," he said to the servants.

They picked up the basket and followed Doihara as he went to meet the mobbing students. Facing them, he held up his hand for silence, and such was his personality that the young men stopped their yelling.

"If you are looking for President Hsu," he shouted so that they could all hear, "I'm afraid you are going to be unlucky. I have just searched the whole palace for him and cannot find him. Oh, just let those men pass through, will you, like good fellows? There's no reason, because you're enjoying a riot, why the laundry should not be done as usual."

His own smile, and the inappropriateness of the laundry basket on this scene, had their effect on the crowd. Laughing, the students opened their ranks and let the servants pass through unimpeded with the laundry basket and President Hsu.

When the basket was safely out of the palace grounds, Doihara addressed the crowd again.

"I would suggest that you appoint leaders and let them come with me and we will search the palace again," he said. "The rest of you stay outside here. If you all come in, the palace wouldn't be fit to live in again. There would be no sense in that, either."

So representatives were appointed, and for two hours they scoured the palace with Doihara. When they returned to their fellows the impetus of their patriotic emotions had lost its thrust and they dispersed quietly, if disappointed.

Meanwhile, President Hsu was in the safety of the Japanese Embassy. When the danger was past he would emerge to continue his efforts to fashion some order out of chaos. But his task would be no easier now than it had been in the past, despite the help and guidance of self-appointed Japanese advisers. Internal factions, corruption, the ambitions of war lords and the obstreperousness of the Five Northern Provinces and of Manchuria were powerful obstacles in the way of anyone trying to draw China into a cohesive whole which would have unity and a degree of power. In the turmoil that distracted him, Hsu did not realize that the Japanese, represented by Honjo and Doihara, were doing all they could to weaken China with their advice, and that as for Manchuria and the Five Northern Provinces, the more they could be encouraged in their recalcitrance, the better would Japan's own ends be served.

The importance of Manchuria for the Japanese lay in the fact that it lay nearest to the home islands in a place which would facilitate the execution of a later phase of their master plan, the domination of southern China; that by the control of it they could build up forces of men and materials there and use it as a springboard for the next step, the conquest of the Five Northern Provinces; and that in its present state of internal insecurity it should fall an easy prey to outside, meaning Japanese, influence.

As time went by, Doihara realized that he was wasting his time in China, for he now believed that he was tackling the problem from the wrong end. He must first work for the annexation of Manchuria. When Manchuria was in Japanese hands, the Five Northern Provinces would not present a great problem.

Even so, he realized that Manchuria could never be absorbed as easily as Korea had been annexed. In spite of its inherent weakness there was an army which was not too badly equipped and supplied; and, just as important, it had a bold and determined leader in Marshal Chang Tso-lin.

Manchuria had always been a kind of buffer state. The Tsarists had cast longing eyes on it and had, in fact, laid predatory hands on it, for they saw that it could blanket any land attack the Japanese might make on them in Asia.

During the Russo-Japanese War Marshal Chang Tso-lin had ranged himself and his forces on the side of the Japanese, and he had helped them considerably by harassing the Russian lines of communication.

When the war was over, the Japanese rewarded their ally by obtaining for him, from the Peking government, a pardon in respect of his previous acts of banditry and the appointment of governor of his native province of Fengtien, in Manchuria.

But Chang was a war lord born and could not be satisfied with the governorship of a province. So in 1922 he left Manchuria with his army and joined in one of those strange and, to Western perception, almost incredible local wars which happened to be raging about Peking at this time.

Unfortunately for whatever he had in mind, he backed the wrong side and his army was defeated by the forces of the war lord Wu Pei-fu. Thereupon Chang retreated to Manchuria to lick his wounds and, declaring the independence of the three eastern provinces, which we now know as Manchukuo, set himself up as a ruler.

He quickly revealed himself as a most admirable administrator though, at the same time, he emerged as a ruthless, pitiless autocrat, destroying everything and everybody who opposed him. Nevertheless, under his rule Manchukuo flourished and was rapidly becoming a very rich prize. To the chagrin of the Japanese, however, Chang now found that he could get along very well without them; and if they were going to be foolish enough to intervene, then he would not hesitate in opposing these former allies.

Doihara had the measure of Chang at once and sought permission from Tokyo to go into action in his own particular way. Before he began, however, it must be clearly understood that he must have *carte blanche* and be sure of the necessary funds.

By this time, Doihara's activities in China had commended him highly in the right Tokyo quarters. Almost automatically Doihara had his way in everything; and it was from this moment on that he began the most amazing phase of his career.

Like Schulmeister, Napoleon's master spy, like Wilhelm Stieber, the founder of Prussian espionage, Colonel Kenji Doihara was a natural spy and spy master. He had the peculiar vision, the tortuous mind, the relentless hardness, the pitilessness, that the successful spy master must have. Soon he was demonstrating to what degree he possessed these qualities.

He formed his own service, or rather, services. The largest was known as the combatant secret service, which was composed of 5,000 criminals who had fled from Russia after the revolution. Other forces were composed of White Russians, and there was a vast army of 80,000 Chinese renegades, called ch'ang mao tao, the long-haired sect, who were willing to carry out Doihara's orders in return for his support. For, while concentrating upon Manchuria, he did not neglect China, and particularly the Five Northern Provinces, which were scheduled next after Manchuria for Japanese tutelage.

Besides these hordes of operatives, who were used more for sabotage, assassination and the stirring up of strife than for purely intelligence purposes, Doihara employed many other nefarious, and in some cases unmentionable, devices.

To his way of thinking, addiction to opium was a virtue, abstention a vice. He converted the Chinese so-called clubs into combinations of saloon, gambling house, brothel and opium den, with the accent on the latter. He employed traffickers in opium who wandered throughout Manchuria and China, visiting every village fair, where they set up booths from which they advertised the sale of a guaranteed cure for tuberculosis. The medicine was either opium or an opium derivative. Once the unfortunate victims had become the slaves of the drug, it was but half a step to becoming the slaves and informers of Doihara, who controlled the supplies of the drug.

Many of those in his pay themselves employed labor. By his directions, these laborers were first paid half in cash and half in opium; and then entirely in opium.

At his request, Japanese cigarette manufacturers began to make a new brand of cigarettes, known as Golden Bat. The sale of Golden Bats was prohibited in the mother country; they were for export only. Doihara controlled their distribution in Manchuria and China. In the mouthpieces were concealed small doses of opium or heroin, and many unsuspecting purchases were thus gathered into Doihara's ever-growing army of addicts.

The more vicious of Oriental gentlemen attain, so they believe, the greatest orgastic release in sexual intercourse with Occidental women. Doihara accepted this imagined perversion as a ready-made weapon with which to weaken further the peoples against whom he was striving.

In Mukden and Harbin and other satisfactory locations he set up brothels in which the prostitutes were all White Russians. The source of supply was a plentiful one, for no fewer than 100,000 White Russians had fled from Siberia into Manchuria and China after the Bolshevik Revolution. They came with nothing; they remained with nothing. Such was their nature that the could not raise themselves out of the depression of mind and spirit into which their fate had plunged them; that they lived, literally, from today to the day after next. In a brothel they were at least sure of their food, and the happy oblivion of opium when they were not on duty. For, for every six pipes of opium they sold to clients they were given one pipe for themselves.

It was a terrible thing that Doihara was doing here. He set about deliberately to destroy half a continent with drugs and depravity of every kind. The success he had was even more terrible.

In 1926, in order to remove Marshal Chang Tso-lin from the Manchurian scene so that they might prepare for their own ends with greater speed, unhindered, the Japanese, through Doihara, persuaded the war lord to have his revenge on Peking. Supported by equipment supplied by them, Chang arrived before Peking and sat himself down there for two years.

But during these two years Kuomintang armies swept over the whole of China. Under the able direction first of the Communists and then of General Chiang Kai-shek, by 1928 they had reached Tsinanfu. By now the Japanese had put a considerable army into China, under their concessions, and were in control of the Tsingtao-Tsinan Railway, and at Tsinanfu they offered considerable resistance to the Kuomintang forces.

Realizing what was happening, Marshal Chang's oldest and best friend, General Wu Shu-chen, whom he had left as regent in Manchuria, begged Chang to return there urgently if he did not wish the Japanese to control his country.

Chang's return was the last thing the Japanese wished to happen, and hearing of General Wu's urgent appeal, on May 19th, 1928, they instructed their ambassador in Peking to warn Chang that he must not return to Manchuria. This opposition removed Chang's hesitation and he made preparations for his journey home.

Now Chang had an agent in Tokyo, an Englishman called Swineheart, and on May 31st he received a message from Swineheart urging him on no account to travel by train to Mukden, as he had it from the most reliable source that Doihara had given an undertaking to the Japanese government that Chang would never reach Manchuria.

Chang, who for some strange reason was completely blind to Doihara's activities in his own country and even looked on him as a friend, was sure that Swineheart was mistaken. He did, however, mention the warning to a Japanese colonel, who at once said that, to set the marshal's mind at rest, he would travel with him, in the same compartment, all the way to Mukden.

On June 4th, General Wu Shu-chen received a message to meet his friend and overlord, Marshal Chang Tso-lin, at a station some twelve miles south of Mukden two days later. He believed that the marshal had made the request while, for his part, Chang was delighted by the courtesy of his friend.

"You were kind to come to meet me, Shu-chen," he said.

"I was happy to come to meet my old friend after so long a time," Wu replied.

And both of them continued to believe, the one in the courtesy, the other in the friendship of old acquaintances.

The marshal and the general talked in general terms only before the barbarian colonel who was keeping his promise to Chang to ride in his compartment with him. Chang was regretting now that he had ever accepted this offer of "protection." Of course, Swineheart had picked one of the myriad rumors with which Tokyo has always swarmed, and always will. In ten minutes the train would be in Mukden and it would all be over. Nothing could happen now.

"In that case, Marshal Chang," said the Japanese colonel, "perhaps you will excuse me while I get my cap and sword from the next compartment."

"Please do," said Chang.

When the colonel had gone along the corridor, Chang said to his friend: "Tell me quickly, how are things?"

"Bad! Bad!" said Wu. "The Japanese are becoming more and more powerful. If we do not join with the Kuomintang they will have us under their rule. Thank the gods you have returned, my . . ."

Wu did not complete his sentence. The compartment in which the two men were sitting was at that moment passing under a bridge. Suddenly a tremendous explosion lifted the carriage from the tracks and simultaneously the collapsing bridge crushed it like match wood. When the debris was removed, Wu and seventeen of Chang's officers traveling in the carriage were dead. Chang died some hours later without regarding consciousness.

Doihara had carried out his promise.

Among the would-be rescuers was the Japanese colonel, who had gone, not to the next compartment, but right to the rear of the train where he had escaped unhurt.

The removal of Marshal Chang and General Wu did not, however, bring the results that the Japanese were sure the assassinations must have. An obscure general rose up in Chang's place, and with the courage of the obscure he refused to give way one pace before the increasing pressure of the Japanese but encouraged his people more and more firmly in the notions and ideals of nationalism.

For the next three years Doihara and his hordes plotted, assassinated, roused riots, dug deeper and wider their wells of depravity in vain.

At last the Japanese government saw that it would achieve its ends only by the direct use of force, and in September 1931 startled the world by their full-scale invasion of Manchuria, which they attempted to cry down by referring to it as the Manchurian Incident.

On September 19th, 1931, they captured Mukden; on February 5th, 1932, Harbin fell to them. A fortnight later they declared the "independence" of Manchuria.

Unfortunately for Japan, what they had done in Manchuria did not look legitimate in the light of international law. It was essential at this stage, for the success of their wider plan, that the rest of the world should not become suspicious of their intentions and be roused to intervene.

Doihara cast about him for a solution and hit upon a possibility. Indeed, it was to turn out to be the only solution. The Japanese should set up a puppet state at whose head, to give it a semblance of independence, should be none other than the unhappy, timid, weak young man, the last emperor of China, Henry Pu-yi.

But here again there were difficulties! The stupid young man, weak and timid though he might be, steadfastly refused to accept the Manchu throne.

And there was no one else!

Doihara was pondering his problem one evening as he paced his room. Convinced now that threats would not move Henry Pu-yi to accept the honor they were offering him, he was at his wits' end to know what to do. A knock on the door interrupted his pacing.

"Come in!" he snapped, pausing in his walking and facing the door.

A servant entered, his eyes fixed on the floor, his whole body trembling a little.

"Well, what is it?" the colonel demanded.

"There is a stranger below, sir," the servant answered. "For two hours he has been here now, demanding to see you. We have told him it is impossible, but at last—" The wretched

man shrugged his shoulders and waited for the rage to burst
on him.

Instead Doihara asked: "What is his name?"

"He will not give his name, sir."

"What sort of man is he?"

"He is a strange man, sir. A Manchu."

"There is nothing strange in that. There are thirty million
Manchus."

"But it's his voice, sir. He speaks like a gentleman, but his
voice is high, sir. As though . . . as though . . . he were a
eunuch."

"There would be nothing so very strange in that, either.
Is he armed?"

"No, sir. He has left his pistols and his dagger on the
table."

"Does he give a hint of what he wants?"

"No, sir."

Intrigued, Doihara made up his mind. Whatever the fellow wanted, it would divert his thoughts for a few moments
from the stupidity of Henry Pu-yi.

"I'll see him," he said. "Bring him up."

While the servant was gone, he drew his sword from its
scabbard and placed it on the table, ready to hand, and put
the table between himself and the door. He had many enemies, he knew. It was as well to be prepared. He disliked
using his pistols; he had never really mastered the weapon
whereas with the sword there was scarcely his equal.

The servant came into the room and stood to one side to
allow a small Manchu to enter.

"What do you want?" Colonel Doihara asked.

"To speak with you alone."

The colonel nodded to the servant and the man went out
shutting the door behind him.

"Well, what is your name?" Doihara said.

"That does not matter for the moment."

"Very well, then what do you want?"

The servant was right; the voice was peculiar. But eunuchs ran rapidly to fat and this young man did not seem to have an ounce of fat on him. Admittedly he was young; too young, in fact, to have been made a eunuch at birth. Those days were too long past.

"I have heard much about you, colonel, and I want to work for you."

"How have you heard?"

"I have my sources."

"The Chinese have sent you!"

The suspicion suddenly came down on Doihara. With a quick movement he had seized his sword and had its point within an inch of his visitor's heart.

"If you make the slightest move, you will be dead before you know what has happened," he threatened. "Now, tell me who sent you."

Whoever the fellow was, he was certainly a brave one. He even had the impertinence to chuckle.

"Your nerves are all on edge, colonel," he said. He was even mocking.

"Who sent you?" Doihara repeated.

"Nobody sent me."

The rage suddenly exploded in the colonel. He would teach the fool a lesson. With a flick of his wrist so quick that his victim did not see it, he ripped up the front of the silk gown, yet left the flesh beneath unscratched.

"Perhaps that will convince you . . ." he began and stopped, his mouth falling open, the point of his sword dropping with a thud to the ground. For the same flick of the sword point that had ripped up the gown ripped up something else besides. The gown gaped open, and slowly, as it did so, a linen band bound tightly round the man's chest was pushed aside and fell apart, revealing the firm, full breasts of a woman.

Doihara passed his hand across his face.

"A woman?" he muttered.

"There is no point now in withholding my name any longer," she said. "I am Princess Yoshiko Kamajama. My father was Prince Su, of the late imperial court."

So Kenji Doihara met this strange woman whose one delight was to go about in men's clothing seeking adventures which normally a woman would shun. He had heard stories about her but had not believed them they were so fantastic.

"I have come to offer my services to you," she said. "But you are weary. If the servants had let me up sooner . . . I will come back tomorrow."

"No . . . stay!" he said.

Next morning he spoke to her of Henry Pu-yi as soon as she awoke.

"Let me persuade him," she suggested. "If what I hear about him is true, it should not be difficult."

If she failed, she could do no harm.

"Very well," he said. "You shall try."

So the Beauty in Male Costume, as she thereafter came to be known among the Chinese opponents of Doihara and his gangs, went to Henry Pu-yi. She was patient, but soon it was apparent that she alone would never persuade him to ascend the Manchu throne. Nor did the bomb she planted in his bed. But the snakes did. After the snakes Henry Pu-yi decided that he might as well die an emperor as a commoner.

His acceptance was Doihara's greatest success to date, and his grateful masters rewarded him with the rank of lieutenant general.

After Henry Pu-yi was settled on the Manchu throne, Princess Yoshiko Kamajama continued to work for Doihara. At the same time she found the opportunity to marry and divorce in quick succession three "princely persons" in the Five Northern Provinces of China.

On the eve of her fourth marriage she was attacked by unknown assailants and stabbed. From the wounds she received any other woman—or man—would have died.

But it was not until November 11th, 1945, that a message

carried by a news agency, under the date line Peiping, announced: "Long-sought-for Beauty in Male Costume arrested today in Peiping by Chinese counterintelligence officers."

With the Manchurian Incident closed, Doihara turned his attention fully to the next phase of the plan. This was to detach the Five Northern Provinces of China from Peking and turn them into a second puppet state which would act as a base for the main project of seizing the whole of China.

He himself went to work on men of high rank. Some of them resisted his bribes and his promises; but some fell for him. Among the latter was Huang-sen, an official of the Central Bank of China.

Doihara operated in Peiping—as Peking was now called—as Ito Soma, a Japanese financier, esthete and patron of the arts. In this role he made friends with Mei Lang-fan, the star of the Chinese theater, who introduced him to Huang-sen.

Ito Soma, Mai Lang-fan and Huang-sen met on nights of the full moon on the steps of the Altar of Heaven to discuss poetry, painting, philosophy and Huang-sen's hobby—goldfish. Ito Soma knew the names and habits of six hundred different kinds of goldfish, and Huang-sen was charmed by him.

Presently, in a conversation about the mating habits of one species of fish, Huang-sen confessed to having another hobby—women. Unfortunately, he was now so acutely embarrassed financially that he could not pursue this hobby as enthusiastically as he would wish. A day or two later he was amazed to receive a gift of 200,000 Chinese dollars. At first he refused the money, but Soma soothed him and the temptation was really too great.

Not very long afterward Huang-sen became the secretary of General Chiang Kai-shek. When the Japanese threats became more violent, Chiang called a council of war, at which were present only General Feng Yu-hsiang, General Pai Tsung-chi and his trusted secretary, Huang-sen.

The generals planned to trap a large flotilla which the Japanese had anchored in the Yangtse River at Hankow. In some way the Japanese got wind of what was going to happen, and when the Chinese forces arrived they found no ships.

Chiang immediately ordered an investigation, and this revealed that his secretary had confided the plan to Ito Soma, alias Kenji Doihara, and he paid the supreme penalty.

It was only by executions and ruthless counterespionage that Chiang was able to resist to any degree the espionage of Doihara. In 1938, after the next phase of the plan had begun to operate, Chiang had to execute eight divisional commanders who were known to be Doihara's agents. It is said by reliable sources that more high-ranking Chinese officers were executed in the first six years of the war for dealings with Doihara than for any other military offense of extreme gravity.

The confusion which this one man spread among the enemies of Japan and the assistance which his own government and armies received from his activities will never be entirely evaluated, since he spread his nets so wide that they could never be pulled in altogether.

Though to call Doihara the Lawrence of Manchuria may be a libel on Lawrence's memory, his achievements exceed in scope and outweigh in importance and results the activities of five Lawrences.

CHAPTER 9

Everyone *Can* Spy: Everyone *Must* Spy

With the successful termination of the Manchurian Incident, Japan completed her first half-century of espionage on the Stieber model. Her development in this aspect of her growth toward a modern power on Western lines had been as remarkable and presented as fascinating a phenomenon as in any other sphere; perhaps even more so.

While Kenji Doihara was exercising his evil genius in Manchuria and China, a West European had already been attempting to make an assessment of this Japanese phenomenon. He was a young German at a loose end. Now not so young, he is still, in 1957, at a loose end, though in a very confined sense, and looks like remaining so for the rest of his natural term unless the mood of the free countries changes and the prisoners of Spandau are debouched upon the cruel world.

His name was Rudolf Hess, who was to rise to a position of great prominence as a particular friend of Adolf Hitler's and was destined to achieve a world reputation, first as a mystery man, and then as a madman, by flying to England from Germany fairly early in World War II in an effort, so he said, to bring hostilities to an end.

In 1925 Hess had enrolled as a student at the School of Geopolitics in Munich. The School of Geopolitics was one of those strange manifestations of elaborately confused thinking which from time to time take seed, sprout and burgeon in Germany.

In the early days after the First World War there had come to Munich a former professional officer of the defeated German Army. He came to Munich in a mood of distinct relief, for conditions were so bad in the fatherland that it was difficult for millions of men trained in industry and the professions to find work, let alone a professional soldier.

Why the rector of Munich University should have offered him the post of lecturer in geography, Karl Haushofer—we have met him before at the beginning of our story as the man who solved Goebels' difficulties with Ruth Kühn—was himself slightly puzzled, when he came to consider all things quietly and dispassionately. But it was true, neverthless, and here he was in the ancient and lovely Bavarian capital, determined to hold down the job even if it meant living poised over the precipice of bluff.

Admittedly, he knew enough about the subject to cope with first-year students. It was the more senior courses that he really feared. It is not possible to deceive adolescents for long—as so many teachers have discovered to their cost—and it would take even less time for his colleagues on the faculty to get his true measure.

But Karl Haushofer was not entirely devoid of brains and he brought to the situation in which he now found himself as a civilian the courage that had marked his career in the Kaiser's army. If he could not long survive as a geographer, he would create his own subject, inventing its theory and its terminology, and then sell it for all he was worth.

Casting about for such a subject, in a sudden flash of inspiration he hit upon a very simple, though at that time new, concept of the relation between geography and politics. Explained very briefly, his contention was this: a country's foreign policy does not determine its history; but rather, a country's history is determined by its geographical position and configuration, since it is these which predetermine its foreign policy.

Now this idea, particularly as developed and expounded by Haushofer, had the great merit that there could be something in it, even if, at first sight, it was difficult to say categorically what that "something" might be. Haushofer was also extremely fortunate in being in the best place for launching his subject, for of all professorial agglomerations, those of the German universities have always been Athenian in their enthusiasm for setting up altars to this -ism and that -ism. Not entirely to his utter surprise, in a very short time Haushofer discovered that he had many disciples. Indeed, so rapidly did his following increase, and so wholeheartedly was his theory embraced, that in a very little while Hauhofer left the staff of Munich University and with a chosen band of his most enthusiastic supporters he founded the School of Geopolitics.

Rudolf Hess was greatly taken with the theories of geopolitics and the founder of geopolitics was greatly taken with him, and they became close friends. As his field of study, Haushofer assigned Japan to Hess; and besides keeping the young man quiet in assigning this particular country to Hess, Haushofer was bestowing upon him a special mark of his favor. For many years Haushofer had been a persistent advocate of an alliance between Germany and Japan. He based his advocacy on the belief that eventually Japan must expand into and control East Asia.

Hess spent two years gathering his material and another two years in writing his paper. But when at last he placed his manuscript of 132 typewritten pages containing some 40,000 words in his master's hands, Haushofer found, to his surprise and initial irritation, that his pupil had limited his studies to Japanese espionage.

Hess set out his thesis under three main headings—the history of Japanese espionage; espionage on a mass basis; the objects of Japanese espionage.

According to Hess, Japanese espionage had had its origins in about 1860. When Commodore Perry had compelled the Japanese to open up their ports to foreign trade, the Japanese had opened their minds to Western civilization. For fifty years the Japanese government sent countless diplomatic, trade and naval missions to gather precious information in Europe and America.

They also sent men who pretended to be in search of training and who were, therefore, admitted to the great engineering works and arsenals of the Old and New Worlds. Manufacturers had to agree to hiring Japanese labor as the price for trading with Japan. But in reality, these laborers were trained engineers who came to discover the industrial secrets of the West. In like manner, economic and industrial espionage was carried on by delegates, students and tourists. Hess then continued with a review of the development of Japan as a world power and her formulation and implementation of her expansionist policy, and then stated the objects of her espionage.

These objects, Hess wrote, were to discover not only industrial and military secrets but to pry into the political and cultural affairs of foreign nations. He proceeded to show that nothing, literally nothing, was outside the scope of Japanese espionage activity, quoting as examples of their thoroughness that the personal habits and weaknesses of responsible officers in the armed forces and of important persons in the industrial defense effort were discovered and listed; that agents would not only study the output of an airplane plant but seek to determine which plants supplied the airplane plant with spare parts, over what routes these spares were shipped and whether there were alternative routes, such information being necessary in order to know exactly where to place a bomb with most effect.

In the diplomatic field they were always looking for secret

agreements and confidential consular reports. They had long
suspected that the United States and Great Britain had entered into secret undertakings with regard to the use of bases
in the Far East against Japan.

Under his second heading, espionage on a mass basis, Hess
observed that espionage was second nature to the Japanese.
For generations they had had what amounted to an internal
system of mass espionage in the operation of which neighbor
spied upon neighbor.

Japanese leaders had always treated their people like children. Since the time of the shogunate, plain-clothes agents
and voluntary or impressed informers had been widely employed, and this had developed in the Japanese as a nation a
penchant for spying that was so ingrained that they pursued
it whenever the opportunity offered, particularly when
traveling abroad. This was not to say that every Japanese
found outside the boundaries of his own country was a
trained spy or an agent of the Japanese intelligence service.
Nor did the Japanese travel so that they might have opportunities of spying which in their intense patriotism they believed would acquire merit for them. Nevertheless, whenever a Japanese saw a chance of spying, he spied, and passed
on whatever information he gathered either to a Japanese
consul or to the police when he returned home.

The sight of a Japanese tourist without a camera was a
very rare one. By and large he was a keen observer, though
he suffered from a deplorable lack of judgment, with the
result that he collected a great mass of useless information
and misinformation which he noted down carefully in travel
diaries and which eventually found its way into the files of
the intelligence.

In Hess's opinion, the most efficient of Japanese amateur
spies were the expatriates. They were not averse to criticiz-
ing their country in the presence of foreigners in order to
gain a confidence if they believed they could acquire information only by a show of false friendship. In fact, the num-

ber of Japanese who really thought ill of their country was so small as to be entirely without significance.

It has long been the tradition of espionage services throughout the world to disclaim any knowledge of a captured agent. The Japanese have never followed this practice and diplomatic and consular representatives have always made forceful attempts to protect their agents. The arrest of an agent invariably drew indignant protests and bail was always immediately forthcoming, though these actions were tantamount to an admission of complicity in the activities of the agents.

The reports of both professional and amateur agents were conveyed to intelligence headquarters in Tokyo generally by one of three methods: through consulates, who passed them on by couriers to the embassies, who in turn sent them to Japan, more often than not in diplomatic bags; or they would be handed to special agent-couriers who were ostensibly on tours of inspection; or they would be handed to the captains of Japanese merchant and passenger ships at the last minute before sailing to Japan.

The Japanese agent had the advantage over the agents of almost every other power in that the difficulty of his language, which prevented all but a few foreigners from learn, ing it, protected him against eavesdroppers. Similarly, the difficulties of the written language permitted him to make notes without having to resort to the use of codes.

The great mass of information that was supplied by all these sources was collected by the army, navy and foreign office intelligence bureaus in Tokyo. It was carefully studied, classified and cross-indexed, and then submitted to staff officers. The latter, as well as the intelligence chiefs, also sent instructions to agents abroad when any specific project was under consideration.

Hess made one serious miscalculation in his assessment of the system. He saw the patriotic societies as jingoistic arrogant secret societies whose belief in Japan's divine mission as the ruler of the world was as irrational as it was fanatic. Nevertheless, he recognized that they were the mainspring of Japan's aggressiveness and that they had an influence on Japanese foreign affairs as great as that of the politicians.

Hess had some forthright remarks to make about the Black Dragon Society, some of which were penetrating and some very wide of the mark. Its recruits, he said, came mainly from among those samurai, the fighting men, who found themselves lordless under the reconstruction of the social order and thus without employment. These samurai were known as ronin, or wave men.

The ronin collaborated fairly closely with army intelligence and were supported, in part, by army funds. The extremist elements of the younger cliques, whose aims coincided with those of the societies, were members of one or another of them. There may have been a certain number of ronin in the ranks of the patriotic societies' agents, but, as we have seen, the agents were picked from every walk of life provided they had outstanding patriotic zeal and were otherwise good "agent material." It is strange to note, as Hess noted, that there is no evidence to be found of any collaboration between the societies and navy intelligence. Indeed, a coolness existed between them which, in the general circumstances, was remarkable.

It is true, as Hess remarked, that many of the patriotic societies' agents on the Asian mainland were seen as the lowest scum, strong-arm thugs, hired assassins, blackmailers and adventurers who lived on compulsory "patriotic" contributions or protection money. Such men were employed, however, because the societies operated in every sphere, and conceited and brazen though they may appear, they were nevertheless courageous. Their role was to provoke brawls and street fights and other incidents which any other power would have been very anxious to conceal. But the Japanese used such incidents as excuses to present demands, exact apologies which inflicted loss of face on those who made them, or pigeonholed them for use in the future as pretexts for opening hostilities.

Hess's study of his subject was a very exhaustive one. The intricate workings of the Japanese system of espionage based on Wilhelm Stieber's pattern, which was the child of a typical German mind and on which the German espionage system had always been, still was and still is firmly founded, was entirely comprehensive and of extreme interest to his own typical German mind.

He recognized, too, how much farther the Japanese had taken their model, expanded it and improved upon it to meet their own specific needs. These needs, as we have seen, were dictated first, by their expansionist policy as laid down in the third tenet of State Shintoism, and second, by the need to make themselves secure in Asia so that their development should neither be impeded nor seized by a foreign nation to enhance its own power.

It was the latter which threatened them in this early period. They recognized Russia to be the first great enemy, and it was against Russia that they directed their main espionage effort until the enemy was rendered ineffective and the immediate threat thereby removed.

But while they were subjecting Russia, not only in Asia but in Europe as well, to invasion by the largest secret army ever put into the field up to this time, they were not unmindful of what may be termed "the follow-up."

Even with Russia no longer a direct threat, the Japanese could never feel themselves entirely secure while China was in a turmoil of decadent disorganization. Such a condition was simply inviting some other power to step in and put China to rights. There were several Western Powers, and most notably the British, who had tremendous interests, industrial and financial, in China.

The British had established a colony at Hong Kong into which many millions of pounds sterling had been poured. They had, also, strong interests in Shanghai and other Chinese ports. China was a good customer for their products. Japan's cotton industry was already threatening the interests of the great Lancashire cotton industry. If Britain saw her position in the Orient undermined by the chaos in China, her previous record made it very plain that she would not hesitate to gain control of China in some form or other. (The fact that she was, in the event, too slow off the mark was not to be foreseen by the Japanese at this time.)

This Japan must avoid at all costs; and it was their early realization of it that prompted, even compelled, the Japanese, at the same time that they were concentrating on removing the threat of Russia, to take preparatory steps to bring China under her own control.

In China, then, in the first fifty years, she built up an espionage organization which, even in its very beginnings, was greater than the organization of any other country altogether, and which was capable of tremendous expansion all the time.

She brought to this section of her secret services all the cunning, the devilishness and the unremitting care which she devoted to all her espionage activities. As an example of this tremendous care, we have notes on the case of an agent called Kotai Kozumi. Kozumi was selected to work in the Moslem provinces of west Asiatic Russia. He first of all spent four years at the Tokyo School of Foreign Languages and at the Military Academy.

When he was considered fit by these two institutions, he was sent to Qurban Ali, president of the Tokyo Islamic Order, who before he came to Japan had had many years of most successful subversive activity to his credit. Qurban Ali was to teach Kozumi not only an impeccable accent but also the right mannerisms. Five more years went by before the teacher was sufficiently satisfied with his pupil to allow him to be sent into the field.

It was this boundless patience, which only the Oriental with his very different conception of time can exert, which is one of the outstanding aspects of Japanese espionage. The care which was taken with the preparation of their agents produced a large proportion of the danger they presented.

By the time that Manchuria had been secured to Japan as a mainland base, the chaos of China had been rendered even more chaotic by the machinations of Japanese agents. By means of bribery, threats, violence and particularly drugs, scarcely a Chinese of any note was not under Japanese influence. With covert support they set the war lords one against the other, and by manipulation made it impossible for any one or combination of war lords to achieve a position in which power to bring China to order might have been achieved. They worked ceaselessly, and with equal cunning, in undermining the morale of the masses by forcing them into dope addiction, and destroyed one of the strongest sets of man's ethical values by the extension of brothels in which they encouraged sexual depravity, on the main principle of Stieber's Green House, but on a scale which makes the mind boggle. At the same time they stirred up unrest by bringing constantly to the surface of the normally fatalistic Chinese mind the extremity of his economic lot.

China alone is a vast area, and they covered it all. But while they were making their preparations there, they were not neglecting an even wider field.

Japanese agents were active in Burma, Siam, India, Indochina, Afghanistan and Malaya. Realizing as early as the eighties that to be masters of the Pacific—and also because they had an old score to pay off: Commodore Perry's actions in 1853—they would sooner or later have to join battle with America, long before the close of the nineteenth century they had agents in Honolulu who were sending weekly reports to Tokyo on American defenses and activities there. This organization operating against the Americans was maintained unremittingly right down to Pearl Harbor. The Philippines, also, were subjected to the same kind of attention.

It is safe to say that by the end of the first fifty years of

its existence, starting from scratch Japanese espionage covered
half the physical surface of the globe and to such a degree
that it is doubtful whether anyone could number exactly
the vast army of the emperor's secret servants.

The other half of the world they had not neglected either.
In all the countries of Europe, in Turkey, Egypt, Abyssinia
and North Africa, and across the Atlantic, small cells of agents
centered mainly on attachés at legations and embassies were
probing, discovering and reporting.

And as yet Japan had not turned her serious attention to
North and Central America, and to the rich preserves of the
Dutch East Indies.

It was a fantastic program. As it developed during the twenties and thirties it was to become more fantastic still. Set beside
the espionage efforts of the two greatest world powers, it
reduces England to an homunculus and the United States to a
disembodied wraith, entirely without substance.

America's espionage history is a strange one, and throws
Japan's efforts into even more horrifying relief.

For the first hundred years after the Declaration of Independence, all efforts of the leaders of the American administration were devoted to internal, domestic development. This
called for neither spies nor counterspies.

In 1898, however, Washington realized with something of
a shock that the tyrannical rule of the Spaniards in Cuba had
seeped into the knowledge of Americans and that popular
feeling demanded an end to the former entirely introvert
policies.

The war with Cuba lasted only four months and ended in
a victory for American arms and consciences. But it also meant
more. By the American annexation of Guam, Porto Rico and
the Philippines, and later in the year, of the Hawaiian Islands,
America became an "overseas power"—dare one say it?—
imperialist.

At the time, Japan was building up all her efforts for a
knockout blow at Russia, which she delivered successfully in

1905. This and her closed-door policy in Manchuria led to a definite deterioration in Japanese-American relations, which became so aggravated by precautionary American anti-Japanese measures on the Pacific coast that in 1907 there was a most serious threat of war.

President Theodore Roosevelt, however, met the situation by a combination of a show of force and appeasement, and two agreements were signed with Tokyo in 1907 and 1908. The Japanese, foolishly, read the appeasement to mean that their special position in Manchuria was recognized by the United States, and were rudely disabused when Washington proposed that the Manchurian railways should be internationalized. Nothing came of the idea, but in disappointed retaliation Japan signed a treaty with her late adversary, Russia, in which both parties undertook to help one another in defense of their interests.

The First World War, and Japan's alliance with the Western Powers, seemed to remove the threat of Japanese opposition, at least for the time being. But when Japanese militarism flared up in the twenties and thirties, one would have thought that America would have realized that she was "on the list." The antidote would have been espionage and counterespionage systems which would have kept Japanese at home and their activities abroad under constant and strict surveillance. But on the contrary, the American leaders appeared to spurn the aid of spies and counterspies.

Until the First World War, America had possessed no corps of intelligence police. Such a corps was formed on her entry into the war and developed rapidly. In January 1918 it was decided to increase its strength by degrees to 750, but the armistice and demobilization foiled this intention, and between the two wars the corps shrank to such ludicrous proportions that it can hardly be said to have existed at all.

This state of affairs lasted until June 1939, when, in view of continued reports that Japanese and Nazi spies were active in Panama, Hawaii and the Philippines, President F. D. Roosevelt issued a proclamation declaring that all matters of an espionage, counterespionage and sabotage nature would be in the hands of the Federal Bureau of Investigation, the Military Intelligence Division and the Office of Naval Intelligence.

The directors of these three agencies were to form a committee to coordinate their activities. In 1940 the directors drew up an agreement which defined the jurisdiction of each agency, with particular emphasis on foreign operations, and renewed this agreement in 1942. The Corps of Intelligence Police was resuscitated in 1940 and rapidly expanded until its eventual total strength reached 4,431 noncommissioned officers.

It is true that during the inter-war years, the Military Intelligence Division, the Office of Naval Intelligence and the F.B.I. had been functioning, but they were so sparsely manned that they were quite unable to cope with espionage in America except to a pathetically meager extent.

Perhaps the best way to illustrate how pathetically meager American espionage and counterespionage effort was is to compare the secret service budgets for the middle thirties of Japan, Great Britain and America.

In 1934–35 the Japanese secret service was allowed an appropriation of 13,814,000 yen, the equivalent at the then rate of exchange of 4,000,000 American dollars. At the same time Great Britain was spending 800,000 dollars and the United States 50,000 dollars.

The gap was to widen still farther, until in 1938–39, the Japanese allotted 25,000,000 dollars, while the whole of the British Empire was spending only 1,000,000 dollars and the United States government 240,000 dollars on their espionage and counterespionage services.

The Japanese began serious espionage activities in the United States in 1927. By that year she was also deeply involved underground with Russia. Incidents, shootings, betrayals, alarms and widespread bribery were the order of the day on the Amur River frontier, in Korea, Manchuria, Outer Mongolia and Inner Mongolia, and elsewhere.

In the American and British spheres of interest they were already expanding their activities in the Philippines and in Hong Kong, Singapore and Malaya, and in other parts affecting the Western Powers such as the Dutch East Indies, French Indochina and Siam. It will be noted that all these areas were to be occupied fifteen years later and that they had been the object of long-term preparatory espionage.

The Japanese were still working on the Stieber model, which had long since become outmoded, for it had been proved by the Western Powers to be too top-heavy. But if the model were outmoded it is still strange to the layman that the United States, in view of all the circumstances, should be at the other extreme.

Nor was this shown only in the virtual nonexistence of espionage and counterespionage organizations, but in the outlook of the administration on foreign espionage within the borders of America.

In 1939, for example, the maximum penalty for spying in the United States was the ridiculously light one of two years' hard labor; and when in the previous year a federal grand jury had indicted eighteen German agents, four of whom were in custody, and it was revealed that the Japanese and German secret services were collaborating in America, the State Department vetoed the disclosure of this information to the public for fear of the effect it might have on international relations.

Nevertheless, when specific Japanese activities in the United States come to be considered, it will be seen that providence favored America. For all their monstrous army of spies, the vast Japanese Goliath of espionage was routed by the minute American David of counterespionage. But with adequate forces much of the interim damage could have been avoided, as we shall see.

CHAPTER **10**

Everyone in the Card Index

One of the things about Japanese espionage which had struck Rudolf Hess most forcibly was the intense interest which the ordinary man in the street took in it.

In his report Hess says: "Every Japanese when he goes abroad considers himself to be a spy; and when he is at home he takes upon himself the role of spy catcher. I suggest that this preoccupation with espionage is ingrained in the Japanese, since for very many years under the shogunate a system of secret police was extensively active whose main task was to secure the shoguns against plots on their lives and against their positions."

Hess was quite right in his first observation. Whether his suggestion that it was ingrained by long subjection to the activities of secret police is correct or not, the Japanese authorities worked upon and whipped the interest of the ordinary Japanese deliberately and continuously by well-planned assaults which increased in intensity as Pearl Harbor approached.

Behind Japanese espionage toward the end of its first half-century and well into its second fifty years were the ostensible directors of military and naval intelligence, General Eiki Tojo and Admiral Kiyoshi Noda. In fact, the *eminence grise* of all undercover organizations was General Jiro Minami, a veteran in his middle sixties.

Minami, who was descended from a long line of samurai, was a patient, resourceful plotter. When the puppet state of Manchukuo was set up after the conquest of Manchuria, he asked for and received the appointment of Japanese ambassador to the court of Emperor Henry Pu-yi. About this time, he organized with that other veteran, Lieutenant General Kenji Doihara, the Great Asia Association, which had as its ultimate goal the conquest of all East Asia and the Pacific.

From Manchukuo, Minami moved into Korea which, it is said, he ruled "with an inflexible will, and all Japan by telephone."

Encouraged by Minami and his subordinates, the people of Japan were led to see espionage activity in every move made by any nation in the Pacific, particularly the United States. Thus, when Colonel Lindbergh and his wife made a flying tour of the Kurile Islands in 1931, the American air ace was denounced as a spy.

People like the retired Lieutenant General Kiokatsu Sato were applauded when they made pronouncements such as this one of Sato's: "It is our duty to detest and loathe the people of the United States." And Japanese approval was strengthened, if this were necessary, by the approval of Germany and Italy.

Not only were foreigners treated with suspicion, but Japanese who had social and commercial contacts with foreigners became the objects of intensified police attention. Any foreign tourist carrying a camera was inviting arrest, while the Tokyo personnel of the Soviet news agency, Tass, were the most intensely watched men in Japan.

Then there was the German, Dr. Walter Donath, whose life was made wretched in the interest which the *Kempei tai* took in him.

Dr. Donath was the chief of the German Cultural Institute in Japan, a body set up by the mutual interest of the two governments as a part of the deep and abiding friendship which they had for one another. This being so, one would have thought that the doctor would have been immune from surveillance; but in fact he could not move about Tokyo, and certainly not farther afield, without a secret service "shadow."

One day Dr. Donath decided that he would pay a visit to a branch of the institute on the island of Shikoku, about sixty miles from Kobe, to see how it was faring and to dispense encouragement. As it was in the manner of being a business trip, Donath decided to take with him a Japanese student, whose expenses would be met by the institute, to help him over any language difficulties which might arise.

An overnight boat brought them from Kobe to Takamatsu, in Shikoku, very early in the morning. As they stepped onto the jetty, a plain-clothes policeman stopped them and questioned the doctor closely about his business and his plans for the day. The doctor gave him every detail.

From the jetty they went to the hotel where they had made reservations, and while they were at breakfast, yet another *Kempei tai* agent arrived and questioned Donath at great length about his antecedents, his occupation, his feelings toward and his opinions on the Japanese people, about war in general, and the chances that the Japanese might have in a war with America. Then he, too, had to be provided with the doctor's itinerary for the day.

After spending a useful morning in Takamatsu, Donath and the student took an early afternoon train to another town on the island in accordance with their plan. At the new station they were met by yet another plain-clothes man who escorted them to where they wished to go and waited for them while they did their business in order to take them back to the station.

The following morning at breakfast yet another agent disturbed them with a request for the new day's itinerary and asking the same questions with the express purpose of seeing if the answers would be the same today as they had been the day before. When the man had gone, Donath paid a visit to a factory. As he was sitting in a waiting room there until the man he had come to see could receive him, the police telephoned to warn him that on his return to Kobe he would be passing through a fortified zone and that if he took photographs while traversing it he would be arrested.

The agent who had visited him at breakfast had already warned him about this. In any case, Donath knew that the police were aware that he had no camera; whoever had searched his room and his baggage at the hotel the previous evening had been very maladroit and left signs of his activities everywhere.

As Donath and the student left the factory for their hotel they were stopped by yet another agent, who told them which bus they must take. On another bus which took them from their hotel to their point of embarkation, on a motorboat which took them across the narrow strait to another island and on a second bus which transported them to the boat for Kobe, they were accompanied by yet another agent, who waited with them until the boat sailed.

During the two days that Donath had been away from his base he had rarely been out of sight of the police, who knew —and noted down on their card index, which was most rigorously kept—every move he had made, and had (seriously) kept a tally of the number of times he had performed his most intimate functions in public conveniences.

The extent to which the spy mania was carried is well illustrated by the action of the police in banning the sale of copies of the famous drawings of the Straits of Naruto—which were then being fortified—by the well-known Japanese woodblock etcher, Hiroshige. This appears to be quite a logical action, until it is known that the artist died in 1853.

In 1939 a new antiespionage law was passed by the Diet which provided for a much wider application of the death penalty. Simultaneously there was a tremendous expansion of the counterespionage services.

The public was educated to an even higher pitch of the awareness of the danger of spies by means of exhibitions which displayed what the Japanese believed to be the devious and criminal methods and activities of foreign spies. Hundreds of posters papered the streets, and antispy weeks and even antispy days were promoted. Antiespionage slogans were printed on matchboxes, and there was scarcely a shop window which did not exhibit either a slogan or a poster. The press, the radio and the speeches of officials constantly encouraged every Japanese man, woman and child to be on the lookout for foreign spies and to report the smallest suspicious incident. By these means the whole population was lashed into an unprecedented hatred of all foreigners. And behind it all was the *Kempei tai*, the secret military police, or counterespionage service.

The *Kempei tai*, like the Nazi Gestapo, had always been the most powerful, the most hated and the most feared of all Japanese institutions, both by the Japanese at home, and later by the peoples of the occupied territories. It derived its power, for the most part, from the semi-independent position which it held within the army.

Though it was organized as a combat arm of the army, it was commanded by a provost marshal general, who was directly responsible only to the minister of war. In Japan itself, though its authority ran directly from the minister of war to the commander, the ministries of the interior and justice had occasional and not very serious supervisory powers. Of the rest of the authorities, the navy alone appeared able to keep a check on it, for we find the minister of the navy issuing instructions dealing with the *Kempei tai* control of navy personnel.

All the members of the *Kempei tai* were hand-picked volunteers from the army, and in peacetime were required to have six years' military service before they could be eligible to make application. The standards of intelligence, education, facility in the learning and speaking of languages and of health and physique were extraordinarily high. Since successful counterespionage requires an intimate knowledge of enemy countries, candidates were often drawn from foreign office, embassy and consulate staffs.

Those fortunate enough to be honored by membership in the *Kempei tai* were given one year's training at special schools. The instruction given in these schools was comprehensive, and among the courses provided were law, languages, espionage and counterespionage methods, horsemanship, fencing and unarmed combat, invisible writing, shadowing and entering and leaving buildings.

There was also equally extensive field training. Students were sent to carry out exhaustive investigations of the organization and production methods of Japanese industries, from which they were expected to return undetected. As a further test of their skill, they were made to disguise themselves and to go to places where they were well known.

In 1945 it was estimated by American intelligence that the *Kempei tai*, including the occupied territories, was comprised of 70,000 men, of whom 24,000 were officers. These figures applied only to Japanese members, and if the numbers of native recruits in the occupied territories were added, the total would probably be doubled.

The *Kempei tai* were entitled to wear regular army uniform with special insignia, which consisted of a flowerlike star surrounded by leaves. When working in plain-clothes, the agents frequently wore a button resembling a chrysanthemum on the underside of a coat lapel.

Besides its counterespionage functions, the *Kempei tai* was responsible for army discipline, and in this it had supreme power. A member of the force could arrest a member of the army up to three ranks higher than himself. He could decide and carry out punishment in the field. To demonstrate his superiority he might dress with a complete disregard of uniform regulations and refuse to salute; and to emphasize his special standing he was released from all routine duties.

Wherever the *Kempei tai* was, whether in the home islands or in the occupied territories, its most important function was counterespionage. To perform this function efficiently in their view, its members haunted all hotels, post offices, railway stations, piers and other public places. They supervised photographic supply shops, cafes, brothels, theaters and cinemas and, perhaps rather curiously, sweet shops.

They regulated the sale of electrical appliances, arms, drugs and explosives. They kept tab on canteen waiters, government contractors and the employees of all the important industrial undertakings. They kept a constant shadow on every foreigner who entered the country from the moment he stepped ashore to the moment he left, and they did this so thoroughly that they boasted that they could tell, if asked, how many times an individual went to the lavatory in one day. They exercised a censorship of press, radio, literature and the theater.

Bearing all these many and varied functions in mind, it can readily be understood why the membership of the *Kempei tai* had to be so vast. But for all its many thousands of agents, it could not function with anything like a hundred per cent efficiency without outside help.

As Rudolf Hess discovered, they used informers, who either volunteered or were pressed into service, and controlled them by threats or blackmail. Yet like the Gestapo's reputation when it was at its peak, the reputation of the *Kempei tai* seems to have been founded largely on the myth which it deliberately built up around itself of being omnipresent and omniscient.

Thus, then, stood Japanese espionage and counterespionage when they entered upon their second half-century of existence. Vast beyond the dreams of any spy master in the history of espionage anywhere in the world up to 1930, both arms of the service, and particularly the espionage arm, were to become even more vast as the tempo toward the final showdown in the Pacific, which would include the United States, Central America, the Dutch East Indies, Malaya and Burma as well as the American possessions in the Pacific, as the scene of military endeavor.

CHAPTER **11**

The Plan Goes into the Last Phase

The plan to set up a puppet state in the Five Northern Provinces of China did not go according to plan, so Japan thereupon turned her attention to controlling the whole of the country. Hostilities broke out between the two countries in 1937.

Despite Japanese victories and the loss of almost the whole of her coastline, railways and river systems, China was still resisting when the local war merged into the Second World War.

While all this had been going on, the internal condition of Japan had been subjected to many vagaries, which included an economic slump, political, military and social unrest, and a series of incidents which had resulted in a new order being imposed on the country. This new order was a one-party political system based largely on the fascist model.

And through all this there began to emerge the real intentions of Japan. As early as January 1934 the foreign minister, Koki Hirota, had proclaimed that "Japan bore the entire burden of responsibility for peace in East Asia." Three months later, in April, what was to become known as the Annam

Statement, warned foreign powers against giving China any sort of aid.

In 1935 she signed the Anti-Comintern Pact with Germany and Italy. She had left the League of Nations in 1933 as a result of the Manchurian Incident, and had become somewhat diplomatically isolated, and it was the appreciation of this which made her seek an ostensible friendship with the Anti-Comintern powers.

In December 1935 she abrogated the Washington Naval Treaty, which had established a naval ratio for the United States, England and Japan of 5:5:3. Though in effect this pact was advantageous to Japan, and was accepted at the time as being so, in her new arrogance she found that the arrangement damaged her prestige, though her motives went much deeper. A month later, in January 1936, she walked out of the London naval conference.

The Anti-Comintern Pact brought Japan into conflict with the U.S.S.R. She was actually in the middle of a large-scale battle with Russian forces over Manchukuo's claim to Outer Mongolia when news arrived of Germany's signing of a non-aggression pact with Russia. Unwilling to bear the brunt of the whole weight of Russia, she settled the incident, and though by signing the pact Germany had proved false to her friends, nevertheless, in the following year Japan was content to become a full member of the Axis by joining the Tripartite Pact in September 1940.

There can be no doubt that Germany's resounding victories in Europe up to this time had convinced Japan that the time was now ripe for her to get rid of her enemies in the Pacific and East Asia.

To immunize Russia, a five-year pact of neutrality was signed in April 1941. This, coming after a year of preparations which had included pressure on the Netherlands to supply specific amounts of raw material, agreement by the Vichy government to allow Japanese troops to be stationed in Indochina to help in the war against China and the intervention in the French-Siamese War which broke out in the autumn of 1940, was more than a straw in the wind.

The Japanese plan, to which all indications pointed, was to seize China and all Southeast Asia and the Pacific. In China and the Pacific the main obstacle to the plan was the United States of America. America was giving material and moral aid to Chiang Kai-shek and encouraging the Dutch to resist Japanese demands in the Indies.

Since 1938 the policy of the State Department toward Japan had been growing increasingly tougher. In 1939 the twenty-eight-year-old commercial treaty had been terminated, and in its place had been introduced a licensing system for a variety of petroleum and metal products for export to Japan. The effect of this measure was to place Japan in an economic predicament and the Japanese government realized that unless they were to be thwarted altogether in their plans, some agreement must be reached with America.

A new ambassador was sent to Washington in the spring of 1941. As soon as Admiral Nomura arrived he entered into conversations with Secretary of State Cordell Hull. The negotiations dragged on inconclusively until July, for the United States government put forward plans designed to contain Japan and obstinately refused to give way one inch.

On July 2nd Japan decided to carry out her plans with regard to Indochina even if this meant war with America and England. The Americans had broken the Japanese diplomatic code and learned of this intention. They immediately froze all Japanese assets in the United States, and Canada and England did likewise, while the Netherlands introduced a licensing system. Thus Japan was cut off from all vital supplies of war material imports. Nevertheless, she went ahead with her plan and occupied Indochina.

Early in August Japan, still hoping to immunize America as she had immunized Russia, submitted new proposals, among which she guaranteed the safety of the Philippines, and asking in return that the United States should persuade Chiang Kai-shek to end his resistance in China, lift the embargo on war materials and stop her military preparations in the area. Naturally, these proposals were promptly rejected.

At another conference in September, the Japanese government decided that they would go so far and no farther, and that if the Americans still refused, they would go to war. America rejected these new proposals on October 2nd.

But still the Japanese did not give up hope that the State Department would weaken, and really final terms were put forward.

Admiral Nomura and a special envoy, Saburo Kurusu, were warned, however, that the terms must be accepted by November 25th or "things are automatically going to happen."

The deadline was then changed to November 29th, but on November 26th Cordell Hull returned yet another no.

On December 2nd the Japanese issued orders to the naval forces, which had already been despatched to meet the contingency, should it arise, that Pearl Harbor was to be attacked.

Against this background of events had been imposed longterm policies of espionage in the Dutch East Indies beginning as far back as 1931, and in the United States for almost as long a period. We shall now see, first, how the Dutch were defeated before the first Japanese soldier landed in the Indies, and then America's own strange behavior during her spy invasion.

CHAPTER 12

The Ten-Year Plan in the Dutch East Indies

The chief of the Java police looked across his desk at his second-in-command and from him to the young detective sitting beside him.

"Well," he said, "I don't know what to think! If you had told me this about anyone else in the Indies, I might have believed you. But Tomegoro Yoshizumi . . . well . . . it's unbelievable!"

He stood up and began to pace about his office.

The young detective watched him for a moment or two, a slight uncertainty and unhappiness in his gaze. Then he turned and looked at the assistant chief at his side. The assistant chief's eye quickly opened and closed. Had he winked, or merely blinked?

"I know, sir," the assistant chief said. "It does seem incredible. However, Peters here has produced the evidence."

"But I've known Yoshizumi for years!" the chief exclaimed. "He was here before I was."

"He came to the island in 1932, sir. He's been here for five years," the assistant chief said.

"And all that time he's built up his business and become

a highly thought of member of the community. Why, I've dined at his house a dozen times! I like the little fellow."

"I like him, too, sir," the assistant chief remarked. "But all the same, while he's been taking us all in with his politeness and his dinners and his honesty in business, he's quietly been making a—a kind of inventory of all the raw materials and the commercial values and sending it off to Tokyo. And not just here in Java, sir, but throughout the whole of the Dutch East Indies. He's had his agents everywhere who have kept his information up-to-date for him."

"You really believe he's the head of this organization, Peters?"

The young man nodded.

"Yes, sir. There's no doubt about it. When I found this fellow with a knife in his back—three weeks ago it is now—he had a whole batch of reports on him and he kept muttering Yoshizumi's name."

The chief brightened.

"That's what makes me suspicious," he said. "A chap like that wouldn't tell the police his chief's name. It's a plant."

Peters answered quietly but firmly. "He didn't know I was a policeman, sir. He didn't know what he was saying. He was light-headed from loss of blood."

When the man had died and Peters had been trying to discover his identity, he had come upon the packet of papers in a belt strapped to his waist next to his skin. Luckily he had broken the seals of the packet carefully. The significance of the lists had not been obvious at once. It was only as he pondered them that he realized what they were. Then he had had them photographed and had made up the packet again as it had been.

Peters was fairly new to the Indies. He knew Yoshizumi by reputation as a leading Japanese merchant and had heard that he was highly thought of. But Peters was also young and had an eye on promotion.

He had gone to his chief and told him his theories, and

his chief had laughed at him as though he were out of his mind. But when the young man had asked for permission to keep an eye on the Japanese merchant, he had agreed.

"It will be good practice for you, at all events, and keep you out of mischief," he had said.

The first thing Peters had done was to pay a visit to the merchant. Yoshizumi had agreed to view the body. The dead man was a stranger to him. On a table in the morgue the clothes and possessions of the corpse had been laid out. The package was prominently displayed among them.

"I'm sorry I cannot help you," the merchant had said politely.

The day after Yoshizumi's visit, when Peters had gone to the morgue to give the morgue keeper instructions about the disposal of the body, the man had said casually that on arriving that morning he had found the door unlocked, though he was sure he had locked it before going home the evening before.

"Missed anything?" Peters asked.

"Not a thing!"

Peters examined the lock.

"Have you ever forced this lock with the point of a sharp knife?" he asked.

"Why should I? If I mislay one key there's always another at police headquarters."

Around the interior of the keyhole the agent had observed some small scratches. They were bright, as if newly made.

Peters went back into the morgue and looked at the dead man's things still lying on the table. They were all there.

For some odd reason Peters picked up the package. The seals were intact, but as unaccountably as he had been prompted to pick it up, he now opened the package. His first glance told him that these innocent figures were not those on the lists he had first seen. Back at headquarters a comparison with the photographs settled the matter. There had been a secret visitor to the morgue in the night, and he had substituted this package for the one the dead man had carried.

Peters now put a shadow on Yoshizumi and a record was kept of all his movements and contacts. His house was also watched twenty-four hours a day, and within a week he had received two secret callers, men not unlike the dead man, men whom a prominent member of the community would not normally receive at his home, even secretly.

All Yoshizumi's private and commercial incoming and outgoing mail also received attention. It was a business letter addressed to a firm of instrument makers in Yokohama which revealed Yoshizumi's great secret. Instead of an inquiry or an order, the outer envelope enclosed an inner one, and in this was one of Yoshizumi's periodic reports, an up-to-the-minute census of the bulk and value of the Indies' raw materials.

The chief of police, compelled to action by the irrefutable evidence produced by Peters, took counsel with his superiors. They were as reluctant to believe the story as he had been, and though the evidence could not be denied they were quite firm that, because of Yoshizumi's reputation and position in the Indies, and especially in the commercial life of Java, there must be no scandal.

He was sent for and confronted with the evidence. Then he was told that he would be kept inconspicuously under house arrest and must board the next ship bound for Japan and never return to the Indies.

So, quietly, Yoshizumi withdrew from Java, and in time, if he was remembered at all, it was by elderly reminiscent gentlemen deploring the bad new days, hankering after the good old ones.

2

Japanese espionage in the Dutch East Indies provides an excellent example of foresight and planning.

The Indies are rich in those raw materials which Japan yearly found essential for her industries in ever increasing quantities. They lay within the Pacific and South Asian sphere of that phase of her expansionist plans designed to make her the master of the Orient.

Execution of the espionage plan for the Dutch East Indies was begun in 1932. It was a comprehensive plan, having for its objective the determining of the strengths and weaknesses of every single aspect of the life of the islands. In order to achieve this objective every espionage device known to the Japanese was brought into play. There were also to be two innovations introduced before the plan was complete and the Japanese armies landed to take over from the emperor's secret servants.

Among their devices for learning what they could of the military secrets of the Dutch, the Japanese opened brothels in which the prostitutes were trained in wheedling military information from their clients. They also set up throughout the Indies a chain of hotels managed by highly trained agents who were skilled in this kind of activity.

The majority of the Dutch forces stationed for tours of two or three years had left their families at home in Holland. When leave came round, there was neither the money nor the time to get home or to venture far afield outside the Indies themselves. It became a custom, therefore, for a large number of the men to visit a neighboring island, or a distant part of the island in which they were stationed, and to enjoy for a few days not only a change of scene but a change of environment in the luxuries of civilization to be found in hotels.

The Japanese hotels were cheap, clean, extremely comfortable after the hard bareness of barracks and provided good food and abundant drink. It was the cheapness which first attracted the attention of the Dutchman, brought initially to his notice by circular and advertisement. What attracted him to make his second, third or fourth visit was another amenity offered by the hotels at no extra charge.

Lieutenant van Joost, stationed in Java, decided to spend

his first leave in Sumatra. He was pleased to be getting away from the communal life of the barracks into quieter and more civilized surroundings, and remembering a card which he had received one day shortly after his arrival—and had fortunately put by for future reference—he reserved a room in the Lotus Hotel at Palembang.

When he arrived at the hotel he was surprised to find that it was much more comfortable and pleasant than he could ever have hoped for at the price.

His bag was carried up to his room by a silent, smiling, white-coated porter, while the assistant manager who showed him up hoped he would find everything he needed; but if anything had been overlooked, he had only to ask.

After an excellent dinner van Joost went to the lounge, attracted by the orchestra which had already begun to play for dancing. Thoughtfully, the management had provided partners for lonely young men like the lieutenant, and not partners who were continually pestering for drinks to be bought for them. The evening soon became a very pleasant one. The atmosphere was friendly and the quiet gaiety dispersed all memories of the barracks and the tedious round of military life in Java. At one point van Joost left the lounge and as he was returning he was met by the assistant manager who had shown him to his rom.

"Have you everything you need, lieutenant?" he smiled.

"Thank you—yes."

"You are enjoying yourself?"

"Very much."

"You could not enjoy yourself more, if, for instance . . ." The assistant manager drew him to one side, and spoke to him in a low voice.

"But isn't it expensive?" van Joost asked presently.

"It is included in the daily charge. All you have to do . . ." And his voice sank to a whisper again.

When the orchestra put away its instruments at midnight, van Joost had one last drink at the bar and went up to his room. He was happy; he felt comfortable inside. But the smile on his face as he climbed the stairs was faintly sceptical. However, when he opened the door of his room his scepticism vanished.

Before the end of his leave it seemed to van Joost that he had known his companion a long time. There was no doubt that she had put the final perfect touch to his leave. She was gay, always happy and intelligent. She seemed genuinely interested in him, too. She wanted to know what he did in the Dutch Army in Java. How long would he be in the Indies? Did he ever practice shooting his guns? Was it a good gun? What sort was it? Did they ever make him go out on exercises like they did the troops in Sumatra, poor things? What did he do when he went on an exercise? Were they going to send more soldiers to the Indies? The interest she took in him made him feel a person. It was good to be made to feel a person when one was so long time a soldier.

Was he young and innocent? Perhaps. But his companion had been very skillful. She had asked her questions one at a time, choosing the moment carefully, so that the memory of them was quickly blotted out by other memories.

Unfortunately there were few among the Dutch security forces, whether military or civilian, who possessed the awareness of the young Detective Peters. What was happening to officers and men going on leave appeared to escape the notice of the authorities altogether.

So did the activities of blackmailers and extortioners, who worked mainly upon the more prosperous Chinese expatriates who had relatives in China within the influence of the Japanese there. These agents, who became extremely active after the outbreak of the China Incident, used their weapons to get information regarding those Dutch with whom their victims came into contact.

The authorities could not remain unaware, however, of the results of the activities of another type of agent. These were the agitators who skillfully worked among the poor, urging them to throw off the yoke of the Dutch oppressors, who were draining the wealth of the Indies, which rightly belonged to the natives of the islands, into their own pockets. When demonstrations and riots broke out the Dutch administrators knew that the natives were being provoked, but they did not know that the *provocateurs* had been trained and sent by the Japanese. As a final outcome of these activities the Japanese scored an outstanding victory, even in the darkest hour of their defeat, for it was their pupils who led the revolt against the Dutch when the war was over, though this had not been quite the way in which Tokyo had envisaged the end.

Had the Dutch known what yet another kind of agent was doing they might have been deeply concerned. But in this case the Dutch had an excuse, for the medical spy was a completely new adjunct to espionage. A number of specially trained medical officers of the Japanese Army Medical Corps were sent to the Indies. Working as laborers, waiters and clerks both in their work and particularly in their leisure they set themselves to study the sanitation and general health conditions of the islands, so that when the Japanese armies arrived they would know exactly what must be done to prevent the outbreak of epidemics.

The moving force in all this glut of espionage was a certain Dr. Tsubota. It was he who invented the second innovation which the Japanese introduced into the technique of spying in this period.

As the time drew near for the invasion of the Indies, it became more and more imperative for the Japanese to know more and more of Dutch military plans. But when the Japanese, after the start of the China war, in their great need for raw material, began arrogantly to threaten the Indies if they did not supply them, the Dutch unaccountably stiffened. Security was tightened and a new awareness of what was happening produced a serious threat to Japanese espionage. Dutch officers and men no longer patronized the Japanese hotels. Even the prostitute spies in the ordinary brothels found their clients to be extremely ignorant all of a sudden of what was going on.

It was at this time that Dr. Tsubota conceived his novel idea. Large numbers of the clerks in the employment of the Dutch military administration were Javanese. Always intelligent, often high-born, a prominent proportion of them were homosexuals, which has not the significance in that part of the world that it has in the West. These Javanese clerks, in whom the Dutch had great confidence, by the very nature of their work would be in possession of many of those secrets the Japanese wished to learn. Dr. Tsubota therefore groomed yet another entirely new type of agent to whom he gave the name of "male Mata Hari." Since the Japanese were in possession of the bulk of intelligence when they landed in the Indies, Tsubota's scheme could not have been so farfetched as it might seem to Occidental minds.

3

Seven months after the respected Japanese merchant Tomegoro Yoshizumi had been discreetly deported from Java, Detective Sergeant Peters burst unceremoniously into his chief's office.

"They've got him!" he shouted.

"Who are you talking about?" his chief demanded.

"Yoshizumi, naturally."

A smile spread over the chief's face.

"Where?" he asked.

"Here, in Batavia!"

On his arrival in Tokyo, to regain face Yoshizumi had volunteered to return to the Indies and his offer had been accepted.

This time he came to the islands not as a respected merchant but as a native; and as a native, he picked up almost where he had left off, though he changed his technique a little. Within a few weeks of his arrival the Dutch police had heard of his insolent return. A disgruntled contact had provided the information. But though the whole of the force had been alerted, their quarry had been able to elude them. Now at last they had found him. Faced with a fat wad of 57,000 guilders—the balance of the sum provided by Tokyo—he confirmed his identity. This time there was no discreet deportation, but trial and imprisonment.

It was one of the very few successes the weak Dutch counterespionage had. Perhaps the blame does not lie entirely at their door, for they were enveloped in a web of spying such as has rarely been spun by any nation.

And on the other side of the Pacific this same nation was simultaneously spinning another web, not so completely enveloping to be sure, but faced with an almost equally counterespionage-weak victim—the United States and Central America.

CHAPTER 13

The Assault on Central America

The assault on the North American continent would
be a very different matter from the assault on the Asian mainland, if only by reason of the four thousand miles of ocean
separating Japan from her objective. Even for her attack on
both Russia and China, Japan had foreseen the wisdom of
having a base where men and materials might be built up in
sufficient quantities to assure success from the first moment of
joining battle.

The securing of such a base presupposes certain conditions.
If the country to be used is not so friendly that it will submit
to an amicable arrangement being reached, then it must be so
weak that it cannot argue effectively when you set about establishing yourself there without permission. It must also
border on the country which is your ultimate objective. It
must be supplied with communications of a sort which will
facilitate your movement toward your objective should you
have to make that move quickly because your enemy has
interpreted your plan. It must have reasonable landing facilities
so that you are not impeded by physical considerations in the
difficult operation of speedily building up your strength. These

173

are ideal conditions; sometimes the gods favor you and provide them. Since the gods not only favored the Japanese plan for "bringing the whole world under one roof" but had laid it upon the people with strict injunction, it would have been thoughtless of them not to provide such bases.

A SKETCH MAP
of MEXICO
Showing Centers of
Japanese Interest
Railway ++++++++
Road ━━━━━━━

And indeed they had. For the assaults on the Asian mainland, there had been Korea and Manchuria, the former taken without a blow, the latter weak and amenable to cunning undermining. Not surprisingly, therefore, the base was to hand for the assault on the American continent.

A glance at the map will immediately reveal the physical suitability of Mexico.

The Gulf of California is an excellently sheltered inland sea, approximately eight hundred miles in length, with an average width of one hundred miles. Comparatively free of reefs and rocks, it has a central channel some fifty miles in breadth and seven hundred miles in length which is 6,000 feet deep.

It is, therefore, a ready-made, natural harborage capable of accommodating a vast fleet. It could be made as impregnable as any base might be by fortifying San Gabriel, at the southern tip of Lower California, and Mazatlan, on the Mexican mainland opposite San Gabriel.

Roughly halfway up the Mexican coast of the gulf is the port of Guaymas. As ports go, it is not a modern port, but equipment transported with the first waves of supplies could soon remedy that. Guaymas, however, has a strategic importance. The main west Mexican highway starts only a few miles away and runs up to the border of Arizona. Almost parallel with it runs the Southern Pacific Railway.

Parts of Mexico are flat, sufficiently so to provide airstrips as bases for assault aircraft. On the other side of the Central American isthmus is the Panama Canal, a waterway as vital to America, and especially an America at war in the Pacific, as the Suez Canal is to the Eastern Hemisphere. Control the Panama Canal and you take away at once half the enemy's sea strength.

If physically Central America had its attractions, its ethnological attractions were no less. The people of Central America are innately lackadaisical; the climate of their country and their heredity are too strong for them to be otherwise. True, they had some armed forces, but numerically they presented no problem and their equipment even less of one. Not only that, their leaders at this crucial time were susceptible to bribery and corruption, and there was constant internal friction in every one of them, which not only weakened their governments but their whole structure.

As a base for such reasons as the Japanese wanted it, it

could not have been much improved. It was a pity, no doubt, that it was such a long way from the home base, but that aspect could be provided for.

So a major part of Japanese espionage preparations was directed toward Central America, and here we shall see the extraordinary adaptability which was one of the prominent features of their syping.

Certainly they had learned well the main principles of spying—that the spy must have a good ostensible reason for being where he is; that he must make himself inconspicuous and dissolve as much into his background as possible; and that neither by word nor deed must he attract the suspicions of the inhabitants toward himself.

So while you will find both in Central America and on the West Coast of the United States the full exploitation of sex which the Japanese used as one of their main weapons of espionage when most other nations shied away from it as they would from a case of bubonic plague, you will not find peddlers of pornographic pictures and literature, no dope peddling, no paneceac medicines, no priests or monks, no traveling salesmen of ribbons and laces, buckles and fans. Instead you will find small farmers, dentists, barbers, language students, shirt sellers, soda water bottlers, doctors and thousands upon thousands of fishermen.

In their espionage invasion of America the Japanese came up against their greatest handicap when spying in an Occidental country—their physical characteristics, which they cannot disguise and which mark them down, not only as foreigners, but as Japanese. Here they met the problem in all its force, for according to their ideas if their spying was to be effective they must use the same vast numbers here that they used elsewhere; and it was not possible for them to coerce sufficient numbers of natives to enter their service. So they had to choose roles for their agents which would allow them to operate without suspicion. As we shall see, they chose those roles well and with considerable ingenuity.

We have seen this ingenuity at work in the efforts of Dr. Tsubota in Java, who coped with a difficult situation by employing an entirely new type of agent, his male Mata Haris. But it is doubtful whether any nation except Japan would have opened an espionage campaign, even in Central America, by attempting to teach the Mexicans to fish *scientifically*.

One of the experts in the Japanese conception of scientific fishing was Dr. Yochuchi Matsui, who arrived in Mexico in 1935 by a special arrangement between the Japanese and Mexican governments. Matsui may have intended to give the Mexican Pacific fishermen the benefit of his knowledge, but he had another and, for the Japanese, more important reason for coming to Mexico. When he had paved the way he was to attempt to persuade the Mexican government to give permission for the establishment of a colony of Japanese fishermen at San Gabriel Bay, on the southernmost tip of the peninsula of Lower California.

Not long after his arrival, Dr. Matsui made the acquaintance of Captain Manuel Camiro. Camiro was already aware of the doctor's chief assignment and undertook to act as his intermediary with the Mexican government.

Finding his first attempts at explaining scientific fishing met with little success with the Mexican fishermen, who had no fault to find with their own methods which their grandfathers and great-grandfathers had used for centuries before them, he decided to concentrate his efforts on achieving his primary assignment. So, with Camiro, he moved to Guaymas, the little fishing port about midway up the east coast of the Gulf of California.

At Guaymas, Matsui and Camiro began to entertain the local officials in a comparatively lavish style to prepare the ground for meeting more important and influential government officials. But when the latter were encountered they proved to be disappointingly uncooperative.

Their lack of cooperation had its springboard in the fact that in San Gabriel Bay a considerable number of Mexican pearl fishers were already engaged in a not unlucrative business. Not unnaturally, the pearl fishers themselves saw in the Japanese proposal a threat to their own livelihood, and the government divined that it would most certainly mean a loss of revenue for them. By an arrangement between the pearl fishers and the government, the pearl fishers made a most vigorous protest of which the government was bound to take notice officially.

But Camiro and Matsui were persistent and patient men, and for three years they entertained and bribed, but were no nearer to reaching their goal than they had been at the beginning.

It was Camiro who lost interest first, and this loss of interest was prompted by a message conveyed to him by the San Gabriel Bay Pearl Fishers Associatian. A full meeting of this body was held on December 19th, 1938, and resolved unanimously that if Captain Camiro continued his efforts on behalf of Dr. Masui he should be permanently removed, and that this decision should be immediately conveyed to the captain. Knowing his countrymen very well, Camiro at once left Guaymas and wisely never showed himself there again.

Matsui, however, stayed on, for Guaymas had for some years been the headquarters of Japanese espionage on the west coast of Central America.

At 323 Avenida XIV, Guaymas, in 1930, a Japanese called F. Matsumiya had set himself up as a bottler of soda water. His little factory soon became so popular that there was scarcely a master of all of the many Japanese fishing boats and other types of vessels that used the port who did not visit it as soon as they stepped ashore, even before they went to report to the shipping office.

Matsumiya was a self-sufficient man. He made no Mexican friends nor did he take part in the social life of other Japanese residents in Guaymas and nearby Empalme. But besides the masters of fishing boats he did receive other visitors, who came alone and departed almost as soon as they arrived.

One of the largest of Japanese fishing boat companies was the *Nippon Suisan Kaisha*. Approximately eighty per cent of the stock of this company, which was interlocked with the great Matsui arms combine, was owned by the Japanese government.

Nippon Suisan Kaisha had a branch office in Guaymas the assistant manager of which was a man named Edisioka. Anyone wishing to make contact with the captain of a fishing boat first approached Edisioka; but he was unable to give a definite answer until he had consulted the soda water bottler of Avenida XIV. If a matter required the cooperation of superiors, Matsumiya would telephone to S. Imamura, the manager of *Nippon Suisan Kaisha*'s head office in Mexico City. Imamura was known on several occasions to postpone appointments with high Mexican officials in order to attend to soda water bottler Matsumiya's requests without delay. Every Sunday afternoon Edisioka went to Empalme to visit a friend, José Gokoku.

Gokoku—which means "for the nation"—had first come to Empalme in 1935, where he had opened up a restaurant next door to the Roman Catholic Church. When his business was progressing he sent for his wife and son to join him.

Now, there were other considerations of importance to the Japanese in laying their plans besides the eminent suitability of the Gulf of California as a harborage. For example, any invasion force destined for the United States could be landed at Guaymas and march north toward Arizona along the main road connecting Mexico with the American southwest states, or, better still, be conveyed by the Southern Pacific Railway, which provided the only means of transport on the west coast of Mexico in the rainy season. The most important marshaling yard and repair shops of the S.P.R. were situated at Empalme.

Edisioka was not Gokoku's only visitor on Sunday afternoons. Working in the marshaling yard and repair shops at this time were at least a dozen Japanese mechanics who, with four or five compatriots from Guaymas, formed Gokoku's entire clientele.

At five o'clock on Sunday afternoons all of them would meet at the restaurant. Gokoku's son, a young man of about twenty, would squat outside the door and remain there until the first of his father's customers began to leave, which was usually around midnight.

Though Gokoku provided refreshment, eating was only a subsidiary function of the gathering. Seated on hard chairs facing Gokoku and Edisioka, each of those present would make his report for the week.

In the course of their duties as mechanics, the S.P.R.'s Japanese employees traversed every inch of the permanent way. But besides carrying out repairs to the line, with magnificent Leica cameras fitted with tele-lenses they explored every road and trail between the railway and the coast and every mountain and desert track between the railway and the interior.

This group was also in contact with the Yaqui Indians. Early in April 1939, Urbalejo, chief of the Yaquis, and his second-in-command, Joe Mattus, held a secret meeting with Nazi agents at Yuma, Arizona, which was arranged by Edisioka's men.

At the Sunday afternoon gathering there would also be one or more Japanese who lived in the towns and cities of Sonora, the province of Mexico in which Empalme and Guaymas are situated. The most frequent of these visitors were L. Z. Okamura, from Cananea, up near the United States border, and Dr. Iwamoto. These two would arrive on Saturday at Edisioka's house, accompany him to Empalme on Sunday and return home on Monday.

Gokoku's restaurant was certainly not a financial success. Nevertheless, in November 1937 he became the owner of a Ford V-8 truck, which had been presented to him, as a matter of fact, by Edisioka. Thereafter, whenever a Japanese fishing boat put in at Guaymas for fueling or repairs, Gokoku and his truck would disappear for two or three days. He would explain to inquisitive neighbors that he was foraging for vegetables for his restaurant, but they noticed that he very rarely had any success.

On these journeys he most frequently took a northerly direction. Occasionally, however, he would go south to Mayo River Valley and would be away for at least a week. On January 9th, 1938, he traveled 150 miles to Navajoa to visit a compatriot called Imukahi, who owned an ice-making plant and 500 acres of level ground there; another called Morimoto, the owner of a small corn-milling business; a third, Tanada, a barkeeper; and a Japanese dentist, Ieda, from Topolobampo.

Gokoku was not the only Japanese around Guaymas to become the proud owner of a new Ford V-8 truck. Every farmer, fisherman and restaurant keeper in the area was also presented with one at the same time. Like Gokoku, these men were transporting arms and ammunition from Japanese boats and caching them at such centers as Huatabampo, Topolobampo and Los Mochio.

Until February 11th, 1938, a small house in Calle 22, Guaymas, was used as a temporary depot for arms. On this day, however, a crate of fish which was being unloaded by a Japanese fisherman crashed to the ground and split open. True a few score of fish scattered in all directions, but so did boxes of ammunition. When Mexican labor union officials visited the house the following day, having heard of what had happened from a member who saw the incident, it was empty.

Dr. Matsui never did get his scientific fishing colony at San Gabriel and he eventually turned his attention to Turtle Bay, on the west coast of Lower California. Turtle Bay was what might be called the headquarters of the largest invasion fleet ever to operate in peacetime, and it was here that a handsome young Japanese fisherman broke the heart of Carmencita.

There had put into Turtle Bay one day a Japanese fishing boat, called the *Taiyo Maru No. 3*, for repairs to her engine.

Some part had had to be brought from Mexico City, so she had stayed nearly a fortnight.

On her very first evening in port several members of her crew had come into the tavern. Among them was a handsome dark bright-eyed young man. As Carmencita handed him the drink he had ordered, accidentally their hands had touched. They had looked at one another and then dropped their eyes.

When the tavern closed and Carmencita left to go home, she found him waiting for her. Shyly he asked if he might see her home. Almost as shyly she gave her permission.

By the end of ten days Carmencita was deeply in love, and on the night before the *Taiyo Maru No. 3* sailed, Shoichi clung to her as desperately as she clung to him and begged her to have no eyes for any other man. He would be back in two months. Would she wait for him? Impatiently.

And yesterday the *Taiyo Maru No. 3* had sailed back into Turtle Bay.

As soon as she heard the news, Carmencita ran down to the harbor.

"Is Shoichi there?" she had called up to a Japanese sailor swabbing the deck.

He smiled at her. "Shoichi who?" he asked.

"Shoichi Motomura."

He shook his head. "No, he's not here. He's not with the ship any longer."

She had not believed him. He was teasing her. She had stood by the gangplank for hours scanning the faces of every sailor who came ashore. It was dark before she was convinced that Shoichi was not on board. And not only Shoichi but any other member of the crew who had served the *Taiyo Maru No. 3* when she was last in Turtle Bay.

"Oh, well," one ignorant fisherman was laughing now. "Let it be a lesson to our girls not to fall in love with Japanese fishermen. The local boys are always here."

The *Taiyo Maru No. 3* was only one of five hundred Japanese fishing boats operating off the coasts of California and Central America. The Japanese had first started coming to these waters in the late twenties and had gone on increasing in numbers until in 1939, out of the 1,000 foreign-owned fishing boats working the American fishing grounds, fifty per cent were owned by Japanese masters or fishing companies.

In the early years of this invasion, a large number of the Japanese boats were British ex-coast guard vessels, bought cheaply and refitted in Japan. But when the refitting was carried out the three-inch gun and machine gun mountings were not removed. They were left *in situ*, and it would be only the work of a few minutes for the guns to be back in place should a fishing boat ever be required to turn raider.

When new fishing boats were constructed in Japan, gun mountings were also included. This was not due to the "slavish copying" of which the Japanese have always been guilty.

In size the boats ranged from a maximum of 2,000 tons down to eighty tons. The larger ones had a cruising range of 6,000 miles, and it was no uncommon occurrence for them to put into port after a trip lasting several months with their unusually large holds quite empty. The hulls of these larger vessels were often constructed of tempered steel. This is an unusual feature in any type of bona fide fishing boat. At a time when ship-to-shore telephones were the very latest word in nautical communications and many large passenger liners did not possess them, all the larger and a prominent number of the smaller Japanese fishing boats were equipped with them. They were also equipped with the most up-to-date diesel engines and with radios.

Under the pretense of fishing for bait, the fishermen were constantly taking soundings of the approaches to harbors, and of the harbors themselves. Practically all the members of the crews possessed expensive Leica cameras with which they photographed harbor installations and the coastline, even going so far as to use infra-red cameras at night.

Half the crews of fishing boats flying the American flag

but under Japanese control were Nisei, or American-born Japanese. The other half were alien Japanese. The regulations governing the landing of alien seamen were strangely lax. No record of their landings and departures was ever made, and Japanese agents were quick to perceive the advantages of a state of affairs which would allow them to go ashore disguised as a fisherman, carry out their missions and return aboard without any note being made of their entrances and their exits. The majority of the alien Japanese seamen were officers in the imperial navy.

They were prone to strange actions. In November and December 1938, for example, there was a glut of tuna, and most of the fishing boats in Turtle Bay were laid up. The glut continued into January 1939, but when in that month the American Pacific fleet put into San Pedro and San Diego for maneuvers, there was not a single fishing boat that did not up anchor.

The majority of the boats in Turtle Bay were owned by the Southern Commercial Company, whose manager was a Japanese called T. Abbe. As soon as the fleet had finished its maneuvers, Abbe made for Japan on a flying visit—taking a consolidated report on all that the fleet had been engaged in doing.

The Mexican fishermen who made fun of Carmencita and her lover who did not return in the *Taiyo Maru No. 3* entirely missed the significance of the situation. The *Taiyo Maru No. 3* had not put in at any American port while she had been away from Turtle Bay; nor had she had time to go to Japan and back. Yet the whole of her crew had been changed!

The *Minato Maru* specialized in changing her master. On November 30th, 1935, flying the Tobata flag and carrying a crew of eight officers and twenty-eight men, she set out for San Diego commanded by Captain F. Fukino. But on December 20th she arrived at Balboa, at the entrance to the Panama

Canal, thousands of miles off course and in the opposite direction from San Diego.

Two days later she left Balboa, giving her destination as San Pedro. On January 17th, 1936, she put in at Salina Cruz, in Mexico, having changed her Tobata flag for that of Tokyo. On March 14th she stopped at Guaymas, where Captain Fukino visited Matsumiyo, the soda water bottler. Eventually she did reach San Pedro, but now no longer flying the Tokyo flag but the Shimonoseki flag; and her master was no longer Captain Fukino, but Captain Suekichi Imamura.

After staying four days in San Pedro, the *Minato Maru* sailed to Mazatlan. Once every four months she was scheduled to call at San Pedro. When she arrived there on September 19th, Suekichi Imamura had been replaced by Captain Yukio Yamashita. On her next visit at the end of December, Yamashita in his turn had been replaced by Yukatsu Okomoto.

The *Minato Maru* was not alone subject to these strange happenings. The *Sendai Maru, Bansiu Maru* and *Taiyo Maru Nos. 1, 2, 4, 5* and *6* could all have reported similar experiences.

None of them put in at any port on their way to and from San Pedro; nor had they had time to go to Japan. The changes had, in fact, been made in midocean from Japanese warships; for all these masters were lieutenant commanders of the Japanese Navy, and leaders of groups of spies.

Japanese fishermen spies were by far the most numerous of all the various types of spies operating both in Central America and on the west coast of the United States. It is estimated that at peak they must have numbered almost ten thousand. The results achieved by them warranted only a small fraction of this number. But it was a Japanese idiosyncrasy to work with astronomical figures. They were doing exactly the same thing in the vital Panama Canal Zone, though there the agents were not fishermen or coolies or soda water bottlers.

In 1937, there were no less than forty-seven Japanese barbers in Panama City and eight in Colón. Panama City is at the Pacific entrance to the Panama Canal; Colón is at the Atlantic entrance. In Panama City they were concentrated round the highly select and exorbitantly expensive Avenida Central and the Calle Carlos A. Mendoza. There were so many of them that they formed a union, the Barbers' Association, to which no barber who was not Japanese was admitted, though Japanese fishermen were made welcome at the meetings! The meetings were held in a second-story room at 58 Calle Carlos A. Mendoza. The founder of the Barbers' Association was not even a shopowner, but a barber's assistant named A. Sonada.

The Japanese consul in Panama, Tetsuo Umemoto, attended the meetings regularly, and he and Sonada sat side by side, facing the rest of the members. Sonada's real position could be partially gauged from the fact that Umemoto never sat down until the barber's assistant was seated. But whenever another member was present, neither Umemoto nor Sonada would sit down until he was sitting, but would stand and bow very low until a sign indicated that they too might be seated. This man's name was T. Takano, and he owned a very small business in a less wealthy district, at 10 Avenida B.

Another important member of the association was Katarino Kabayama, a gentle-voiced, placid-countenanced business-man in late middle age who lived at 11 Calle Colón. Kaba-yama had not always been a businessman. In his younger days he had been a barefoot, tattered fisherman. But even then, when he had gone aboard a Japanese warship visiting Panama, not bothering to change out of his tatters, he had been piped aboard, while the assembled crew had come to a smart salute. When he had left, after a two-hour interview with the com-mander, he had been piped over the side. Then he had rowed back to his fishing boat.

Kabayama was a close associate of the consul. Whenever Takano visited the captains of Japanese ships calling at

Panama, Kabayama invariably accompanied him. If asked, he would say that he was doing business with the mess stewards.

But he was not the only businessman who found it worth his while to operate in the canal zone. One of the others was a certain T. Tahara, who came as the traveling representative of the newly formed Official Japanese Association of Importers and Exporters for Latin America. He rented a room in the offices of Boyd Brothers, the shipping agency, in Panama. For the big businessman he made himself out to be, his mail was curiously insignificant in bulk. This gave rise to speculation. His superiors felt that he had thus been compromised and recalled him to Tokyo.

Before he set up his experimental cotton station in Costa Rica, Takahiro Wakabayashi had also operated in Panama as the representative of the Federation of Japanese Importers and Exporters, which was really the O.J.A.I.E.L.A., Tahara's organization, under a slightly changed name.

With disarming audacity, Wakabayashi established himself in the Tivoli Hotel, which was run by the United States government. Very soon he was extremely active negotiating for manganese. He saved time by traveling in a private charter aircraft. The amounts of manganese he bought were trifling, but he was very successful with the photographs of military installations throughout the Canal Zone which he took from his airplane.

Rather out of the usual run was a shirt shop which used to be on Calle Loa, between the Avenida Herrera and the Avenida Amador Guerrero. The owner was an attractive Oriental lady who called herself Lola Osawa.

Lola's real name was Chiyo Morasawa, and she had arrived at Balboa from Yokohama as long ago as May 24th, 1929, in the liner *Anyo Maru*. As soon as she landed she disappeared from the public view, and it was not until a year later that she reappeared at the other end of the canal, in her shirt shop.

Lola's husband lived with her in rooms over the shop. He had entered Panama illegally, for his passport contained no visa. He gave out that he was a merchant. In fact, he was a reserve officer in the Japanese Navy. He and Lola specialized in photographing all objects of military importance in the Canal Zone, and they operated without interruption for more than ten years.

When the Axis countries agreed to collaborate in espionage, the Canal Zone became one of their most vital points of interest. Control of the canal, which automatically entailed command of the zone, could cripple the movement of the United States fleet. So they set about wooing the republics on either side of the Republic of Panama, Italy serenading Costa Rica and Nicaragua, while Germany exerted all her charm on Colombia.

But the Japanese had their own ideas. At Corinto, in the Cauca Valley, thirty miles from Cali and two hours' flying time from the canal, they established a colony of several hundred of their countrymen on terrain that was long, level and flat and which could be transformed in a few hours to an airstrip capable of accommodating aircraft landed from carriers or assembled on the spot.

In 1934 the Japanese increased their efforts to obtain a base near the Pacific entrance to the canal. Permission was sought to set up a refrigeration plant on Taboga, a small island facing Panama, not to be confused with the British-owned island of Tobago, in the Lesser Antilles. Taboga would have been an excellent vantage point from which to observe the canal's Pacific defenses.

When permission was refused, and a rumor became current that the authorities were considering banning all foreign fishing in Panama waters, a Japanese store owner in Panama, Yoshitaro Amano, was so undismayed that he formed a new company called Amano Fisheries Ltd. The "flagship" of Amano Fisheries was the *Amano Maru*. Built in Japan in July 1937, it was the largest and most luxuriously appointed fishing boat in the world at that time. When in September 1937 it became known that the United States was contemplating excavating another canal through Nicaragua, and that some out-of-the-ordinary fortifications were being built in the military zone at Managua, Amano lost no time in going to investigate.

He arrived in the area at 8 A.M. on October 7th, 1937. At 8:30 A.M. he was under arrest, charged with suspected sabotage and taking photographs in a prohibited area. As happened when he went to visit Wakabayashi in Costa Rica and was arrested there on similar charges, and as happened when he repeated the experience in Colombia, he was acquitted. There are some who hint that the fact that he rated as a millionaire in Panama may have had some bearing on these verdicts.

The Japanese who arrived in Panama were well provided with passports, which enabled them to change their names from time to time. On June 7th, 1934, for example, the Japanese Foreign Office issued passport No. 255,875 to Masakazu Yokoi. Though he had permission to visit all the Central and South American countries, he applied only for a Panamanian visa. He arrived in Panama on September 28th, 1934, and did nothing but consort with fishermen and barbers. On July 11th, 1936, while on a return visit to Tokyo, he was issued with another passport, this time in the name of Shoichi Yokoi, and thereafter traveled on whichever of the two documents seemed to offer him the greater safety at the moment.

Since professional men are not expected to maintain regular office hours, the dental profession was a favorite "cover" for Japanese agents. In Panama City and Colón they were not so numerous as the barbers. In fact, Mexico, and especially its western provinces, was the particular hunting ground for dentists.

The strategic importance of the Southern Pacific Railway has already been noted. There was also an equally important highway leading to the United States, which began in Guaymas and passed through the border town of Nogales.

At 40 Calle Granja, Nogales, lived the dentist, Dr. Hoiyo Takaichi. Hoiyo was not an outstanding member of his profession, but no Japanese tourist or businessman entering the United States from Mexico would consider going on his way without having first visited him. Among his "patients" he counted at least thirty Japanese scattered at various points along the highway carrying on a variety of poorly paid occupations. Yet each was the owner of an expensive camera.

In the town of Hermosillo, placed strategically at the other end of the highway, was another dentist, Dr. L. M. Iwamoto, who had his consulting room and surgery at 81 Calle Serdan. Iwamoto had his own little band of twenty or so agents, who were employed in barbershops, ice cream parlors and restaurants in the town.

From the very rare attendances which he made at his surgery Iwamoto did not seem to have his heart in his professional work. He preferred making visits to Guaymas, where he never failed to call on Matsumiyo, the soda water bottler.

The liner *Tyoko Maru* called at Guaymas on a monthly schedule. Each month, a few days before the departure of the *Tyoko Maru* on her return to Japan, Iwamoto would drive to the Japanese farming colony in the Mayo River Valley. He would inspect there, not the colonists' teeth, but the progress they were making on the long, level acres they were "cultivating." He would then return to the soda water factory, and when the captain of the *Tyoko Maru* called to say farewell to the soda water bottler, he would be handed the latest report of the Mayo River Valley project.

So the barbers, dentists, farmers, traveling salesmen, shirt sellers, consular officials and fishermen watched over the defenses of the Panama Canal and prepared Central America for the day when the fleet of Japanese transports and supply vessels would sail into the Gulf of California and set up in Mexico and Costa Rica and Nicaragua the bases from which they would humble the great United States of America.

In the meantime, in those same United States, other secret servants of the divine emperor were spinning their webs in preparation for the day when the earthly armies of the sun goddess would march over the border of Mexico into Arizona.

CHAPTER **14**

The Student of English at Stanford

On August 13th, 1936, a Japanese fishing boat, one of the *Taiyo Marus*, tied up at a dock in San Francisco. Presently down the gangway came a dapper little Japanese, well-dressed and carrying an expensive piece of baggage. He was directed at once to the United States immigration officers who took his passport and looked through it.

"Ever been in the United States before, Mr. Ohtani?" the official asked.

The passport had been recently issued, and except for the one visa and the particulars of the holder, it was in its pristine state. But Mr. Ohtani might have had another passport before this one, and that passport might have run out.

Mr. Ohtani shook his head.

"No, sir," he told the official. "I have never been in the United States before."

"What is the object of your visit, Mr. Ohtani?"

"I am coming to study English at Stanford University."

"You seem to talk English all right to me," the official smiled.

"I wish to speak English perfectly."

192

"A good many of your compatriots come here to learn English."

"So I believe."

"Well good luck, Mr. Ohtani. Enjoy your visit to the States."

The little Japanese picked up his suitcase, pocketed his passport and moved toward the pier entrance.

The immigration official looked after him and remarked to a colleague: "Funny people those little Japs."

"I know," replied his friend. "But what makes you pass that judicially considered judgment at this moment?"

"Well," said the official, "look at his clothes and look at that bag he's carrying, and he's coming to Stanford to learn English. He could obviously afford to come first class on a luxury liner, and yet he's come the 4,000 odd miles from Tokyo in a stinking fishing boat."

To which his friend replied, since he was of Scots descent: "And very commendable too. He'll have saved at least half the fare of a luxury liner."

"I didn't know the Japs were so thrifty."

"I couldn't say whether they are as a nation. Not all Scotsmen, not even all Aberdonians, are thrifty. But there's a leaven of good in all nations, and that little man belongs to the leaven."

"Yeah, I suppose you're right."

What the official did not know was that Mr. Ohtani had traveled in the *Taiyo Maru* for sentimental reasons—he had once been a member of her crew, despite the fact that he was actually a lieutenant commander in the Imperial Navy of Japan, and the *Taiyo Maru* was a fishing boat. Nor did he know that when Mr. Ohtani had said that he had never been in the United States before he was lying; nor that he never intended to enroll as a language student at Stanford University or any other academic institution.

Mr. Ohtani went from the docks straight to the railway terminus and took the first express to Los Angeles. On arrival at Los Angeles he was driven to the Tia Juana, the Japanese quarter, to a brothel called the Molino Rojo, the Red Mill. Mr. Ohtani stayed in the Red Mill only ten minutes, and when he emerged he hailed another cab and told the driver to take him to the Olympic Hotel.

Within a day or two of settling in, Mr. Ohtani realized that his stay in Los Angeles would be protracted and that he might as well make himself as comfortable as possible. So dressing carefully, he went out to the Japanese quarter, to a restaurant called the Kawafuku Tei, one of the best-known Japanese restaurants in Los Angeles.

He had not been in the bar for half an hour when he had already made the acquaintance of a young compatriot as charming as she was beautiful. Inao Ohtani was alone; Chieko Nagai was alone. What could be more natural than that the dapper little gentleman with his deeply penetrating eyes which turned on a smile whenever he looked at you should ask a very attractive young lady to dine with him, and that she should accept the invitation?

After dinner he suggested that they should go to a night club to dance. Long before midnight they could have believed themselves to be old friends. Before they parted they had become more than old friends.

Ohtani was charmed by his little mistress, and when any woman charmed him, he could prove himself generous. If the immigration officials could have seen the couple as they made the rounds of the Los Angeles night spots and could have appraised the jewelry which adorned Chieko Nagai's slender throat and tapering fingers and the silken sheaths in which she was swathed from throat to toe, they would have changed their minds about the thrift of a language student who saved money by traveling 4,000 miles from Japan to San Francisco in a stinking fishing vessel.

With his private life satisfactorily arranged, Inao Ohtani could apply himself to the task which had brought him to the United States. If he conducted his leisure moments with

Chieko Nagai with a certain ostentation, he went about his other activities with such circumspection that there was no one on the west coast of California, even at the United States naval bases at nearby San Pedro and San Diego, who could have told you what those activities were.

No one who knew the couple even saw anything strange in Ohtani's twice or thrice weekly visits to the Red Mill, sometimes immediately after he had come from his mistress. They certainly did not seem to worry or hurt her.

But when Inao Ohtani visited the Red Mill he did not pass the two hours he spent there in upstairs dalliance. Every moment he was in serious discussion in the bolted and sound proof office of the proprietor, So Yasahura.

One day in June 1937 Ohtani suddenly announced casually to Chieko Nagai that he was going to take a vacation. He thought he ought to see New York. He did not ask her to accompany him and she did not suggest it. Once he had told her, she was not even surprised that he planned to travel to San Francisco on the midday plane.

His decision had not been so sudden as it might have seemed to Chieko. The night before he had visited the Red Mill and there So Yasahura had handed him a sealed envelope in which was a brief note signed by the Japanese naval attaché in Washington.

So he came to New York, but his stay there was brief. After a rapid glance at the Empire State Building and the Rockefeller Plaza, he returned to the Pennsylvania Station, and four and a half hours later was entering a cab outside the Union Station in Washington D.C.

"The Alban Towers," he told the driver.

The Alban Towers is a magnificent block of modern apartments, one of which, at this time, was rented permanently by the Japanese Embassy to house the naval attaché, who was the Japanese chief of naval intelligence in the United States.

When he left the Alban Towers in the early hours of the morning, Ohtani carried with him a small bag which he had not had when he arrived. At his hotel he undressed wearily and getting into bed he took the bag with him under the covers.

Two days later he was back in Los Angeles. In the train and in the aircraft he nursed the small bag on his knees all the time. Now he drove straight to the Red Mill. As So Yasahura transferred the bundles of American dollars from the bag to the safe, Ohtani talked, and three hours passed before he left for the Olympic Hotel and Chieko Nagai.

For almost another year Ohtani took exercise in San Pedro and San Diego and danced in the night clubs of Los Angeles and Hollywood. From all points of view they were a gratifying eleven months.

On May 3rd, 1938, another summons came from him from Washington. This time he did not tell Chieko Nagai to her face, but left a note for her saying briefly that he had had to go on a journey.

When at last he returned, at six o'clock on the evening of May 27th, he was driving a 1937 Chevrolet carrying a District of Columbia license plate, number 57-512.

In the lounge of the hotel Chieko ran to meet him, all her Japanese restraint forsaking her.

"You're leaving me," the porter heard her say.

Ohtani hushed her and hurried her to the lift. In his apartment, he had to confess that she was right. Yes, he had to go back to Japan, but he would not be leaving for some weeks.

At eleven o'clock in the morning of May 30th, three days after his return from Washington, Ohtani stood by the reception desk of the Olympic Hotel. From time to time he looked at his watch and from his watch to the clock which was on the wall above the desk. Presently through the doors into the lobby came another Japanese, slightly taller than Ohtani, and bespectacled. Ohtani hurried forward to meet him.

"Ko Nagasawa?" he asked.

"Yes."

"I am Ohtani—Inao Ohtani."

The little men bowed gravely to one another.

When Nagasawa had registered and Ohtani was accompanying him to his apartment, he suggested that if Nagasawa were not too tired from his journey they might play a game of golf after luncheon. Nagasawa replied that nothing would give him greater pleasure.

So at half past two, the two Japanese gentlemen, looking slightly ridiculous in plus-fours and white cloth caps—the *costume de rigeur* of the American golfer—with bags of golf clubs almost as tall as themselves slung over shoulders, passed through the lobby to Ohtani's 1937 Chevrolet.

Their play was not good. The professional undoubtedly would have told them not to talk so much and to concentrate more on the game. And they took an unconscionable time to go around. Again and again they stood aside to let following twosomes and foursomes through; and then they stood silent, impassive and polite. But as soon as they were sure the other players were out of earshot they broke into conversation even more voluble than before.

Had you understood Japanese and been near enough to overhear what the little men were saying, you would no longer have been surprised by the length of their conversation, for Cheiko Nagai's lover was none other than the chief of Japanese naval espionage for southern California, which included the farmers and the fishermen operating in Mexico. Naturally, it took a long time to brief his successor in that post, Lieutenant Commander Ko Nagasawa.

On the next and following days, Inao Ohtani introduced the new chief to his principal operatives. They were an odd assortment.

First among them was a photographer, N. Kamakura, with no visible means of support but whose purse was always well lined. Then there was a striking Japanese woman with the unlikely name of Beby O'Hara. Beby had been dismissed from her situation as stewardess in the *Tabuta Maru*, a Japanese luxury liner, for an indiscreet love affair with a passenger. She had settled—on her savings, she said—at the Miyako Hotel and had invested in a course of beauty culture. She was acquainted, but only acquainted, with another Japanese guest at the Miyako. He was K. Yamakashi, a more intimate friend of his chief's, whose photographs he developed with his own in his hotel bedroom.

At this precise moment there had occurred a most unfortunate rift between Yamakashi and his current mistress. The wretched woman had been unwise enough to call on her lover unannounced, while he was using his bedroom as a darkroom. When she let herself in with the key he had provided for her, she also let in the light and ruined all the films which were being processed. The next thing she knew was that she was sprawling on the floor of the corridor outside the room, where she had been placed with unnecessary violence by an enraged and outraged K. Yamakashi.

It says something for the discipline of K. Yamakashi that at this time, when he might have sought a more intimate acquaintance with Beby O'Hara, he should introduce her to Ko Nagasawa, and thereafter had to watch the new and beautiful friendship which developed rapidly between the newcomer and the slant-eyed woman with the Irish name.

On June 16th, 1938, Ko Nagasawa was sitting in the lounge of the Olympic reading the Japanese language newspaper published in America, the *Rafo Shimpo*. This was his first task as soon as he came down in the morning. He was not attracted by the banner headlines on the first page but would turn at once to the market lists. If he was satisfied with what he found in the lists, then he would come back to the front page.

This morning he found something which made him hurry at once to the telephone and ring up Beby O'Hara to cancel their date for the evening. He gave no explanation and allowed her no opportunity to question him. Putting down the receiver, he hurried up to Ohtani's apartment. Within the hour the two lieutenant commanders were on their way to Washington, summoned there by the price of green peppers. They were away from Los Angeles for a fortnight. The greater part of this time was accounted for by the round-about route by which they returned. This took them via Yosemite, Yellowstone and Mount Rainier, where they visited groups of Japanese laborers.

Arrived in Los Angeles, they drove directly to the Red Mill, where they remained closeted with the proprietor for several hours. The immediate outcome of these discussions was the decision of the Nippon Suisan Kaisha, a Japanese shipping firm, to open a branch office in Los Angeles.

A gentleman called Y. Takimitsu was appointed manager of this branch office. Anyone with any real knowledge of that kind of business in Los Angeles could have told them before they opened up that they would be wasting money and time. But lack of business did not worry Takimitsu. He was a keen fisherman and was delighted with the opportunities his new job gave him of indulging his hobby, which he always made sure of doing in waters close to places of strategic naval interest.

At the beginning of July, Inao Ohtani said farewell to Chieko Nagai. It was not such a tearful parting as he had supposed it might be. He did not know that since he had introduced her to Y. Takimitsu a fortnight earlier she and the manager of the Los Angeles branch of the Nippon Suisan Kaisha had arrived at an understanding.

In San Francisco, Ohtani went down to the docks and after he had cleared with the immigration officials and his passport had been stamped he boarded the *Taiyo Maru* which had brought him two years all but a few weeks earlier through the Golden Gate. Back in Tokyo he became one of the outstanding officers at headquarters of Japanese Navy Intelligence.

Ko Nagasawa remained at his post in Los Angeles until

shortly before Pearl Harbor, carrying on the work so ably performed by his predecessor.

Ohtani, Nagasawa and Yamakashi were not the only Japanese agents who posed as language students. Had you scratched ten per cent of the Japanese language students in America you would have found a lieutenant commander.

Nor were Yamakashi, Nagasawa and Ohtani the first language students to be sent to the west coast of America. In 1932, four years before Ohtani had arrived, a language student called Torii had been killed while crossing a Los Angeles street.

His death revealed three things: that he was really Lieutenant Commander Torii "on active service"; that the Japanese were using language students as spies, though this meant little, since there were not enough American counterespionage agents to watch them effectively, and that some very strange things were happening at 117½ Weller Street, Los Angeles.

CHAPTER 15

117½ Weller Street, Los Angeles

As he waited for the ambulance to arrive, the patrolman knew that the little Japanese over whom he was bending was dead. But he said nothing to the crowd except to ask them to stand back. Nearby the pale and trembling driver of the car stood looking down at the still body, muttering to himself that there had been nothing he could do. The little man had stepped right out in front of him, almost as if he meant to get knocked down.

From the distance came the crescendoing duet of ambulance and police car sirens. They blared with a sudden strength and stopped, and the crowd gave way before the stretcher-bearers and doctor and the headquarters' men. The doctor knelt beside the body, listening with his stethoscope. Presently he put the instrument away and stood up, nodded at the policemen and made a sign to the stretcher-bearers.

"Take down the particulars," the police lieutenant said to the patrolman, "and report to me." He stooped and picked up a slim leather brief case lying in the road. "Was this his?"

A man in the crowd said he had noticed the Japanese carrying it under his arm just before he stepped off the pavement. The lieutenant carried it with him to the car.

Within a quarter of an hour the spot was cleared and the Los Angeles street returned to normal. Another inhabitant had been killed in a traffic accident. It happened in some street almost every day of the year. It was just another tragedy of this fast-moving age of machines we live in.

On the surface it may have seemed that, but it was not long before the police discovered that though there might be nothing out of the ordinary about the manner of death, there was something strange about the victim. Documents found on the body showed that the Japanese was a language student called Torii. Another document, however, disclosed that besides being a language student Torii was also a lieutenant commander in the Japanese Navy. Even the words "on active service" might not have raised suspicions unduly, because there were a number of legitimate reasons why a Japanese lieutenant commander should be posted to America to perfect his English. It was the contents of the brief case which revealed the dead man to be what he did not appear to be.

The brief case was locked. The police had the identity of the victim and where he lived. There was no necessity for them to examine the contents of the brief case. All that remained to be done was to inform the Japanese consul, arrange the formalities with regard to handing over the body and regiment the evidence for the coroner's inquest. But before any of these things could be done the police received a telephone call from a compatriot of Torii, a Dr. Furusawa, the proprietor of a private nursing home situated at 117½ Weller Street.

There were two things about this call which made the police suspicious. The afternoon editions in which the accident would be reported were not yet on the streets; so how had Dr. Furusawa learned of the accident? The second thing was the anxiety expressed by the doctor, not on account of Torii's death, but for the safety of the brief case.

He was assured that the brief case was safe and that it would be handed in due course to the Japanese consul. It did not require a psychologist to recognize the relief in the doctor's voice when he thanked the police for the news.

But the attention of the police was now focused on the brief case. Why did the doctor regard it as far more important than the life of the unfortunate Torii?

The case was opened, and after a cursory glance through its contents, the Federal Bureau of Investigation was called.

In themselves, the contents of the case did not present a serious threat to the security of the United States. Certainly, to learn that Lieutenant Commander Torii in his role of language student was a spy contained the elements of shock; but it was decided, however, that no action should be taken at this point purely on the basis of the contents of the case. Instead, a little watchfulness might produce more important results. So the contents were photographed, the case relocked and handed over intact to the Japanese consul.

But what was Dr. Furusawa's role? If Torii was a spy, where did the doctor fit in? The investigations of the F.B.I. were to plow up some curious facts.

2

Dr. Takashi Furusawa had lived in the United States for several years. He had, in fact, graduated at Stanford University. While still a student he had met his wife, Sachiko. She was a beautiful woman with an outstanding personality and a lively mind. They had met when she was working as a waitress in a Japanese restaurant in Little Tokyo, the Japanese quarter of San Francisco. How she had come there was part of a pathetic story.

At the age of fifteen, she had married a commander in the Japanese Navy. He was very much older than she, and consequently had a very different outlook on many things which his child bride, perhaps mistakenly, considered important. But besides being beautiful and intellectually alert, Sachiko was a girl of determination and action. After five years of what

were to her dullness and frustration, she left him and took
passage to San Francisco. There she worked first as a cham-
bermaid in an hotel and then became a waitress in the restaurant where Furusawa saw her and fell in love with her. When
she had obtained a divorce from the commander and Furusawa had qualified, they married.

The doctor's early years in his profession were not easy.
Gradually, however, his outstanding ability, both as a physi-
cian and a surgeon, became more and more widely appreci-
ated. He was eventually elected president of the Southern
California Japanese Physicians Association and, not long
afterward, president of the South California Fishing Club, an
honor bestowed in recognition of his prowess as a fisherman,
which only slightly exceeded his prowess at golf. He was,
therefore, a man of high professional reputation, respected
and popular. Just the sort of man to attract a spy master looking for a local cell leader in Los Angeles.

Coming to Los Angeles in 1930, he rented 117½ Weller
Street, which thereafter also became known as the Medical
Building. His establishment was a private nursing home to
which, theoretically, any patient might apply for treatment.
It was perhaps a little strange, therefore, that no resident of
Los Angeles, either American or Japanese, ever became a bed
patient there.

The Medical Building was frequented solely by Japanese,
who arrived from more distant parts of America, stayed at
the nursing home for two or three days only—during which
time they never ventured outside its doors—and when they
did leave, were taken either to Los Angeles or to the San
Francisco docks, where they arrived just in time to board a
Japanese liner sailing for Japan.

Yet, apart from his duties as president of the Japanese Physicians Association and of the Fishing Club, his rounds of golf
and his angling expeditions, Dr. Furusawa's duties at the
Medical Building seemed to preclude his taking a very prominent part in the public and social life of Los Angeles.

Mrs. Furusawa, on the other hand, devoted much time to public works. She was a very active member of the South California Federation of Women's Societies. She was appointed an officer of and an adviser to the Koysan Buddhist Temple Women's Society. She was one of the founders of the Los Angeles Branch of the Women's Patriotic Society of Japan, whose headquarters were at 7425 Franklin Avenue, the official residence of the Japanese consul.

For the time being there were no facts, beyond Furusawa's anxious interest in the spy Torii's brief case, to connect him and his nursing home with Japanese espionage. The F.B.I. was not in a position to devote numbers of personnel to keeping 117½ Weller Street, its inmates and its visitors under constant surveillance. They did, however, set a comparatively tight watch on the place and were to discover a good deal that was as serious as it was important.

It must be remembered that though they made these discoveries and could build up a fair picture of what happened, their field of vision was restricted. This arose from the official attitude toward both espionage and particularly counterespionage, which denied them the necessary facilities for full investigation; and also from the fact that there was no coordination between the F.B.I. and other counterespionage agencies such as, for example, the Office of Naval Intelligence. This agency was working on its own, like the F.B.I. Like the the F.B.I., the O.N.I. also made disquieting discoveries and was instrumental in frustrating some Japanese plots, as we shall see. Not only did this situation allow the Japanese to carry on their undercover work almost unmolested, it often acutely embarrassed the respective agents of the F.B.I. and the O.N.I.

Nevertheless, the death of Lieutenant Commander Torii and the cynical anxiety of Dr. Furusawa, by bringing 117½ Weller Street to the notice of one counterespionage agency, at all events, had, within limitations, important results. One of these results was to disclose a link between German and Japanese agents, and between the east and west coasts.

3

About the time of Torii's death, a certain German count, Hermann von Keitel, was behaving rather peculiarly in New York.

Von Keitel employed a German butler, called Manfred, whom he would invite into his study to drink with him. This seemed to indicate either that the count was an eccentric or that the true relationship between the two men was not that of master and servant.

What was quite clear, however, was the count's interest in Japanese affairs. Certain suave, silent oriental gentlemen were frequent visitors to his apartment; and from time to time he himself made the journey by train to Washington, where he visited Commander Josiuki Itimiya, the Japanese naval attaché, at his home in the Alban Towers.

Near the Hudson Terminal, in the financial district of New York, there was at this time a small stationer's shop, a one-man business which just, but only just, provided a living for its proprietor.

One day the count walked into this shop bent, it seemed, on enhancing his reputation as an eccentric. He announced to the delighted but somewhat surprised proprietor that he would be prepared to place quite a large order for some embossed stationery on the somewhat singular condition that a sample of it should be displayed in the shop window in a certain position, with the surrounding stationery arranged in a certain way.

For the sake of the order the proprietor was prepared to humor his client. He embossed the note paper and arranged a sample in the window in the way stipulated. He did not, however, notice that during the days following Japanese would come to his window, pause, glance in quickly and move away.

The subsequent behavior of the count convinced him that his client was perhaps rather more than eccentric. No normal man would change his address so often or have note paper embossed with the new address each time. But if it meant a pleasant increase in his takings, who was he to object?

Quite suddenly and without warning, however, in the middle of March 1933, the stationer lost his client. But it turned out to be only a temporary loss, for in the following September the count called and announced that he was going to the Pacific coast. He wished some visiting cards to be prepared for him—with a sample displayed as usual—omitting the title, and bearing simply: Hermann von Keitel, 117½ Weller Street, Los Angeles.

It was his arrival at the Medical Building shortly after this which brought the count into the orbit of the F.B.I. But it did not take them long to discover that besides being a count he was also a high-ranking German naval officer.

This discovery aroused sufficient interest for his progress to be followed by F.B.I. agents wherever he went from now on, and it was through him that they discovered the identities of other spies, both German and Japanese.

They looked in on, though from a distance, the party which Dr. and Mrs. Furusawa gave for their guest two days after his arrival at the Kawafuku Tei, that well-known Japanese restaurant in Los Angeles; and they noted that among the other guests were certain Japanese attachés.

Indeed, Japanese attachés appeared to have a particular liking for the count, for during his stay at 117½ Weller Street attachés in Los Angeles, San Francisco, Seattle and Portland—all of which places were important in the life of the United States Navy—visited the Medical Building.

The Furusawas must have felt very secure, because on the eve of von Keitel's departure they gave him another party at which, besides the attachés, was Momotu Okura, commandant of the South California Imperial Veterans Association, a body which was controlled by the Japanese government. Okura was now a citizen of the United States and his son, Kiyoshi P. Okura, was an examiner for the Los Angeles Civil Service Commission.

Von Keitel stayed in Los Angeles, off and on, for about a year before returning permanently to New York. Here, naturally, the F.B.I. continued to watch him. The first thing they discovered was that he was on intimate terms with Roy Akagi, manager of the New York office of the Southern Manchurian Railway. So Akagi was added to the list of those under surveillance, and this uncovered the fact that he was frequently in the company of George Gyssling, the German vice-consul in New York. Gyssling, who was only twenty-eight and a typical Nazi, had made himself extremely unpopular in America for his outspoken criticisms of conditions during the depression.

One evening toward the end of December 1933 Akagi, with the F.B.I. on his tail, went to the Foreign Press Association offices at 110 West 57th Street. He did not go into the building but waited in the entrance where he was presently joined by Chuzo Hagiwara, the New York chief of *Domei*, the official Japanese news agency.

Now, there was nothing extraordinary in two Japanese meeting and spending the evening together. But they did not do this. They went straight to East 66th Street where they entered number 5, which was a very exclusive German club. The watching F.B.I. agents noted that they were admitted without difficulty and concluded that they had been expected. Shortly afterward Gyssling, accompanied by two other Japanese, entered the club, and close on their heels came Count von Keitel.

So the F.B.I. were now able to add to their list of suspects Gyssling, Akagi and Hagiwara. With von Keitel providing the link, it was also clear that there was close collaboration between the east and west coasts.

On the west coast, the Furusawas of Weller Street were being very busy, Mrs. Furusawa particularly so. Whenever a Japanese liner arrived at Los Angeles she would hurry to the pier to welcome, in person, certain Japanese officers, whom she would entertain lavishly at the Kawafuku Tei. Shortly before the liner was due to leave she would hurry down to the pier again and go aboard. Each time she would be carrying a brief case when she went on board, and each time she came ashore she would be empty-handed.

In the early days of his prosperity the famous film star, Charlie Chaplin, had employed a Japanese valet and handyman named Torzichi Kono. In 1933, Kono was no longer in Chaplin's employ; in fact, several years had passed since he had worked for the comedian. But in the intervening years he certainly seemed to have found for himself a much more lucrative source of income.

He was now ensconced in a sumptuous apartment in Bronson Street, Hollywood, and owned two cars, in one or the other of which he would drive up to 117½ Weller Street and have it wait while he was inside. When the American Embassy in Tokyo was asked if they could supply any information about him, they were able to say that he owned a very fine estate on the outskirts of the capital, which he visited for a few months every year.

In May 1934 Kono was one day seen to be in a great hurry; so great, in fact, that he drove through several sets of traffic lights. He did not stop until he had reached the Medical Building.

He stayed with Dr. Furusawa about a quarter of an hour, then at midnight took the express to San Francisco. Next morning he went by taxi to Stanford University and was seen to enter one of the men students' hostels. It was assumed, since he could not be followed inside, that he was visiting a Japanese language student, one of the few who did actually attend a place of learning.

From the university he returned to the station, where he

took the day express back to Los Angeles. He drove straight
to 117½ Weller Street and stayed the night there. Next day
he took a transcontinental limited—an express that makes
a limited number of stops—to Chicago. In Chicago he boarded
an express for New York and there went at once to the apartment of Count von Keitel.

Von Keitel and Kono emerged from the apartment in time
to catch the midnight train to Washington. There they visited
Commander Yoshiaki Ichimiya, the naval attaché, with whom
they stayed for several hours, and then returned to New York
on an overnight train.

On the following day Kono began his journey back to Los
Angeles. Von Keitel accompanied him to the station and
when the train had left went straight to the offices of the
Southern Manchurian Railway, where he stayed some time
with Akagi.

When he left, Akagi visited Hagiwara at *Domei,* and he in
turn went to see Vice-Consul Gyssling. Together Gyssling
and Hagiwara went to the German Club, where they were
presently joined by von Keitel, Akagi and two Japanese attachés.

And the F.B.I. was hamstrung by those two strange factors
—the attitude of the State Department and the lack of coordination between the various intelligence and counterespionage agencies.

4

Fortunately, the F.B.I. was not missing very much. All this
frantic activity was partly a general attempt by the Japanese
to keep abreast of United States Navy development, partly
to find out whether American reaction to the Annam Statement, which warned foreign powers against giving aid of
any sort to China, was likely to include secret naval preparations which might threaten to defy the warning, but mostly
it was a kind of friendly get-together between the Japanese

and their new friends the Germans, in which the Japanese were doing their best to impress their friends with their methods and achievements in the United States.

In 1933 Colonel Eugene Ott, who was an intimate friend and close associate of one of the chiefs of German intelligence, Colonel Walther Nicolai, had been sent to Tokyo, a visit which appears to have been a natural offshoot of a desire in fascist-minded Japanese to make friends with German fascists. This desire had been manifested by a visit of delegates of the Japanese Fascist National Youth Movement to Berlin and by a visit by one of the most important *eminences grises* of Japanese affairs, Prince Tohigawa, to Alfred Rosenberg, the Nazi racial philosopher.

In actual fact Colonel Nicolai, who was later to become director of German military intelligence, had had contact with Sazo Nakamo, one of Japan's leading espionage experts. Nakamo had suggested that there should be cooperation on a world-wide scale between German and Japanese civil and military espionage. So the fiat had gone forth, and Count von Keitel had made the acquaintance of Akagi and Hagiwara and the Furusawas as well as the various Japanese attachés, including the naval attaché in Washington, who was always the chief of Japanese naval espionage in the United States.

The idea behind the suggestion, of course, was the difficulty which the Japanese had in establishing their own agents in Occidental countries on account of their undisguisable facial characteristics. The settlement of many innocent Japanese in America naturally helped them there, and it was there that they had established their most successful and numerous espionage system in any Western country, which they naturally wished to exhibit to their friends.

At the same time, it was mooted that the Japanese should reinforce Germany's espionage in the Far East and Asiatic Russia as a *quid pro quo* for Germany's reinforcement of Japanese espionage in the Western countries.

Despite the great friendliness of the "ring" in America with von Keitel and Gyssling and others, the Germans were not willing to accept such an arrangement out of hand, and Colonel Ott's mission was to study Japanese espionage methods and results and to report by the summer of 1934. He met with great kindness from Japanese officers, and within a few weeks of his arrival was invited to enter the Japanese Army as an observer. He also made the acquaintance of Admiral Nobumasa Suetsugu, a self-confessed admirer of Hitler, and of the Lawrence of Manchuria, General Kenji Doihara.

With the latter he developed a close friendship. Doihara seemed to take to him as he rarely ever took to anyone, even among his own countrymen, and when he went on his journeys he invited Ott to accompany him. Ott also became on very friendly terms with Colonel Hiroshi Oshima, who, at Doihara's request, expounded to him the organization of Japanese military espionage.

It was mainly on the basis of what he learned from Oshima that Ott made his report, the outcome of which was his own return to Tokyo later in 1934 as military attaché and Oshima's posting to Berlin early in 1935 in a similar capacity.

Though the suggestion for collaboration had emanated from the Japanese, it was with the mental reservation that they would impart to the Germans as little information of any consequence as was possible without raising German suspicions. The Germans, on the other hand, were prepared to treat the matter with unwonted honesty. For example, from 1934 onward the Japanese consul in Los Angeles was again and again invited to meet the captains of German vessels, who handed over to him the latest information to come their way.

The closest collaboration between the Germans and the Japanese was in Central and South America. Outstanding among the Japanese agents in these areas were J. Yamashito and Y. Matsui, who reached Mexico in fishing boats and operated in Guaymas, the port on the Gulf of California.

For a time the Germans seemed oblivious of the fact that they were receiving very little information from the Japanese, but eventually the realization emerged. Subordinate German agents in Mexico brought the matter to a head by entering a most vigorous protest. The Japanese bowed and were polite, made promises, but carried on as usual.

But if the Japanese were polite, the Germans were persistent, and on October 5th, 1937, the German minister in Mexico City, Rüdt von Collenberg, called a conference of his Italian and Japanese colleagues. Von Collenberg was a diplomat of the old school and looked askance at becoming involved in espionage, even that of his own country. He went to the meeting scarcely knowing what it was all about. But he had been well briefed by his civilian attaché, Dr. Heinrich Northe, and the arguments he put forward must have been impressive, for the Japanese thenceforward fully collaborated.

This collaboration was particularly successful in Costa Rica, where the chief operators were Takahiro Wakabayashi for Japan, Gerhard Henschke for Germany and Giuseppe Sotanis for Italy, which was now included in the agreement after the signing of the Anti-Comintern Pact.

Sotanis lived at the Grand Hotel in San José, Costa Rica, and was known as an ardent stamp collector. What was not known was that he was an even more ardent collector of arms and ammunition.

To carry forward their plans in this area, the Japanese proposed preparing an airfield which would be camouflaged as a cotton plantation. Wakabayashi was able to purchase an ideal site and Sotanis, who had a certain influence, though a shady one, with the Costa Rican government, obtained a concession for him to plant his cotton. Wakabayashi then brought twenty-one laborers from Chimbota, in Peru, where there was a Japanese colony numbering 20,000.[1] The laborers arrived, bringing with them one bag of cotton seed, and lodged

---

[1] *Note.* Other extensive Japanese colonies in South America were in Colombia, 25,000, Brazil, 40,000 and Paraguay, 15,000.

themselves in one of the best hotels. The bag of seed never left the hotel.

Not long after the conference of diplomats, Yoshitaro Amano, who was the owner of the *Amano Maru*, then the largest fishing boat in the world, came to Costa Rica and made an attempt to contact Wakabayashi's experimental cotton station. Unfortunately, he bungled and was immediately arrested. Gerhard Henschke appears to have heard about Amano's misfortune first, and he at once got in touch with Sotanis, who, in turn, approached his "friend" the president of the republic and obtained Amano's immediate release.

The collaboration did not entirely solve the problem of the Japanese in America and they were constantly on the lookout for disaffected or corruptible Americans whom they could bribe to work for them. Unfortunately they were able to find two, and it was with their discovery that the administration allowed the O.N.I. and F.B.I. to enjoy the fruits of their labors and to bring the traitors to justice.

CHAPTER 16

The Ex-Naval Traitors

"Got a light, pal?"

The young man shook his head. "I don't even have a drag," he said.

The man who had accosted him—he might have been three or four years older—looked at him with intense closeness. "Down on your luck?" he asked. "Wait a minute!"

He turned to ask another passer-by for a light, and when he was drawing on his cigarette he held out a packet of Camels. "Have one," he said.

The young man took a cigarette and lit it from the glowing end held up to him. He took a deep pull, and the unaccustomed bite of smoke in his lungs made his head reel. He swayed, a hand to his eyes.

"Say, what's up?"

"This is my first drag for four days."

"When did you last eat?"

"The day before last—I think."

"Jesus! Here, you'd better come home with me. Hi! Taxi!"

The young man made no protest. He still could not focus his eyes. He allowed himself to be half-helped, half-pushed into the cab.

"Linden Street, Long Beach," he said to the driver.

At his apartment, where he lived by himself, he made coffee and put a loaf of bread, some butter and a hunk of cheese before the pale boy.

"Don't eat too quick," he warned. As the color came creeping back into the boy's cheeks slowly and faintly, he said: "What's your name? I'm Harry Thompson."

"I'm Willard Turntine, from St. Louis."

"Where are you living?"

"On the beach."

"Got any money?"

"One darned solitary nickel."

"You seem a nice enough kid. You'd better stay here with me until we can get something worked out. What are you doing here, anyway?"

"Looking for work."

"Huh!"

The sound was no criticism of the boy, but rather of the times in which they lived.

"Like looking for a needle in a haystack here in Long Beach," he said. "How old are you?"

"Eighteen."

"Well, let's forget it for now. Come on, we'll go some place and get you a decent meal. Then you can stick around."

"Thanks," the boy said, his embarrassment holding him back from saying more.

And that was how Willard Turntine met Harry Thomas Thompson—and thought he had made a friend.

2

Harry Thomas Thompson was in his early twenties. He had been a yeoman in the United States Navy but now, like Turntine, he was unemployed. Unlike Turntine, however, he was not short of money.

There has never been any proof, nor even a suggestion,

that Thompson had any motive other than kindness for a penniless boy when he invited Turntine to come and live with him. Turntine never at any time subsequently hinted that the older man made any physical approach.

Turntine liked Thompson more as he came to know him better, but after a time his curiosity began to be roused by the fact that although Thompson had no work he always had plenty of money, some of which he was pleased to give to the younger man.

Plucking up courage one day, Turntine asked Thompson where his money came from and was given the vague but even more curiosity-rousing answer that he would know some day—perhaps. For it seems that Thompson had by this time developed ideas about Turntine, now that he really knew him.

Though no longer in the navy, Thompson seemed to hanker after his former life aboard the *Colorado*, the *Mississippi* and the *Texas*, the United States battleships in which he had served. For whenever these vessels, and the radio controlled ship *Utah*, in which some of his naval friends now served, put into San Diego and San Pedro, he always went to meet and have a drink with his old associates.

Thompson took Turntine with him on some of these trips and the boy was surprised to hear his friend asking very searching questions about ship movements, developments in equipment and changes in orders.

There is no doubt that of the two Thompson was the dominant character. On the other hand Turntine was no fool, and he was observant. He also possessed courage.

He asked Thompson why, since he had left the service because he did not like it, he made these visits to naval vessels, and received the reply: "I just like to keep in touch with what's going on."

But Turntine was not satisfied. He kept his suspicions to himself, but as each day passed he read more and more sinister implications into his friend's behavior and watched him more and more closely. And so he discovered Thompson's association with a little Japanese.

Choosing his time, he asked Thompson who the Japanese was and what the relationship was between them. As a result of what Thompson said, he knew then that his friend was deep in treachery. Indeed Thompson made no attempt to deny it. "The world owes me a living. O.K.?" he said. "If my country won't give me a living, another country will."

Now that Turntine knew the truth, Thompson saw that for his own safety the boy must also be compromised. He spoke to his Japanese master, and he agreed to see Turntine. The name of the Japanese was Tanni, and a meeting was arranged in Los Angeles. Tanni, however, could not make up his mind.

His secret no longer a secret, Thompson became careless about concealing communications which he received from Tanni from time to time. By Christmas 1934 Turntine's conscience had become so uneasy that he decided that he must go to the authorities.

A suitable opportunity did not occur, however, until the end of January 1935, when Thompson announced that he was going away for a few days. Turntine knew that the flagship, the U.S.S. *Pennsylvania*, was anchored at San Diego. He went to San Diego and by sheer persistence was at last taken before Admiral Joseph M. Reeves. He told Admiral Reeves his story and Reeves was impressed. He told the boy to go back to Long Beach and carry on as usual, taking care not to let Thompson know what he had done.

Admiral Reeves immediately passed Turntine's story to the Office of Naval Intelligence. O.N.I. agents, moving quickly, went to Long Beach and closely interrogated Turntine. They had already checked on the boy and found that he had a clean record.

They were as impressed as the admiral had been, especially when they saw one of the letters from Tanni, which Turntine had been able to cache, and which Thompson in his carelessness had not missed. Giving him the same instructions to carry on as before, they told him that he might hear from them later. They then went away to try to discover the identity of Tanni.

Tanni presented a problem, but eventually he was traced to Palo Alto. This suggested that he might be a language student at Stanford University; and so it turned out to be. By comparing the handwriting of the Tanni letter with the handwriting of the one or two Japanese studying at Stanford, they discovered that Tanni's real name was Toshio Miyazaki.

Miyazaki had entered the United States on August 24th, 1933, and almost immediately had enrolled at Stanford. Though only thirty, he was already a lieutenant commander in the Japanese Navy.

Miyazaki was now permanently shadowed by the O.N.I., who, a day or two after he had been identified, followed him to San Francisco. There he dined well and spent an hour or two in a brothel, leaving just in time to catch the train for Los Angeles, where he took a taxi to 117½ Weller Street. He was Dr. Furusawa's guest until Sunday evening, when he took a taxi to Long Beach and visited Thompson, now returned from his trip, at his apartment on Linden Street.

Thompson was aware of the impending visit. Earlier in the evening he had tossed Turntine a five-dollar bill saying: "Go out and lose yourself for an hour or so, will you? I've got a doll coming."

O.N.I. agents had also installed themselves in the building opposite the apartment building and were able to see into Thompson's room. As soon as Miyazaki arrived he handed Thompson a wad of dollar bills and then took from his brief case a large sheet of paper. The two men bent low over the paper for a quarter of an hour or so and then Thompson went into the bedroom, returning with a sheaf of papers which he handed to Miyazaki one at a time. Each paper was fully discussed, it seemed.

It was after ten o'clock when the Japanese eventually left,

taking Thompson's notes with him. He drove straight back
to Los Angeles by taxi, which took him to the Red Mill
brothel. He was in the brothel for three-quarters of an hour,
and then he caught the night train for San Francisco. On
Monday morning he was attending his lectures at Stanford
University.

The counteragents next discovered that Miyazaki banked
at the Yokohama Specie Bank in San Francisco. His account
revealed that he had been paying Thompson 200 dollars a
month. He was meticulous in meeting his financial commit-
ments with Thompson. Later the following letter from him
to Thompson was to be made public:

> . . . I am very glad to know you are doing very good.
> Don't hurry. Go slow and steady.
>
> Since now your monthly salary will be sent not later
> than the first of each month, and tomorrow 300 dollars
> will be sent. . . . I shall have a very long trip next month,
> and may return in January, but not sure. I will send your
> January salary before I leave here.
>
> Will you send me the schedule of the force tactics
> which will commence from 5th December? If you can
> get it before that time, send me from 3rd December.

(It is said that several phrases in this letter made Miyazaki's
tutors wince.)

The day following Miyazaki's visit to his apartment
Thompson told Turntine that he was rejoining the navy and
bought himself a petty officer's uniform.

Turntine, who was now cooperating fully with the O.N.I.
asked Thompson bluntly whether he, himself, was going to
be given a chance of working for the Japanese. Thompson
told him that Tanni could not find work for him at the moment, and for the first time uttered a threat.

"If you ever tell anyone about what's going on, or that you
met Tanni, you won't live long!"

Dressed in his uniform Thompson went to San Pedro,

where he spent most of his time in the bars, buying drinks for sailors and skillfully questioning them about the fleet's future activities.

The O.N.I. was now fully convinced that Thompson was a dangerous menace. They approached the State Department with the request that both he and Miyazaki should be arrested.

But the State Department was falling over itself at this time not to antagonize Japan in any way, and refused point-blank to authorize Miyazaki's apprehension. All that the O.N.I. could do was to warn sailors not to talk to Thompson.

Thompson masqueraded in his petty officer's uniform for several months. During this time he met Miyazaki frequently either at his own apartment in Linden Street or at the St. Francis Hotel in San Francisco.

When the sailors would no longer talk to him, Thompson had to confess to Miyazaki that he believed there had been a leak and that he suspected Turntine. Miyazaki did not directly order Thompson to remove Turntine permanently, but suggested that this would be the best solution. To protect Turntine, the O.N.I. secured work for him in San Francisco, so that he need no longer live with Thompson.

When Turntine told Thompson that he had got a job as a salesman in a San Franciso department store, Thompson was at once more suspicious than ever. But when Turntine was able to produce letters on headed stationery, Thompson appeared satisfied.

After Turntine left Thompson began to crack up. He took to drinking heavily, his bouts sometimes lasting for several days at a time. His behavior perturbed Miyazaki, who visited him at Linden Street. O.N.I. agents watching from the building opposite surmised from Thompson's demeanor and Miyazaki's gestures that the Japanese was soundly rating his agent. When Miyazaki left Thompson sat down at his table and spent an hour or two trying to compose a letter. It gave him great difficulty. He made several false starts, screwing up the sheets and tossing them into the wastepaper basket. The

O.N.I. could not legally enter Thompson's apartment, but they arranged for the contents of the wastepaper basket to be handed to them. Among the screwed up sheets was found a rough copy of the final draft of the letter he had at last managed.

> My dear Mr. Tanni, I respectfully request that this letter be treated as my resignation from the service of your country and the country of which I have been serving. It is with great reluctance and regret that I tender this resignation to the Japanese government as I can only state that I have enjoyed every moment I have spent in the service of your country, and hope that all information that has come to you through me has amply repaid for the salary paid me.
>
> This resignation is to take effect as of the date of our last meeting. This is my own doing and free will and for the safeguard of my own person and has nothing whatever to do with anything you or your country has done or should do.
>
> In saying goodbye I extend to you my heartiest congratulations and hope that anything you may undertake will prove of a successful nature.
>
> Harry Thomas Thompson.

Miyazaski, realizing that Thompson's usefulness was finished, accepted the resignation. His superiors, anxious lest he might be compromised by the demoralized American, ordered his return to Japan.

The evidence against Thompson was so conclusive that now the Japanese had flown there could be no excuse for postponing his arrest. A brief announcement was made to the public in the press on March 5, 1936. At his subsequent trial, Turntine was the prosecution's star witness, but others showed that Thompson had been in the service of the Japanese since 1933. In July 1936 he was sentenced to fifteen years in the federal penitentiary on McNeil Island.

3

On March 5th, 1936, John S. Farnsworth picked up a copy of the *Washington Post* and quickly scanned its columns. The announcement of Harry Thompson's arrest on charges of spying caught his eye and he read it through carefully.

He shrugged his shoulders, emptied his glass, and pushed it across the counter to the barman. "Same again, Joe!" he said.

He drank his second drink slowly, still looking through the newspaper, and when he had finished, got off the stool and went up to his apartment. He glanced at his watch, got his hat and coat and went out. A short time later, he was in the room of the Japanese naval attaché at the Alban Towers and was regarding the little man, Commander Akira Yamaki, with utter incomprehension.

The commander was pacing the room like a caged animal, his face distorted with a variety of emotions. "It's terrible, terrible!" he repeated over and over again. Then he turned on Farnsworth. "You should not have come here. Go away. See that no one notices you leaving. Drop everything you are doing and do nothing until you hear from me!"

"But, commander," Farnsworth protested, "just because they've caught this dolt it doesn't mean that they've got anything on me. I must say it surprises me that you ever used an uneducated yeoman who had no training and no sense, obviously."

"The risk is too great," the commander insisted. "This is one of the greatest blows Japan has ever suffered."

"Oh, come, commander!" Farnsworth smiled.

"It is true. Now go please, and remember—you are to do nothing until you hear from me."

"Commander, I have no money."

The commander went to his safe and counted out 300 dollars. Farnsworth took the money. But he did not know that it represented the last of a long series of payments he had received from the Japanese over the last three years.

4

John S. Farnsworth was born in Cincinnati and had graduated from high school at the top of his class. During his last years at school he had developed an ambition to enter the navy, and on leaving school he obtained an interview with his congressman, who was impressed by the boy and secured a place for him at the Naval Academy at Annapolis. While at Annapolis, though he seemed to concentrate more on women and drink than he did on his studies, nevertheless he passed out in 1915 with a brilliant mark.

Farnsworth served in destroyers in World War I, but in 1922 his interest turned to flying and he went back to Annapolis to study nautical aviation. From Annapolis, he continued these studies, in 1923, at the Massachusetts Institute of Technology, and when he left there he was promoted to lieutenant commander and posted to a teaching appointment at the Navy Air School at Pensacola, Florida. After a time there, he commanded the squadron base at Norfolk, Virginia.

Farnsworth's charm made him not only very attractive to women but he was popular with a wide circle of people. He married a society girl, well above him in social station, and his attempts to keep her in the style to which she had been accustomed, and to repay the hospitality they received, ran him into debt, and he began to borrow. Getting deeper and deeper into financial difficulties, he eventually borrowed from a naval rating, and when pressed to repay, refused. The result was a court-martial; the verdict—dismissed from the service.

It is one of the unfortunate consequences of cases like this that such an entry in a man's record is indelible. Farnsworth's attempt to obtain civilian employment failed always as soon as he had to confess that he had been dismissed from the navy. It can perhaps be understood that after repeated failures to procure a means of livelihood he felt he was being hounded by the authorities. In desperation, he offered his expert knowledge of aviation to Peru, China, Brazil and Russia. None was interested. Then he turned to Japan. The Japanese were interested, but not in a technical adviser. Perhaps he would consider other employment in which his knowledge and his background would be of great use?

Farnsworth first came to the notice of Captain William Puleston, chief of the Office of Naval Intelligence, early in 1934.

A few days previously Farnsworth had paid a call on a former navy friend, Lieutenant Commander Leslie Gehres, of the Navy Examining Board. For some time now it had been known in navy circles that Farnsworth had been haunting old navy friends hoping, it seemed, that his past might be forgotten and that he might be re-employed.

While Farnsworth was with him Gehres was called from his office for a few moments and when he returned he asked his visitor to excuse him, as he had some urgent work to deal with. Farnsworth took his leave.

Within a short time Gehres found that a copy of *The Service of Information and Security*, a highly confidential document printed especially for a very limited number of high-ranking navy officers, was missing from his desk. Perturbed at not being able to find it, as a last resort, after questioning his staff, he telephoned Farnsworth and asked him if he had by any chance picked up the book by mistake. Farnsworth replied that he had, and would return it the following morning, which he did. Being a good officer, Gehres made out a report of what had happened. It was this report which found its way to the O.N.I.

Captain Puleston called for the Farnsworth dossier and found that since he had left the service he had been divorced, had remarried and that the second marriage was now running into difficulties. But more significant, he also discovered that Farnsworth was no longer short of money but almost any day could be found flashing hundred-dollar bills.

This was strange, because he had confessed to Gehres and other naval friends that he had no employment. How then could he live in the New Willard, a luxury hotel in Washington, for days never getting any farther than the bar? Where did his money come from? His bank account revealed nothing.

O.N.I.'s experience with Harry Thompson caused Captain Puleston to wonder whether Farnsworth might not be getting his money from a similar source. So, when he began to look around for the ex-lieutenant commander's "Tanni," his attention was attracted to the naval attaché, Commander Ichimiya.

From the maids at the Alban Towers he learned that they were never allowed to go into two rooms in the commander's apartment. They also spoke of a strange acrid smell seeping under the doors of these rooms from time to time, which suggested photographic activity.

But Farnsworth and Ichimiya never seemed to meet. Yet, when Ichimiya's bank account was studied it was found that he regularly received large sums of money over and above his normal salary, and whenever he paid in one of these checks he also withdrew the greater part of it in new hundred-dollar bills.

Since the O.N.I. was very much understaffed, Puleston decided to ask the F.B.I. for assistance. The F.B.I. put a twenty-four-hour watch on Farnsworth, but for a time they gathered no evidence that he was in any way connected with the Japanese. But presently they got their break. Farnsworth paid a visit to Annapolis and there called on Lieutenant Commander James E. Mather at his home, staying for more than an hour. When he left F.B.I. agents visited Mather and asked what Farnsworth had wanted.

Both the lieutenant commander and his wife were above reproach. They told the F.B.I. that Farnsworth called on them from time to time, and believing his protests because they were loyal navy people themselves and could understand that the navy was in his blood, they had tried to make him happy by talking about navy affairs. When, however, the F.B.I. agents suggested that Farnsworth might be involved in espionage, though it came as a great shock, the Mathers were able to read sinister implications into his visits to them.

On several occasions, for example, while Mather had been out of the room, Farnsworth had questioned Mrs. Mather closely on various matters affecting the navy which a non-naval, even an ex-naval man, would not have asked. In fact, this had happened on this very visit.

Almost as soon as Farnsworth had arrived he had begun to ask questions about a new destroyer, the U.S.S. *Baddlitt*, very recently commissioned and purported to be the very latest in destroyer construction and equipment. Noticing the deterioration in Farnsworth's physical appearance since the last time he had called, and reading the all too obvious signs of too much drinking, Mather evaded answering the questions. But when, presently, he left his wife alone with Farnsworth for a few minutes, Farnsworth had said to Mrs. Mather: "Please tell me about the *Baddlitt!* I've just got to know!"

Since registering in Annapolis at the Carvell Hall Hotel, Farnsworth had made a telephone call to an unlisted Washington number. This was suspicious; but more suspicious still, he had given the operator a false name. The man who had answered had angrily said that he had the wrong number; but the man had spoken with an unmistakable Japanese accent. When the number was traced, it was found to be that of Commander Ichimiya. But Ichimiya had been recalled to Japan and his apartment in the Alban Towers had been taken over by his successor as naval attaché, Commander Akira Yamaki. And so the F.B.I. learned for the first time definitely of Farnsworth's connection with the Japanese.

Now, the recall of Ichimiya and his replacement by Yamaki had been done with such secrecy that no one in American government circles was aware of the change until Yamaki had installed himself in the Alban Towers. The reason for the secrecy could only be surmised.

Farnsworth's action in telephoning the unlisted Washington number led the F.B.I. to check on his other visits to Annapolis, where he always stayed at the Carvell Hall Hotel. He had been to Annapolis seven times in the last two years, they discovered, and each time he had telephoned this same number at least once a day. On one occasion he had made three calls in four hours. The F.B.I. investigations were now extended, with the result that a picture of Farnsworth's movements over the past three years was built up. He had been to Boston, Philadelphia, Baltimore, Norfolk and New York. In every instance he had called Ichimiya in Washington.

In Boston, early in 1933, he had telephoned a second number, that of a Japanese called Sato, who was officially described as correspondent of *Domei*, the Japanese news agency. He lived in Morrison Street in Washington, and since he was seen only in the highest official circles, he was looked upon as a semi-official representative of the Japanese government. One of Sato's closest companions was Yamaki, it was now discovered. They dined together frequently in the leading restaurants of Washington, but when they parted each went to his own home. Nor were they ever known to meet again the same evening.

Then an F.B.I. agent made one of those chance discoveries which are always appearing in the pages of espionage history and which are almost invariably instrumental in bringing about the downfall of a spy. The agent learned from a maid at the Alban Towers that Sato often called on Yamaki at four o'clock in the morning, using the rear entrance and staying until dawn, Thinking that perhaps Farnsworth might also be using the back door to visit Yamaki, a permanent watch was set on it. But there was no result until the day of Thompson's arrest.

Slowly but inexorably the F.B.I. ground on, and presently they had milled a fine flour of evidence which would be capable of suffocating Farnsworth as a spy. Among the information which came to them was that during the last three years Farns-

worth had constantly visited commercial photostating firms
in Washington. When employees of these firms were questioned they were unable to recall details of the material which
they had processed for him, though they could say definitely
that the work was always connected with naval matters. He
had always waited while the photostating was being done, had
paid on the spot and had taken away with him all the copies
and the originals. Extending this line of inquiry to other cities,
photostat operators in Norfolk and Baltimore recognized
Farnsworth's photograph. They, too, recalled that he described
himself as a naval officer who needed immediate copies of certain official documents.

Remembering the testimony of the maids at the Alban
Towers concerning Ichimiya's ban on their entering two rooms
in his apartment and of the odors which sometimes seeped
under the doors, the F.B.I. began to wonder whether he might
not also have been engaged on such work. With increasing satisfaction they found that within a month of Ichimiya's arrival in
Washington in 1933, two photostating machines had been delivered to him at the Alban Towers.

By this time enough evidence against Farnsworth had been
collected to justify his arrest, for besides the obvious contact
there was between him and certain Japanese, interrogation of
naval ratings and officers who had been approached by him revealed that unwittingly he had been supplied with a great deal
of information. He had been told, for example, the effectiveness of almost every gun in the navy and the vital performance
records of the aircraft carriers *Ranger* and *Saratoga*.

But as in the case of Harry Thompson, the F.B.I. was held
back by the authorities. Eventually, when Farnsworth had to
be arrested to avoid a scandal, he had ceased to be active as a
spy, Commander Yamaki was safely back in Tokyo and Sato
was working innocently in New York.

Commander Yamaki's decision that Farnsworth was no
longer to engage in any espionage activities on behalf of the
Japanese, and even more so his withholding of money from

Farnsworth, were about the biggest blunders the Japanese secret service ever made in America.

The publication in July of the fifteen-year sentence on Harry Thompson had an effect on Farnsworth that his arrest had not had. That night he went out and got very drunk indeed—on money he had had to borrow.

The following morning he went to the National Press Building on Fourteenth Street N.W., where he took the lift to the offices of the Universal News Service, a Hearst subsidiary. There he was interviewed by John Lambert, chief of the Washington office, and was passed on by him to Fulton Lewis Jr.

The entirely impecunious Farnsworth besides being in search of money was now bent on establishing justification for his collaboration with the Japanese. It had at last struck him that he, too, might have been watched by counterespionage agents.

His story was an ingenious one, and had the F.B.I. been unaware at this time of the true damage he had done, they might have been deceived by it. He told Fulton Lewis Jr. that he had been pretending to spy for the Japanese in an attempt to find out the extent of their espionage activities. He had not told the authorities what he was doing because he hoped that if he did a good job it might lead to his reinstatement in the navy. He offered Fulton Lewis Jr. the story for 20,000 dollars. Wisely, Lewis refrained from asking him why he had come to him instead of going to the O.N.I., and playing for time he said that he could not himself authorize the payment of so large a sum as 20,000 dollars but would have to consult his chief. Perhaps Farnsworth would call back the following day?

As soon as Farnsworth had gone Lewis informed the police, and the F.B.I., arguing that it would be dangerous to the security of the nation to leave him at liberty any longer, obtained the consent of the authorities to his arrest. He was taken into custody a few hours after he had left the National Press Building.

It was February 1937 before the United States attorney had his case against Farnsworth ready. The indictment included specific charges of having visited the Navy Department in August 1934 and January 1935 and the Naval Academy at Annapolis in April 1935 for the purpose of obtaining code and signal books, sketches, photographs, blueprints, maps and models.

To his defending attorney and to all who came into contact with him, Farnsworth protested his innocence, as he had done to Fulton Lewis Jr. and the F.B.I. But at the last moment he changed his mind and entered a plea of *nolo contendere*.

On February 23rd, 1937, he was sentenced to four to twenty years in a federal penitentiary.

Fortunately for the people of the United States, there were more patriots like Willard Turntine among them than traitors. Such a one was Kilsoo Haan, a Korean.

CHAPTER 17

The Night Club Owner on the West Coast

Not only did the imprisonment of Thompson and Farnsworth badly frighten the chiefs of Japanese espionage, but it led to a certain reorganization of American counter-espionage. More F.B.I. agents, though still a totally insufficient number to cope with the worm in the damask cheek of the American rose, were detailed for counterspy duties.

Thus the movements of Count von Keitel were noted when he changed his domicile once more from New York to Los Angeles, though still continuing to function as liaison officer between the Japanese and German espionage systems on the east and west coasts. They knew, too, every time Countess von Keitel and the so-called butler Manfred made their frequent trips to New York and Hamburg as couriers. They searched the baggage of these two carefully every time, but the Germans were well versed in security and nothing was found to incriminate them. Manfred led them to other Japanese. These in turn were trailed and it was found that their common contact was Akagi, who, with Vice-Consul Gyssling, now appeared to be in charge of the New York organizations. But it was Kilsoo Haan, a Korean who spoke fluent Chinese and Japanese, who put them on the trail of Yamamoto.

By this time Yamamoto had reached a certain prominence on the west coast. Ostensibly he managed, and owned, a chain of night clubs and brothels. He was a typical gangster type, maintaining a bodyguard without whom he seldom moved, and he had as a very lucrative side line a dope racket, which chiefly peddled opium.

Kilsoo Haan had organized a secret anti-Japanese society called the Sino-Korean Peoples' League. In an attempt to worm his way into the secrets of the Japanese, Haan had approached the Japanese consul at Honolulu with the suggestion that he should be allowed to try to win over the Koreans in Hawaii to the Japanese side. He made his case so convincing that the Japanese agreed to his proposal and arranged a job for him as bellboy in a Honolulu hotel as "cover." Thus strategically placed for overhearing conversations, he concentrated chiefly on what passed between Japanese.

Not long after Farnsworth's conviction, Haan had gathered information from his eavesdropping which enabled him to send the following telegram to the Sino-Korean Peoples' League in Washington:

Have definitely learned through a conversation just overheard in the Japanese Consulate here [Honolulu] that Yamamoto and his organization are about to begin an intensive course of study for the purpose of sabotage in California Oregon and Washington when war comes stop The night clubs operated by Yamamoto are to be the HQ for this training which will include the construction and study of specially built scale models of bridges electric power plants water supply systems railroad yards and other such strategic points stop An NYK liner due San Francisco next Thursday is bringing two men whose names I have been unable to discover with instructions for Y stop

The Sino-Korean Peoples' League passed this information to the F.B.I., and when the liner docked all Japanese disembarking were shadowed. All but two remained in San Francisco. These two, having visited the Japanese consul, went by train to Seattle. In Seattle Yamamoto met them and took them to his hotel suite where they stayed for three days, during which time they did not once emerge. At the end of this time they returned to San Francisco on a train which connected with a Dollar Line ship leaving for Japan. Immediately his guests had departed Yamamoto called a meeting of all his associates in Seattle at his club there and after an all-night session went to Portland, Oregon, where he called another meeting. After this meeting he visited the Japanese consul in Portland before going on to San Francisco, where he repeated the procedure.

Haan's intelligence was certainly reliable. Whatever Yamamoto's men were engaged upon, they dropped it immediately and began to deploy themselves in and around all the strategic naval and military positions along the whole of the west coast. Armed with the indispensable camera, they took photographs of all strategic installations from every conceivable angle. Yamamoto himself had never been so active or covered and recovered so much ground as he did during this period. He was so engaged in his new activities that his addicts and his exchequer suffered from lack of dope.

So many Japanese were engaged on the project that neither the F.B.I. nor the O.N.I. had the resources to keep track of every individual. They were extremely anxious, however, to identify the men who would make the models, so, hoping that these men would sooner or later be attracted by the magnet of Dr. Furusawa's Medical Building at 117½ Weller Street, they put a constant watch on it.

Nor were they disappointed. In April two Japanese arrived at the clinic who had not been there before. The following day Yamamoto flew in from Seattle and went directly to Weller Street where he stayed until evening, when he emerged with the two new arrivals. The three stayed the night at the Japanese Consulate, and in the morning Yamamoto returned to Seattle by air while his companions were trailed to an office in the business section of Los Angeles. This identified them at once as being two of the most prominent Japanese engineers on the whole of the Pacific coast. Whereas previously they had carried on a legitimate business, keeping regular office hours, now they closed their doors, admitting no one and refusing all commissions. A week or so later they began to receive visitors, among whom were the Japanese consul, Dr. Furusawa and various Japanese attachés.

At the end of the first week in May, the engineers began the unusual practice of leaving their office at some hour between 11 P.M. and 3 A.M. On these outings they carried large suitcases and went either to 117½ Weller Street, Yamamoto's well-known Little Tokyo Club or the Japanese Consulate.

One point exercising the minds of the F.B.I. was whether other Japanese were doing similar work in other strategic places like Portland and San Diego and Seattle. When attempts were made to find out they were not successful, but as the F.B.I. was beginning to get very anxious the Los Angeles engineers started to go farther afield.

The activities of Yamamoto's henchmen were of direct importance to the F.B.I. if they were to be able to check any outbreak of hostile behavior, but it was impossible for Americans to break into the gang without raising suspicions. To overcome this difficulty, the F.B.I. approached six American-born Japanese on whose loyalty they could depend and asked for their help. These Nisei undertook the role of F.B.I. agents, and though amateurs, within a few weeks were able to supply the general outline of the Japanese government's plans for sabotage on the Pacific coast when war started.

All Yamamoto's men were receiving an intensive course of instruction in the blowing up of bridges, electric power stations, port installations and all other strategic points the destruction of which would throw American defense on the whole west coast into complete chaos.

Sometimes Yamamoto himself was their instructor. At others, it was the engineers who were the teachers with the aid of their perfect scale models, which they carried about in their suitcases. Whereas Yamamoto dealt with small groups of two or three, there were always large gatherings when the engineers visited the clubs in Portland, Seattle, San Francisco and Los Angeles.

Presently the F.B.I. ran into difficulties. One day Yamamoto was observed leaving hurriedly for the airport in Los Angeles to board an aircraft for San Francisco. At San Francisco he was met by a chauffeur who handed him a note. As soon as Yamamoto read it he lost all his Oriental composure, and in an obvious rage took the next flight back to Los Angeles. His behavior at the Los Angeles airport made the F.B.I. fear the worst. Waving aside his waiting chauffeur he took a taxi, and for the next two hours was involved in the most elaborate evading action, which told the agents that he knew he was being trailed. The F.B.I. immediately warned their Nisei agents, but only four of the six received the warning. The following morning the other two men were found murdered.

For a time Yamamoto and his men lay low, but it was not long before their activities were once more in full swing.

Still the State Department refused to consider taking action until at last, without reference to the State Department, the F.B.I. arrested and jailed Yamamoto—for evasion of income tax.

While all this had been going on, Mrs. Furusawa of 117½ Weller Street, Los Angeles, was becoming busier than she had ever been. She was now head of the Japanese Navy Assistance League, which gave her "cover" to entertain Japanese sailors and naval officers when they visited Los Angeles and to whom she passed information and from whom she received instructions from Tokyo. Through Count von Keitel sha was also a link with the new German consul general in San Francisco. This was Captain Fritz Wiedemann, an intimate friend of Hitler from the earliest days and his personal aide-de-camp. He had held no consular or diplomatic post before he came to San Francisco in 1938, at the same time that General Eugene Ott was appointed to succeed von Dirksen as ambassador in Tokyo.

Taken by itself, Wiedemann's appointment would have been significant. Taken in conjunction with Eugene Ott's appointment to Tokyo and Gyssling's promotion from viceconsul in New York to consul in Los Angeles, it should have prompted the State Department to take really serious countermeasures.

Indeed, Axis and particularly Japanese espionage in America was now being stepped up, with the emphasis on activity on the west coast. But here again the Japanese were destined to meet yet another American patriot who was to foil several important plans.

CHAPTER 18

It Began with Nude Girls

There are few aspects of the American scene and of American thought and behavior more puzzling to the foreigner than the seeming inconsistency in connection with the display of the naked human figure. This is not the place to expatiate on this point, and one Englishman, at all events, seriously wonders whether any pattern of logic could be found however long and however deep he probed. But there was, at the San Francisco World's Fair in 1940, a side show which could have been put on exhibition in very few other countries, if any. It was called *The Candid Camera Artists' Model Studio*. For a small fee an amateur photographer might enter and take photographs of the attractive nude girls provided for this purpose.

The man who had conceived the idea and who was employed to be personally in charge of it at the fair was a well-known American entertainer named Al Blake. Blake had a most remarkable muscle control and would often pose in the windows of tailors' shops alongside the dummies and the public would be asked, with a prize as bait, to identify the living model. His ability to control his movements in this way had earned him the title of King of the Robots.

One afternoon in 1940 there came into *The Candid Camera Artists' Model Studio* a thickset, fiftyish Japanese with the inevitable camera slung round his neck. He took his quota of photographs and then walked over to Blake and reminded him that they had met in 1917, when Blake was appearing in Charlie Chaplin's film, *Shoulder Arms*. Without this reminder Blake would not have recognized Chaplin's former valet, Torzichi Kono, whom we already know through his connection with Dr. Furusawa's Medical Building and Count Hermann von Keitel.

The two men exchanged personal histories for a few moments and as Kono was on the point of leaving he said: "It's a pity you're not in the navy now, Mr. Blake. You could make a lot of money." Before Blake could ask him what he meant, the little man had gone.

Puzzled by Kono's remark, Blake tried to find out where the Japanese was living but had no success. Then one day in March 1941 they ran into one another accidentally on Santa Monica Boulevard, in Hollywood. They walked along together for a short distance and Blake, carefully watching Kono for any reaction, casually remarked that conditions on the American stage being what they were, he was seriously thinking of rejoining the navy, particularly as it seemed that the United States must sooner or later be drawn into the war. Kono showed considerable interest in Blake's proposal and asked him if he had friends in the navy who would help him to get back. On the spur of the moment Blake invented a very good friend aboard the flagship U.S.S. *Pennsylvania*, at that time stationed at Hawaii. After a little more conversation Kono invited Blake to dine with him that evening at his apartment on Bronson Street. Not wishing to overplay his eagerness, Blake pleaded a pretended prior engagement and eventually agreed to lunch with Kono two days later at the now familiar Kawafuku Tei. At luncheon Kono probed Blake more deeply on his intention of rejoining the navy and Blake, who was shrewd as well as being a good actor, played up, commenting how much he admired the Japanese for their characteristic good qualities. Kono then asked Blake the name of his friend in the *Pennsylvania*, and after a show of reluctance Blake said: "Jimmie Campbell," and under continued pressure described Campbell's smartness, shrewdness and his service.

That same evening Kono telephoned Blake and asked him to meet him in a furniture store the next morning. Puzzled still, but now excited, Blake agreed to do so, and at that meeting, after a good deal of spy-fiction precautions, Kono told him to be without fail at Sunset Boulevard and Wilton Street at noon, where "a very important man would speak to him."

When Blake arrived at the rendezvous he found Kono already there, but he studiously avoided making any sign of recognition. Presently a large sedan drew up to the curb on which they were standing and at the faintest sign from the Japanese Blake got into the rear seat followed by the ex-valet. At the wheel was another Japanese who introduced himself, as he drove them out to the Hollywood hills, as Yamamoto. He said he was interested in Blake's proposal to return to the navy and asked Blake to tell him as much as he could about Jimmie Campbell.

At first Blake refused to answer. Who was Yamamoto anyway? Why should he answer questions put to him by a complete stranger? Calmly Kono soothed and reassured him, and appearing to be satisfied, Blake insisted that if he agreed to join forces with the Japanese there must be definite arrangements, particularly with regard to money.

The driver was silent for a few moments after Blake's outburst, then asked if he would be prepared to go to Hawaii. Blake replied that he was ready to go anywhere provided there was satisfactory money in it. Yamamoto said that Kono would arrange the financial details, but that all he would have to do would be to go to Hawaii and persuade Campbell to give him certain information. They then drove back to

Hollywood. "You'll be hearing from me shortly, Al," Kono remarked as they parted.

During the next few days Blake became aware that the Japanese were being serious. Everywhere he went he was being tailed by them. With the realization of this, it also came to him with some force that he had got himself into quite a difficult position. For an amateur and a civilian to get himself embroiled in what was undoubtedly foreign espionage was not very clever unless he intended to be a traitor, which Blake did not.

He was now faced with the problem of getting in touch with the Office of Naval Intelligence without letting the Japanese know. His followers were persistent, and he was unable to shake them off by any means that his amateur imagination could devise. He thought of the telephone, until he discovered that a dictaphone had been planted in an armchair in the sitting room of his apartment. So while the telephone was out of the question, he became more resolved than ever to contact the O.N.I.

Before he could shake off his "shadows," Kono telephoned to arrange a second meeting and suggested that if he were prepared to leave for Honolulu within the week he should receive 2,500 dollars and all expenses. A further 5,000 dollars would be paid to him when he had delivered the information Yamamoto wished him to obtain from Campbell.

These proposals made contact with the O.N.I. more imperative than ever. But as soon as he got into the street he saw that the Japanese were still there, ready to fall in behind him.

But his pondering of his problem had not been in vain and now he had a sudden flash of inspiration. He went to a movie, and making sure from the foyer that the Japanese did not intend to follow him inside, he asked to see the manager, to whom he briefly told what was happening, and asked him to let him out by a side door.

At the Office of Naval Intelligence Blake told Lieutenant Leo P. Stanley all that had happened. Stanley, who had been impressed from the beginning by Blake's sincerity, asked if he were prepared to cooperate with the O.N.I. by doing whatever the Japanese asked him to do. Blake agreed, and Stanley said that the O.N.I. would at once put an agent aboard the *Pennsylvania* to impersonate the nonexistent Campbell. When they had laid such further plans as were possible at that point, Blake returned to the theater by the side door, remained for the rest of the performance and when he came again into the street saw that the patient Japanese were still sitting in their car waiting for him.

Later the same evening Kono telephoned and instructed him to make a reservation in the Clipper flying next day to Honolulu. The O.N.I., who were now tapping Blake's line, needing more time to install their agent in the flagship, intervened with the airline and Blake was told that there was no seat available. When Blake immediately telephoned Kono and told him of this, Kono arranged for him to meet Yamamoto again at once. At the meeting Yamamoto varied Blake's instructions. He was now to leave for Honolulu by the *Matsonia*, due out of San Francisco two days later.

By this time the O.N.I. had been able to identify Yamamoto. His real name was Commander Itaru Tachibaka of the Japanese Navy. He had been educated at the Japanese Naval Academy and the Naval War College in Tokyo, had been commissioned as a lieutenant commander and rapidly promoted to commander. He had arrived in the United States in 1930 and had enrolled at the University of Pennsylvania, where he had studied American history and American foreign relations. When he had completed these courses he transferred to the University of Southern California in Los Angeles. For several years now he had been traveling constantly up and down the Pacific coast meeting prominent Japanese.

When Blake arrived in San Francisco and called at the shipping office he was told that the *Matsonia* was full and that the next liner sailing for Honolulu would not be leaving for another week. Blake was not particularly worried, believing

that this was another delaying tactic of the O.N.I. But as he
left the office a Japanese fell in beside him for a few paces
and whispered to him to follow him. He led Blake to a restaurant, where he surreptitiously handed him an envelope which
contained a ticket for a passage on the *President Garfield*, of
the Dollar Line.

Two days before Blake was due to sail, back in Los Angeles Yamamoto had met Kono, again under fictional circumstances in a hat shop, and while they had tried on hats they
had held a whispered conversation. Leaving the shop sepa-
rately, Yamamoto returned to the Japanese Consulate, from
which he had come, while Kono had gone to 117½ Weller
Street, where he remained until it was dark and then emerged
accompanied by two other Japanese. The three men had then
gone straight to the Red Mill brothel, which they left just in
time to catch the overnight train for San Francisco. In San
Francisco Kono's companions had met two Germans, and
with them had boarded the *President Garfield* shortly before
she sailed with Blake aboard.

Now deeply involved in something for which he had had
no training, Blake had become somewhat apprehensive. Lieutenant Stanley had promised to get in touch with him to tell
him what to do when he got to Honolulu. But because of the
dictaphone in Blake's apartment the O.N.I. had not been
able to telephone him and the Japanese had kept such a close
watch on him that personal contact had been out of the
question.

On the *President Garfield*, it did not take Blake long to
realize that he was being carefully surveilled by the two Germans and the two Japanese. If he sat or strolled on deck, the
Japanese were not far away; if he went down to the bar, the
Germans were already there drinking.

There was also on board a hardware dealer from the Middle West who was making a cruise for health reasons. He
and his wife were listed as Mr. and Mrs. Horner. Mr. Horner,
it would seem, was well on the way to becoming a chronic

alcoholic, for he rarely moved from the bar. He was not a pleasant alcoholic. He spent most of the time when he was not holding a glass to his lips in truculently provoking people to speak to him and then, when they did, even more truculently disagreeing with them.

The day before the *President Garfield* was due to dock at Honolulu Mr. Horner turned his unpleasant attentions to the now very worried Blake, who had no idea how he was to get in touch with "Campbell." Horner was more than usually disagreeable, and when Blake said something to which he took particular exception, he attempted to attack him physically. But before he could get near enough to the actor he slipped and fell and lay still on the floor. His wife began to fuss over him and implored Blake to help her get him to their stateroom. In the stateroom, while Mrs. Horner was fetching the ship's doctor, Horner miraculously regained consciousness.

"When you get to Honolulu," he whispered rapidly, "call the *Pennsylvania* from your hotel and ask to speak to Campbell. Arrange for him to meet you at the hotel. You'll be able to identify him by a tear in the left breast of his uniform tunic. Beware of dictaphones!"

As Mrs. Horner and the doctor came into the stateroom Mr. Horner relapsed easily into unconsciousness, but Blake thought he could detect a reassuring smile on the hardware dealer's lips.

Arrived at the hotel, Blake telephoned the flagship and arranged for Campbell to come to his room as soon as he came off duty that evening. When the time for Campbell's visit Blake had located a microphone carefully concealed near the table on which the telephone stood.

The two men greeted one another as old friends and Blake maneuvered Campbell close to the microphone, which he revealed silently. Then lowering his voice, but speaking close to the microphone, he made his proposals. At first Campbell appeared shocked by the suggestions, but gradually allowed himself to be persuaded. He left arranging to meet Blake again the next evening, saying that he would give a definite answer then. But an hour before he was due he telephoned to say that he could not come; and for the next week he played these delaying tactics.

Blake had not been to Honolulu before and spent much of the daytime sightseeing. He noticed that whenever he left the hotel the two Germans were not far behind. Both they and the two Japanese had registered at the same hotel as Blake, and by a further "coincidence" the Germans had been given a room on one side of Blake's while the Japanese were in the room on the other side.

The first thing the two Japanese had done after unpacking had been to call at the beauty parlor run by the German, Ruth Kühn.

When at last Blake and Campbell did meet, Campbell flatly refused to hand over any information until he saw "the color of your money." Blake, playing his part with equal skill, refused to buy "a pig in a poke."

"How do I know what the information is worth until I've seen it?" he demanded.

But Campbell would not change his mind, and the men parted not on the best of terms.

As Blake was preparing to go to bed an envelope was pushed under his door. Inside it was a thousand-dollar bill and a message which read: "You are doing very well. Give to your friend this as a down payment. Act quickly."

Blake knew that Campbell always called at a certain bar for a last drink on his way back to the *Pennsylvania*. He at once telephoned the bar and was able to reach Campbell and ask him to return to the hotel. When Campbell saw the thousand-dollar bill he exclaimed: "For money like this I'll turn over the whole goddamned fleet!"

From then on the negotiations went smoothly and by degrees Campbell handed over an amazing collection of "information," which had been concocted, not without some difficulty, by the O.N.I. They knew that it would be assessed by

Japanese naval experts, so it had to have the appearance of being genuine while being sufficiently wide of the truth to make it quite useless when it came to be used. The skill with which it was done may be judged by the fact that the Japanese accepted every word of it.

Inevitably the time came when Campbell, as a source of information, dried up. The Japanese then instructed Blake to return with it to the United States. While he was on this journey all the O.N.I.'s work was almost ruined by the F.B.I. in circumstances which threw into the arc light of incomprehension the fact that there was no coordination between the O.N.I. and the F.B.I. at this time, which was only a few months before Pearl Harbor!

Having negotiated the customs at San Francisco successfully, Blake made for the airport, where he was to take the plane for Los Angeles to hand over his information to Kono and Yamamoto. On the way to the airport Blake realized that he was being followed by a young American. At Santa Barbara the young man approached Blake, identified himself as an F.B.I. agent and asked him to accompany him to the airport security office. Blake was, of course, cleared as soon as the F.B.I. had contacted the O.N.I., but he was worried lest the incident should have been seen by a Japanese agent, for in Japanese eyes this would at once have compromised him. However, Yamamoto's excitement when he saw Campbell's "information" seemed to indicate that all was well.

Yamamoto asked Blake to return to Honolulu at once, explaining that he would receive instructions when he got there through the Japanese Consulate. His suspicions were slightly roused, however, when Yamamoto began to haggle about payment; but he did agree to return.

By means of a dark movie and a double, Blake was able to contact Lieutenant Stanley personally, to be told by him that the O.N.I. had discovered that now his usefulness to them was finished, the Japanese proposed to liquidate him in Honolulu. It was necessary for Blake to return there, however, so that the Japanese should not yet become suspicious of the "information."

When he arrived back in Honolulu, Blake found that the two Germans were still at the hotel, but that whereas before they had taken only a passing interest in him after he had contacted "Campbell," now they were never far away whenever he went out.

Yamamoto had told him that he would receive his new instructions in Honolulu. It had occurred to him that in order to lull him into a sense of false security some chore would be given to him. But the days went by without any word at all from the Japanese; and everywhere he went he was dogged by the Germans!

As the days passed he began to feel intuitively that it was to the Germans that the task of liquidating him had been allotted. He believed that as soon as they caught him in some secluded spot they would attack. They made no attempt to lure him to such a place; they were content to bide their time.

When the days of waiting became weeks the strain of his situation began to tell on Blake. But he was anxious to do nothing which would be contrary to the wishes of the O.N.I., who desired that the Japanese should remain unsuspicious of the genuineness of the material he had passed them for as long as possible. Soon, however, he was to reach the point where he could no longer support the strain. He pondered how he might escape and still not betray the true nature of his information and, with a resourcefulness extraordinary in a man completely untrained in espionage, eventually worked out a plan.

One morning he went down to the hotel vestibule and, making sure that one of the ever-present Germans could overhear what he was saying, he asked the clerk at the desk to arrange for a taxi to take him that afternoon to a spot outside the town which, while noted for its beauty, was unfrequented.

At the time arranged he came down into the hall and

noted, as he had hoped he would be able to do, that the Germans were nowhere to be seen. They had gone on ahead to the place, which by its nature was eminently suited for what they had to do.

Now Blake had chosen his time carefully. Shortly before there was a customary delivery of mail. Within half an hour of the time he was due to leave the hotel a plane for the United States was scheduled to take off. Because of the microphone in his bedroom he had not dared to make a reservation on the flight, but he hoped that he would have no difficulty in obtaining one at the last moment.

Coming down to the hall with his bag, he explained to the clerk that he had just received a letter from home informing him that his mother was very ill, so he was going to try to get a reservation on the afternoon plane. Might he, therefore, have his bill?

While the clerk commiserated and made out the bill Blake kept up a flow of worried conversation. His mother was all he had; if anything happened to her he did not know what he would do. He hoped he would be able to get a seat on the plane. Were they often fully booked? When would be the next plane out if he were unsuccessful? His object in all this was to impress the reason for his going on the clerk, so that if the Japanese should make any inquiries about him they would be sure to learn the reason. At the airport, where he arrived fifteen minutes before the plane was timed to take off, he made his inquiries and gave his reasons for leaving in equally emphatic terms, with the same object in mind.

He had no difficulty in getting a reservation and was soon high above the Pacific heading for safety; and the Japanese were not to learn of the tricks he had played on them for some time to come.

Now, the Japanese had sent Blake all the way to Honolulu for one specific purpose—to obtain information about the speed, equipment, armament and performance of one battleship of the United States Navy. On the face of it, it appears

to be a tremendous expenditure of time and effort compared
with the results that could possibly accrue from it, even supposing he were entirely successful. Yet this episode is indica-
tive of all Japanese espionage effort in the United States.
Their language students, night club owners, Thompsons,
Farnsworths, doctors, brothel keepers—all were engaged in
exactly the same kind of activity. They had been planted
there, in their hundreds, not to find out any closely guarded
top secret of the United States Army, Navy or Air Force.
Were something of this order to be achieved, so much the
better, but the main object of Japanese espionage in the
United States was to gather a mass of information about every
conceivable facet of American naval and military accomp-
plishment and intention. No matter how trivial it might be,
it must be collected, reported, classified and filed for future
reference.

Collecting, reporting, classifying and filing are, of course,
a feature of all intelligence work. It is the small, probably
unimportant-seeming pieces on their own which, when collected together, form the essential, all important completed
mosaic. But the individual agent must be trained to recognize
until it becomes an instinct the correct interpretation of isolated minutiae.

The Japanese failed to do this. They collected, apparently
being more interested in bulk than quality, vast mountains of
trivia which, however they might be put together, could
never amount to anything of importance. A large proportion
of their material was not only unimportant but based upon
misinformation. This led often to really vital items being lost
in an ocean of uselessness.

But they kept at it in the United States, fondly believing
that because Russia and Manchuria had proved to be successes
arising out of intensive espionage preparations, the same success would be gained in America. It was not so much the
times that had changed—their success in the Dutch East Indies
was soon to prove that it was not that—but that the Americans

are not an Oriental or a Slav people, and were therefore not fully understood by the Japanese. It was this which was to save America from any great harm in the long run. And yet, despite all this, the Japanese were to achieve one of the really great espionage successes of all time on the very site of Blake's success—Pearl Harbor.

Everything was now gathering a momentum which would increase daily and hourly right up to 7:55 A.M. on the morning of December 7th, 1941. And only a few brief weeks before this date, in a naval base as important to the British as Pearl Harbor was to the Americans, another Japanese spy was on the eve of being rendered ineffective, though only after he had done great damage.

CHAPTER **19**

The Steward of Singapore

As the summer of 1941 dissolved into autumn the
tension in the great British naval base of Singapore mounted
with daily impetus. To those who could read the signs at all
it would not be long before the Japanese made yet another
move in the Pacific; and this would involve Singapore in ca-
tastrophe, for whatever the politicians at home might say
about the impregnability of the defenses of the base, those on
the spot knew just how weak those defenses were.

With the future looming thus alarmingly and ominously,
one would have thought that there would have been a strict
tightening up of security and that the most severe penalties
would have been meted out for any breach of it. Yet those
who ought best to have known better—the British officers—
were among the worst offenders, and the place where they
committed their crime most was the British officers' club.

One day in October a young American guest, Captain
Anderson, was discussing this very point with a British colleague, Major Ross. Ross had first mentioned his anxiety, and
the American had agreed with him. "You know," Ross had
said. "If I were the big boy of Japanese espionage I would

plant one good spy in this club, and be sure that he would be able to supply me with news of everything of military and naval importance happening in the colony."

Anderson looked round at the silent and efficient servants and nodded his agreement. Not one of them was white. All of them had the pronounced facial features of Malays and Chinese.

"Do you know the man I'd go for first?" Anderson asked. "That steward, Shawan."

But Ross did not agree. "Oh, good lord no!" he said pleasantly but firmly. "Shawan has been here for years. If he weren't here the club would cease to function. He's more pro-British than I am. Damned useful too! Engages all the servants, sees that we aren't cheated over the price of food and makes it his most sacred point of honor to see that we never run out of Scotch."

Anderson said no more about Shawan, but he was not convinced.

Suddenly Ross said: "Let's conduct a little experiment. I'll give a dinner party for a few of my pals. I'll choose them well, and I'll tell them that while we're feeding they are to discuss all those things which security conscious officers should not discuss, but they're to invent them. Then we'll keep a sharp eye on the waiters and see if any of them act suspiciously. Mind you, it'll only be a game, but it'll relieve the tedium of these exciting days."

So Ross announced that he had a birthday coming up and that he intended to give a small dinner party to a select few of his particular friends. He consulted with Shawan about the food and the wines and emphasized that he wanted the party to be one which his guests would remember affectionately for many years to come. Shawan bowed and smiled his very distant smile and replied that if they did not, it would be through no fault of his.

Before the dinner Major Ross entertained his guests in the bar, and he entertained them so well that when they went to the private room which Shawan had suggested as being more agreeable than a table under the vulgar gaze in the dining room, they were all happy and more than ordinarily loquacious. The conversation at dinner might have induced Major Ross's death from shock had he not known that all that was being said was invention.

"I must say," said one of his guests loudly, "that those forty Free French companies will be jolly welcome reinforcements. They left Trincomalee four days ago, so we can expect them any time now."

"My dear chap," exclaimed a fellow guest, "I shall be much happier when those twenty-nine Free French mechanized units get here. I'm told they'll arrive by the end of the month."

At the other end of the table another guest was saying: "Well, speaking as a loyal Scot, you can keep your Free French, I shall not sleep peacefully in my bed until we've built up our Scottish forces."

"Then that will be very soon," said his neighbor. "Old Archie Macfarlane told me today that they're sending us another six or seven battalions of your countrymen. I don't know what regiments, but they'll be here by the second week of November for certain."

In the middle of the table two other guests were uninhibitedly discussing the strength of the antiaircraft units.

"If only we had more Boforses," said one. "Out of the dozen and a half we've got, only twelve will function properly."

As this very indiscreet conversation was bandied back and forth, Captain Anderson wrote two words on a scrap of paper which he tore from a used envelope, and asked a waiter to give the folded message to his host.

Ross unfolded the paper and read: "Watch Shawan."

The steward was standing by a table on which he had arrayed the wine. As Ross looked he saw Shawan tear the corner off a wine list and fumble for a few minutes with what looked like his suspenders. But not only that, he was doing something with a stub of pencil on the wine list itself.

For the time being Major Ross did nothing, but when at last the port was circulating he sent a message to the staff security officer asking him to join the party. He had seen the major in the bar with a guest before dinner. He worded his message so that the major could not refuse.

When the major arrived Ross behaved in a suprising manner. "Shawan," he said, "tell the waiters to get out. You can serve us if we need anything."

When the last waiter had gone, Ross said: "Shawan, come here!"

The steward approached him. "Sir?"

But instead of giving him an order, Ross seized his suspenders. On the under side of one, he found a small, specially made pocket, and from it he took the torn off corner of the wine list. On it was written: "P.W. end Nov." which being interpreted meant: "The *Prince of Wales* (England's most invulnerable warship) due to arrive Singapore at the end of November."

Meanwhile Captain Anderson had gone to the wine table and picked up the wine list which Shawan had been using. Against the cognac were lightly penciled 40 and 29, the numbers respectively of the Free French infantry and mechanized companies which had been mentioned in conversation. Against the Scotch was 6 or 7, the numbers of Highland battalions said to be on their way as reinforcements. Against the akvavit were the figures 12:18; twelve of a dozen and a half Bofors A-A guns serviceable.

When Shawan was investigated it was discovered that his real name was Colonel Tsugunori Kadomatsu of the Japanese Army, who, in 1930, had paid a visit to West Point to study American training organization. But instead of being stationed in the United States he had been sent by Japanese army intelligence to Singapore, from where he had kept his headquarters in Tokyo fully conversant with British military strength in the all-important base for the past half dozen years.

Of all those amazed by the revelation, perhaps Major Ross was the most surprised. But he echoed the general view when he said: "I'd always thought the blighter was Chinese!"

It was views like these, carelessness like this, which had made it possible for Colonel Kadomatsu to make his contribution to Japanese espionage efforts which were to be crowned at Pearl Harbor. The colonel himself might not be aware yet of the significance of Pearl Harbor; neither the British, the Dutch nor the Americans themselves might be aware of it, until it happened. But an ally of the British and the Dutch was to know about it seven full weeks before it happened. How they learned of it is as fantastic a story of espionage economy as the whole history of Japanese espionage is a story of prodigality *in excelsis*.

Ironically, it was the first enemy of the Japanese, the Russians, who acquired the information; and even more ironically, it was one of Wilhelm Stieber's countrymen who obtained it for them.

CHAPTER 20

Colonel Osaki's Defeat in Success

One evening toward the end of September 1941 Colonel Osaki, the chief of Japanese counterespionage, sat in a Tokyo night club with an acquaintance. Presently the acquaintance remarked: "Here he is!" and called out: "Hello, Richard, come and have a drink!"

Richard Sorge, a German foreign correspondent who had lived in Tokyo for the past seven years, came over to the table and, having been introduced to Colonel Osaki, sat down gratefully.

Now, Colonel Osaki had engineered this meeting because he had devised a plan by which he was certain he would be able to confirm or eliminate certain suspicions he harbored against Sorge. It had all begun two years previously, toward the end of 1939, when the colonel's radio experts had begun to intercept radio transmissions in a code they were unable to identify or break; and his direction-finding apparatus was equally unable to give even an approximate pinpoint for the transmitter, though they could say definitely, from the strength of the signal, that is was in Tokyo.

The problem had remained with Colonel Osaki throughout

the next two years; and the transmitter had remained in Tokyo. Driven almost out of his wits by frustration, pride and the proddings of his superiors, Osaki had eventually hit upon an idea. He asked the Foreign Intelligence Department to instruct their agents abroad to indicate if the countries in which they worked gave the impression of being aware of Japanese policies in advance of those policies being announced. When the consolidated report was placed before him, he had his first clue.

With a great deal of painstaking Osaki drew up a list of all those who might for some reason or other have had either official or unofficial access to advance information regarding Japan's expansionist plans over the last four years. His first list of suspects, as he called it, besides including officers, civil servants, officials and certain foreign representatives, also included the names of three foreign correspondents: a Japanese called Ozaki (not to be confused with the colonel), a German, Richard Sorge and a Yugoslav working for the French, called Voukelitch.

Though these last three names were "possibles" only, he submitted them to the same tests as the others. To his surprise, when the rest were eliminated these three remained. But he had no evidence against any of them. He had arranged this meeting with Sorge in the hope that he would, in time, get the evidence he sought, or be assured of Sorge's innocence.

With consummate skill he brought the conversation around to women. Sorge had a Tokyo-wide reputation on account of his sexual activities.

"Have you seen the new dancer here, Herr Sorge?" the colonel asked.

Sorge shook his head.

Osaki went on: "She's one of the most beautiful women I've ever seen; and I'm told quite one of the most unapproachable."

He was watching Sorge closely and saw the quick glance he shot at him as he said the last words.

"No woman is unapproachable," Sorge growled. "The more beautiful they are, the easier they fall. But women don't interest me any more."

"Oh, come, Herr Sorge," the colonel laughed. "Wait until you see Kiyomi."

They had not long to wait. Presently the lights in the room were dimmed and there appeared in a spotlight a young Japanese woman who went through all the movements of the traditional Rice Dance.

Within a few moments Osaki knew that Sorge's interest in women had been revived. "It's a pity she is so unapproachable," he whispered in Sorge's ear.

On the evening of October 3rd Sorge sat in the night club alone at his table watching his latest mistress dance the traditional Rice Dance. But his mind was not on either the woman or her dancing. He was worried. He had not seen one of his friends, an artist called Miyagi, for more than a week and did not know what he was doing or where he was. Another friend, Voukelitch, the foreign correspondent, had shut himself up in the French Embassy and refused to move out of the protection of its extra-territorial rights. He himself was now almost certain that Colonel Osaki had discovered what he was really doing and was only waiting to pounce.

Presently he called for his bill. When the waiter brought it he brought also another scrap of paper folded in such a way that he knew it came from Miyagi. It was a message saying that he, Miyagi, and some of their other friends were being watched.

Through her mask Kiyomi saw Sorge read the paper, and as soon as her dance was finished she telephoned to her chief and told him what she had seen. A quick check by Colonel Osaki revealed that the waiter, who was a known Communist, had on several occasions been seen visiting the offices of the journalist Ozaki. Colonel Osaki was well satisfied.

For his part, Sorge had decided that the time had come for him and his friends to stop their private—and secret—work.

But there was one last coup he must pull off before this happened: he must find out, if possible, the date on which the Japanese intended to attack Pearl Harbor.

On the evening of October 14th Sorge was again sitting at his table in the Fuji night club. Kiyomi was again dancing the traditional Rice Dance. She saw a man pass in front of Sorge's table and drop a small pellet of paper on it. Sorge looked up to see who it was and recognized Miyagi.

Sorge had arranged to call for his mistress after her dance, but she hoped that before he came to her dressing room she would be able to telephone Colonel Osaki. But Sorge was too quick for her.

As Sorge drove out into the country on his way to a small seaside chalet which he rented, he stopped the car and began to make love to her. After a time he drew from his pocket two cigarettes. But his lighter refused to light and he threw the cigarettes out of the car. He then produced the scrap of paper, tore it into fragments and threw them after the cigarettes, and then drove on. At the first public telephone booth Kiyomi asked him to stop so that she might telephone her family that she would not be home until next day. Sorge stayed in the car, apparently quite unsuspicious, while Kiyomi telephoned Colonel Osaki.

When she was sitting by his side again, they drove on to the chalet. There he told her to prepare something to eat while he went out to look at the fishing boat which he kept moored in the bay. On board he found another friend, a German called Max Klausen, whom he had warned previously to be there. Within a few moments Klausen had tapped out a message in Morse on the transmitter which was hidden in a secret compartment on the boat, and intelligence headquarters in Moscow was acknowledging the message which read:

"Japanese carrier force attacking United States Navy at Pearl Harbor probably dawn 6 December source reliable."

When they had locked the secret compartment Sorge shook

hands with Klausen. "That's the last message," he said. "You must get out of Japan as quickly as you can."

Sorge returned to the chalet, ate the food Kiyomi had prepared, and as if he had some premonition that this would be the last time that he would ever make love to a woman, his appetite that night seemed insatiable. Dawn was breaking before at last he fell asleep.

But his sleep was shallow and toward eight o'clock he got up and mixed himself a drink. Before he could raise the glass to his lips there was a knock on the door. He opened it to admit Colonel Osaki. Osaki said nothing, but held out to him the scraps of paper which Sorge had thrown out by the roadside. They were neatly pasted together, and the words on them read:

"Japanese carrier air force attacking United States Navy at Pearl Harbor probably dawn 6 December source reliable Joe." Joe was Miyagi's pseudonym.

At noon, the German ambassador received a courteous note from the Japanese minister of war, General Tojo. It informed him that two Germans had been arrested as spies. Their names were Dr. Richard Sorge and Max Klausen. The French ambassador received a similar note naming Voukelitch, who had left the embassy to pack his belongings on the previous evening. The prime minister was informed of the arrests of Ozaki, the journalist, and Miyagi, the artist.

It was Colonel Osaki's proudest day!

Richard Sorge was the grandson of Alexander Sorge, who was at one time the private secretary of Karl Marx. In 1914, at the age of nineteen, Richard joined the kaiser's army and was three times wounded. His experiences in the army and conditions in postwar Germany made him turn to communism in his disillusionment.

Having graduated as a doctor of political science, a sequence of experiences brought him to Moscow, where he met Dimitri Manuilsky. Through Manuilsky he was led to take up an occupation which he was to follow with outstanding success for the rest of his life—spying for Russia.

He was a remarkable linguist and became fluent in Russian, English, French and in certain of the Chinese and Japanese dialects. He studied carefully the historical and cultural backgrounds of the countries to which he was assigned, and since he regarded all other men as his enemies he exercised the same care in getting to know as thoroughly all those with whom his work brought him into contact.

By 1933 Sorge had become such an outstanding agent that the Russians had complete confidence in him, and when they decided that they must have a first-class spy in Tokyo it was Sorge they sent, giving him—which was very rare in Russian espionage history—*carte blanche* as to choice of agents and an almost unlimited budget.

Before he came to Tokyo he had paid a return visit to Germany, and there had completely hoodwinked many of the highest in the Nazi hierarchy into believing him to be a loyal National Socialist. He came to Japan with the full confidence of the German leaders, which automatically made him *persona grata* with the German embassy officials from the ambassador down.

He was not a stranger to the Orient. He had already organized Russia's so-called "China Unit" on the mainland of Asia, and it was one of his agents in this unit whom he transferred with him to Tokyo. Ozaki Hozumi, a young Japanese journalist, was to become, after Sorge, the most valuable member of the Tokyo cell.

Sorge's other colleagues, whom he had himself selected, were Max Klausen, another German, and the finest radio operator in the Russian secret service; Branko de Voukelitch, a former officer in the Yugoslav Army; and Yotoku Miyagi, a Japanese artist, whom Sorge had found in the Little Tokyo quarter of San Francisco.

As cover, Sorge was the accredited Japanese correspondent of no less than three leading German newspapers; Klausen was the representative of two or three German industrial undertakings, though none of them was very prominent; Voukelitch was the accredited Japanese correspondent of a French review and a Yugoslav newspaper; Ozaki was political correspondent of the Japanese *Asah Shimbun;* while Miyagi followed his profession as an artist.

The fact that Sorge, Voukelitch and Ozaki were bona fide correspondents made it possible for the three men to meet naturally in Tokyo and for their intercourse to raise no suspicions. Sorge did not rush the initial operation of his ring, but by meetings in cafes, restaurants and bars, at first casual and then arranged, he allowed it to appear that the relationship which ultimately developed had done so gradually.

Sorge's occupation also took him to the German Embassy, where he made it appear that he was meeting Max Klausen for the first time. It seemed to onlookers, too, quite natural that the eccentric correspondent should take pity on the lonely German salesman and invite him to join his circle.

Miyagi was brought in in much the same way. Sorge and Voukelitch were in the Uneo Art Museum one day when Voukelitch recognized a Japanese artist friend. He introduced him to Sorge and a discussion between the two men developed concerning the merits of Eastern and Western art, and Miyagi was invited to continue it at a cafe frequented by artists and journalists.

A base from which to operate is essential to any spy ring, and it must be a base to which all members may go openly, with ostensibly legitimate reasons for their visits and yet safe and secure from eavesdroppers. Sorge chose as his base a ramshackle house, the rent of which was well within his salary as a foreign correspondent.

Installed in his house, Sorge gave a party which shocked both his respectable neighbors and the members of the diplomatic corps who had been invited along with journalists, artists, young Japanese army officers and a sprinkling of Japanese businessmen. When the less intimate of the guests left about ten o'clock, a number of geisha girls were summoned to the house and for the next few hours the noises emanating from the rickety structure testified to the orgy going on within. The neighborhood listened unhappily until the early hours, when the girls left accompanied by the majority of the remaining guests, all, that is, except Voukelitch, Ozaki, Klausen and Miyagi, whom Sorge pressed to finish the last bottle with him. In the comparative quiet that followed, and before the four guests eventually left with the first light, Sorge had given his spies their first briefing.

Sorge's parties soon became the talk of Tokyo, and if watching *Kempei tai* agents noticed that his four best friends always stayed after the other guests had left, they saw nothing suspicious in that.

A spy normally draws the least possible attention to himself. Sorge worked from the other extreme. Not only were his wild parties the talk of Tokyo, but his relationships with women became notorious. He was a very highly sexed individual, and his attitude toward the unfortunate women who fell under the spell of his great charm and consummate wooing was fundamentally one of contempt. He soon grew bored with his victims, and within a few weeks of the opening of an affair he cast them off and looked around for new excitement. This reputation also served him as "cover." Any man who attracted so much attention to himself could not be a spy, seems to have been the argument.

With his ring well established Sorge went to work, and it was not long before he was justifying the confidence which his Moscow masters had placed in him by a series of brilliant espionage coups.

The first of these coups was achieved by the agency of Ozaki, whose family background and his work as a political correspondent for Japan's most influential newspaper gave him the entrée to high political circles. His political acumen and his tremendous knowledge of Chinese affairs were such that when, toward the end of 1935, the foreign minister prepared a report for the cabinet on Japan's economic and political aims for 1936, Prince Konoye, the prime minister, readily agreed to a proposal that he should be allowed to see a draft copy and to give his independent views of those sections referring to China.

Ozaki was permitted to study the document for the greater part of a day in a private room at the Foreign Office. Completely undisturbed, he photographed it page by page. The report made it quite clear that Japan had no intention of attacking Russia in the near future and that the invasion of south China would depend on the development of heavy industries in Manchuria.

In search for confirmatory evidence, Sorge obtained a private interview with the German ambassador, Dr. Herbert von Dirksen, on the excuse of writing a report for his newspapers. By clever questioning he learned that the Japanese high command had hinted to the German military attaché that the withdrawal of German officers instructing the Chinese armies would be taken as a sign of friendship.

At the same time Miyagi discovered from a Japanese staff colonel, whose portrait he was painting, that large-scale models of certain parts of south China were being constructed for practice purposes.

All this information taken in conjunction satisfied Moscow that their spy had supplied them with material of truly vital importance; and if before they had acknowledged him as a master, they were now prepared to promote him to miracle worker.

Such a coup so early in his career might have influenced another spy to rest upon his laurels. For Sorge it merely set the standard for his future activities.

Realizing the importance of Ozaki's contacts in high political circles—he presently became the private and confidential adviser of the prime minister himself—he set about acquiring similar contacts himself at the German Embassy. There he soon became the confidant of the military attaché,

Colonel Eugene Ott, who was later to become much more valuable when he replaced von Dirksen as ambassador.

Voukelitch also consolidated his own position at the French Embassy while Miyagi extended his friendships with the younger military clique, with whom his work was popular.

Sorge's path was not always smooth. His involvement with women at times threatened his security. Klausen, though a first-rate radio operator, was not good agent material, and on more than one occasion narrowly escaped arrest.

But in some strange way the *Kempei tai* remained deceived. For seven years Sorge and his ring operated, pulling off coup after coup, each more brilliant than the last. He warned Russia of the impending German attack on the U.S.S.R. and, as we have seen, brought his career to a climax by obtaining the approximate date for the attack on Pearl Harbor.

He had been in prison awaiting trial less than seven weeks when his cell door opened one morning and the guard brought in his breakfast. As the man set down the bowl he said: "This morning our air force destroyed the American fleet in Pearl Harbor."

The prisoner looked at the homemade calendar he had scratched on the wall. It was December 8th. He had told Moscow it would be December 6th. But he was only one day out, for in Honolulu, because of the International Date Line, today would be December 7th!

CHAPTER 21

The Smoke and Noise of Climax

Normally the aircraft warning station at Pearl Harbor closed down at 7 A.M. On December 7th, 1941, however, two private soldiers under training who were operating a set on the north shoulder of Oahu decided they would carry on until their relief arrived.

At two minutes past seven they picked up on their instrument indications that a large formation of aircraft was flying on a bearing almost due north of them at a distance of roughly 130 miles, but rapidly approaching. Their first reaction was that something was wrong with their apparatus. But when they checked all was in order.

They telephoned the central station. It had shut down dead at its customary time and they could get no reply. Eventually they did manage to contact the air lieutenant in command, who told them to forget about it; it might be merely some aircraft coming in from the mainland.

The soldiers plotted the aircraft until they were so close that the echoes from the sea and the surrounding hills blotted out the echoes of the engines. Then they, too, closed down.

Thirty-two minutes before the soldiers had picked up the

flight of aircraft the U.S.S. *Ward* had sighted a small submarine in the prohibited area outside Pearl Harbor. For fifteen minutes she stalked her prey and at 6:45 A.M. attacked with her four-inch guns and depth charges. The incident was noted in the destroyer's log, timed 6:53 A.M., and a warning was sent to shore.

No action was taken, no alert sounded and not even the antitorpedo net protecting the harbor was closed, with the result that at least two Japanese submarines got right inside the harbor net defenses without being seen.

The fact was that a lack of cooperation between the military and naval comanders at Hawaii had led to a complete disregard for the defense of Pearl Harbor. On this Sunday morning in December 1941 the army's aircraft warning system was not operating; no regular reconnaissance or inshore patrols were maintained either by the army or the navy; the antiaircraft and coastal batteries were unmanned, and if they had been manned they would have been absolutely ineffective because not one of them was supplied with ammunition.

True, the likelihood of an attack by Japanese submarines and possible sabotage had crossed the minds of Admiral Kimmel and Lieutenant General Short; but it would seem that they were not impressed by the risk and had promulgated the taking of only a few minor precautions. Warnings had been issued from Washington, where negotiations between Japanese representatives and the secretary of state had been dragging out for weeks but, for some reason or other, these, too, were ineffective.

Fifty-three minutes after the soldiers had picked up the approaching aircraft they arrived over Pearl Harbor, where no less than seven of the eight battleships of the United States Pacific Fleet was moored along the shore of Ford Island and over eighty other warships—cruisers, destroyers, minelayers, minesweepers and auxiliaries—were at anchor. The formation consisted of forty torpedo bombers, fifty-one dive bombers, forty-eight horizontal bombers and forty-three fighters. Their first objective was to put out of action the fighter aircraft packed tightly at the moorings in Kaneohe Bay and on Wheeler and Hickham airfields. Their second objective was the ships in Pearl Harbor.

These objectives they reached and those attacking the aircraft obtained success beyond their own expectations. The survivors of the Americans were for the most part rendered ineffectual by the cratering of the runways, which prevented their taking off, but a few planes were able to take off and joined forces with seven patrol aircraft which were in the air when the engagement began.

By a fortunate coincidence Admiral Halsey, in the aircraft-carrier *Enterprise,* was returning from an exercise and immediately put his planes in the air. Four of these were shot down and one was so badly damaged that it had to withdraw.

In the attack on the ships in the harbor the Japanese made eight runs. In the first, one of the battleships opened up immediately with machine-gun fire and accounted for two of the torpedo planes. Within ten minutes of the opening of the attack, all ship-borne antiaircraft batteries had come into action.

The Japanese pressed their attack until 8:25. Then they drew off and there was a lull until 8:40. Dive bombing and precision bombing attacks were then made on the port and airfield installations and completely destroyed them. For another hour and five minutes the battle raged until, at 9:45, the Japanese finally broke off.

When they had gone, the American Pacific Fleet had had all its battleships knocked out, and a large proportion of its other forces. Almost 2,500 men had lost their lives, nearly a thousand were missing, and more than 1,200 were wounded. American sea strength in the Pacific was for the time being but a tiny fraction of the power it had been one hour and three-quarters before.

For the greater part of this time, up in her attic Ruth Kühn was watching the results of the attack through her binoculars, and her father, at her side, was flashing with his signal lamp the information she gave him.

Pearl Harbor was to be the climax of Japanese espionage against America. It has been suggested that the reason why Japan did not take immediate advantage of the great success she achieved that day was that the magnitude of it took her by surprise. Whatever may be the reason, all the work of her spies in the United States and in Central America was to be of no avail. There was to be no base in Mexico, no seizure of the Panama Canal, no landing on the California coast. All the work of years, the efforts of the language students, the brothel keepers, the dentists, the barbers, the soda water bottlers, the coolies, the farmers, the doctors and fishermen was to be put to no account.

To call Pearl Harbor the climax of Japanese espionage is not to impute too great importance to the work of their intelligence. It was undoubtedly a coincidence that so great a proportion of the Pacific Fleet should be in Pearl Harbor on December 7th, 1941, but the Kühns had been plotting the movements and locations of all the units of the fleet for weeks, and at the moment of attack the Japanese knew exactly what their target was, though it was then too late to make preparations to follow their attack up as logic demanded. It was the climax of the Kühns's spying, too. Even had they escaped, nothing in the future could have been quite so successful.

Fate seems to have a penchant for tying up loose ends. With the part played by the Kühns at Pearl Harbor, the greatest achievement of Japanese espionage, the denouement was neater than any man-devised denouement could ever have been, for at the most crucial time and in the most crucial spot it was countrymen of Wilhelm Stieber's who made the victory possible, just as it had been Stieber's precepts and tuition which had been the basis for all Japan's spying.

With the American Pacific Fleet powerless the Dutch East Indies were easy prey, defeated by espionage before the Japanese invasion though they were in any case. The Pacific islands were equally at Japan's mercy. So were Singapore, Malaya and Burma.

As the armies of the divine emperor spread over a quarter of the globe and took possession of the lands they had formerly secretly invaded, the role of espionage lost in importance and gradually its great force was retracted. Then as the tide turned and Japan began to fight for her life, it was no longer a case of preparation for attack; and retreat needs no preparation by espionage.

So, brilliant as her first fifty years of espionage had been, Japan was to see herself destroyed before the second fifty years were completed; and in that destruction espionage had played a major if indirect role. For had she not used espionage to prepare for her attack, and if she had not attacked, she would not herself have felt the blast of atom bombs on Nagasaki and Hiroshima.

Post-Mortem

It is not usually difficult to be wise after the event; and post-mortems cannot change the result of the game. But standing back from events in time places us in a position from which we can see what was happening, events, trends, failures and successes unable to be seen at once by those involved because of their very nearness to them, or if seen, not in the right perspective because, again, too close proximity throws them out of focus.

Whatever happened in the past, whatever may happen in the future, the meteoric development of Japanese espionage will always remain a phenomenon not only in the records of espionage but in the wider field of history.

Had the perpetrators of State Shintoism been asked and had been prepared to give an honest answer, they would have explained that the third tent—"to bring the whole world under one roof"—was originally designed not as a basis for expansionist policy but as an instrument for stirring the pride of the individual Japanese and diverting it into a channel where it might operate for the good of the country. A people used to discipline, as the Japanese had been under their feudal struc-

271

ture, is lost if that discipline is relaxed, and rapidly degenerates
into a goal-less people without ambition or direction. Such a
development in Japan would have automatically removed
every possibility of the nation's benefiting from its new contact with Western civilization.

The industrial and economic, political and military growth
of Japan presents a phenomenon of no less proportions than
her espionage. In it is revealed a flair for organization and
imitation unsurpassed so far by any other nation in the world.
Though it is easy to sneer at the imitation, it is nevertheless
a fact that this imitation was responsible for converting Japan
into a great power in the space of a generation and a half.

It was this conversion to power, rather than the third tenet
of State Shintoism, which made it absolutely essential for Japan
to secure her position in Eastern Asia, and it was this necessity which gave rise to the need for espionage. Only later,
when the rulers were imbued with fascist arrogance, was the
third tenet of Shintoism taken as the basis for policy. The
doctrine of the Master Race, the need for *lebensraum* and the
creation of slave nations were as much part and parcel of the
credo of the Japanese leaders of the thirties as they were of
the contemporary leaders of the Third Reich. But whether
the necessity to secure her position or the third tenet of State
Shintoism was the motive or excuse, Japan's resulting actions
were the same.

In seeking to establish her position in Asia securely, Japan
saw herself faced with the need for controlling immense
physical areas. Siberia, Eastern and Central Asia cover a vast
proportion of the earth's surface. Accepting the theory of espionage preparation being essential for success in war, it appeared to Japanese leaders that large numbers of spies were
required to cover the area of operations.

It was, perhaps, fortuitous that the most up-to-date system
of espionage at that time should also be based on the use of
vast numbers of agents. This point certainly gave the Stieber
system an added appeal in the eyes of the Japanese. Indeed, it

is doubtful whether any other system would have suited their purpose.

So enthusiastically did they take to espionage, and so greatly were they encouraged by the ease with which their spies operated on account of the lack of opposition everywhere, that they let themselves be run away with by the idea of numbers. The defeat of Russia and the conquest of Manchuria were first-rank espionage successes, but there is no doubt that they could have been no less brilliant had one-third of the agents been used.

The Japanese became obsessed by espionage, and if *total war* was an invention of their National Socialist German friends, the original concept of *total espionage* must certainly be conceded to the leaders of Japan. In essence, their theories were right. The infiltration of the Moslem Russian minorities of Central and Western Asia by agents who fomented a state of constant unrest which made the minorities a sword point constantly tickling the ribs of Russia had everything to commend it in theory. The Nazis were not too proud to copy and use the method with great effect in Danzig, with the Sudeten Germans in Czechoslovakia and, after the Second World War began, the Croats in Yugoslavia. But exactly how much good accrued to Japan from these efforts is not easy to define. Had she occupied Central and Western Asiatic Russia, then her activities there would have been fully justified. As it was, she seemed to have involved large numbers of men and spent many millions of dollars in these distant areas merely to keep Russia preoccupied. She could have achieved the same result with fewer men, and at far less expense, in Siberia itself.

So it was in every field in which she was involved, particularly in China, where the chaotic state of the government and of the economy produced already a mature condition for the imposition of foreign control. With a hundred or two agents, instead of the thousands actually employed there, carefully and cunningly placed, she could have kept the China caldron on the boil.

Nevertheless, it would be wrong to denigrate the brilliance of Japan's espionage achievement, when reckoned in terms of the implementation of national policies, during the first fifty years of spying. It is the next fifty years which surprise, almost bewilder, certainly mystify.

When Japan turned her attention to the American continent, she turned on it the same weight of espionage which has already been described. Granted that preparing Mexico as a base might require the efforts of many men, as the years passed it must have become only too obvious that the achievement there was falling far below expectations.

There was, however, a very different set of conditions facing the Japanese in America from those which aided her in Asia, the Dutch East Indies and elsewhere. Here the economic structure was sound and there was no national unrest. This called for different tactics, and the only tactics which she could devise—and which American military activity, or the lack of it, allowed—were the tactics of ordinary, straightforward espionage. She did not understand, however, that this type of spying is impeded rather than helped by large numbers.

In California and the Panama Canal Zone she was working very closely to Stieber's methods when he was preparing France for the Prussian invasion of 1870. Her spies were instructed to discover and report every small detail, not only in connection of the armed forces, but concerning the economic and structural potential of the destined area of invasion. But in doing this she outdid Stieber in the number of spies she employed, with the effect that three-quarters of the information she received when it was not misinformation was unimportant, and far better results would have been achieved with a few highly trained, highly organized, strategically placed cells.

Nothing points the ineffectiveness of the vast armies of Japan's secret servants with greater emphasis than the successes, against the vast organization of the *Kempei tai* in

Japan, of Richard Sorge and his four companions; and even more so, the achievement on their behalf of the trio of Kühns in Honolulu. Had they worked on similar principles of operation elsewhere they would surely have gained more for less effort and expense.

The more one considers it the more is one impelled to the conclusion that Rudolf Hess was right when he suggested that spying is ingrained in the whole Japanese nation. This being so, even without Stieber's model the Japanese leaders would probably have organized their espionage on a grand scale, since they would know that every subject of the emperor was prepared to be his divine and imperial majesty's secret servant. In such circumstances, the temptation might have been too great to resist.

But if Hess was right, are there in the suggestion any implications for the future?

Under the instrument of capitulation the Japanese were forbidden to operate a secret service. But the questions nag for an answer: can a people in whom the principles of espionage are so deeply ingrained ever be compelled to refrain from spying by an injunction placed upon them?

Bibliography

The following are original documents from the Japanese Foreign Office archives which have been consulted:

1. Investigation of the military preparedness of Honolulu, Sections 1 to 4, March 1907 to December 1926.
2. Intelligence from the Japanese Naval General Staff, November 1922.
3. Weekly reports from the Army Intelligence Bureau at Hawaii.
4. Miscellaneous documents relating to proposals by foreigners concerning the sale of documents containing military secrets, September 1908 to September 1922.
5. Miscellaneous documents relating to the movement of Russian forces, June 1897 to April 1903.
6. Documents relating to the despatch of Tsuruok Nagataro, Yamane Takusaburo and Ioya Toyoto of the Japanese Legation in China to investigate the movements of the Russian Army in the hinterland of Manchuria, April 1903 to February 1904.
7. Diary of Lieutenant Colonel Morita's travels in Inner Mongolia, March 1908.
8. Reports from intelligence agents in connection with the Russo-Japanese War, October 1897 to April 1906.
9. Documents relating to the investigations of intelligence offices in various foreign countries, June 1936 to March 1938.
10. Documents relating to appointments of Japanese army officers for intelligence work in the U.S.S.R.
11. Documents relating to the eastward journey of the Russian Baltic

Fleet at the time of the Russo-Japanese War, June to November 1904.

12. Documents relating to secret information, August 1930 to September 1931.

Other documents consulted are:

1. Records of the patriotic societies.
2. Documents relating to Japanese espionage in the Dutch East Indies.
3. The report on Japanese espionage compiled by Rudolf Hess.
4. The papers of the trial of the Kühn family in Honolulu, 1942.
5. The files of various American national newspapers for the trials of Thompson and Farnsworth.

The following is a list of printed works consulted, to which the author acknowledges his indebtedness.

1. *Honorable Spy* by J. L. Spivak (1939)
2. *Secret Service in America* by H. O. Yardley (1940)
3. *Total Espionage* by Curt Reiss (1941)
4. *Betrayal from the East* by Alan Hynd (1943)
5. *Passport to Treason* by Alan Hynd (1943)
6. *Japan's Secret Service in the Hawaiian Islands* by K. D. Singer (1944)
7. *Japanese Attempts at Infiltration among the Muslims in Russia* (U.S. Office of Strategic Services, 1944)
8. *Japanese Infiltration among the Muslims in China* (U.S. Office of Strategic Services, 1944)
9. *Hearings on American Aspects of the Richard Sorge Case* (U.S. Congressional Committee on Un-American Activities, 1951)
10. *History and Mission of the Counter Intelligence Corps in World War II.* (U.S. Counter Intelligence Corps School, 1951)